Modern Biology®

Study Guide

HOLT, RINEHART AND WINSTON

A Harcourt Education Company

Orlando • **Austin** • New York • San Diego • Toronto • London

About the *Modern Biology* Study Guide

The Section Review worksheets can be used in a number of ways to guide you through your textbook: as a pre-reading guide to each section, as a review of the chapter's main concepts after you read each section, or even as test preparation for your biology exams. No matter how your teacher chooses to use these worksheets, the *Modern Biology* Study Guide will help you succeed in your study of biology.

In each Section Review worksheet, you will encounter four types of exercises:

Vocabulary Review exercises help you to review important terms in each section.

Multiple Choice questions test your understanding of important concepts and terms introduced in each section.

Short Answer (with Critical Thinking) questions help you to synthesize and write your own conclusions using information in the section.

Structures and Functions questions provide opportunities to label major structures and processes or to interpret data or figures in order to examine the section material in a larger context.

ISBN 978-0-03-036718-2
16 17 18 19 0982 15 14 13 12
4500371514

CONTENTS

SECTION 1-1 REVIEW

THE WORLD OF BIOLOGY

VOCABULARY REVIEW Define the following terms.

1. development _____

_____

2. reproduction _____

_____

3. organ _____

_____

4. tissue _____

_____

MULTIPLE CHOICE Write the correct letter in the blank.

_____ 1. Biology is the study of

    a. animals.   **c.** all living things.

    b. plants and animals.   **d.** energy transfer.

_____ 2. A short segment of DNA that contains instructions for the development of a single trait of an organism is known as a

    a. DNA loop.   **b.** gene.   **c.** library.   **d.** membrane.

_____ 3. As the cells in a multicellular organism multiply, they become specialized for different functions in a process called

    a. sexual reproduction.   **c.** photosynthesis.

    b. descent with modification.   **d.** cell differentiation.

_____ 4. Homeostasis refers to the

    a. organization of cellular structures.

    b. stable level of internal conditions in organisms.

    c. organized structure of crystals.

    d. destruction of tropical rain forests.

_____ 5. Photosynthesis is part of a plant's

    a. metabolism.   **c.** development.

    b. homeostasis.   **d.** response to stimuli.

SHORT ANSWER Answer the questions in the space provided.

1. Explain why the cell is called the basic unit of life. _____

   _____

2. Give a specific example of homeostasis. _____

   _____

3. Why is it important to study biology? _____

   _____

4. Contrast the reproduction of bacteria with that of frogs. _____

   _____

   _____

5. **Critical Thinking** The organization of a rock is much simpler than that of living things.

   By what other criteria can a rock be distinguished from living things? _____

   _____

   _____

STRUCTURES AND FUNCTIONS Explain how the drawing below illustrates the characteristics of life.

_____

_____

_____

_____

_____

SECTION 1-2 REVIEW

THEMES IN BIOLOGY

VOCABULARY REVIEW Distinguish between the terms in each of the following groups of terms.

1. domain, kingdom _____

_____

2. diversity of life, unity of life _____

_____

3. adaptations, evolution _____

_____

4. ecosystem, ecology _____

_____

MULTIPLE CHOICE Write the correct letter in the blank.

_____ 1. A "tree of life" explains

    a. how organisms are related to each other.
    b. how organisms differ from each other.
    c. the lineages of various organisms.
    d. All of the above

_____ 2. Which of the following is NOT an important unifying theme in biology?

    a. the diversity and unity of life
    b. the relationship between organisms and society
    c. the interdependence of living organisms
    d. the evolution of life

_____ 3. An example of a domain is

    a. Animalia.   **b.** Protista.   **c.** Fungi.   **d.** Eukarya.

_____ 4. A trait that improves an individual's ability to survive and reproduce is a(n)

    a. mutation.   **b.** natural selection   **c.** adaptation.   **d.** domain.

_____ 5. Which of the following statements is *true*?

    a. Destruction of rain forests has no effect on living things.
    b. Destruction of rain forests increases the rate of evolution of rainforest organisms.
    c. Humans have had no impact on the world's environment.
    d. Humans have had a large impact on the world's environment.

SHORT ANSWER Answer the questions in the space provided.

1. Give an example of how two organisms are interdependent. _____

_____

2. Why must an adaptation be inheritable if it is to cause a population to evolve? _____

_____

3. What is natural selection? _____

_____

4. If two organisms share the same kingdom, must they also share the same domain? Explain.

_____

_____

5. **Critical Thinking** A female frog has a genetic trait that prevents it from producing eggs. How likely is it that this trait will spread through the frog population? Explain your answer.

_____

_____

STRUCTURES AND FUNCTIONS Briefly describe the interactions among the panther, the deer, and the grass in the drawing below.

_____

_____

_____

SECTION 1-3 REVIEW

THE STUDY OF BIOLOGY

VOCABULARY REVIEW Define the following terms.

1. prediction _____

_____

2. control group _____

_____

3. dependent variable _____

_____

4. independent variable _____

_____

5. theory _____

_____

MULTIPLE CHOICE Write the correct letter in the blank.

_____ 1. A field biologist who studies the behavior of birds in a rain forest most likely collects
data through

  a. experimenting.   **b.** modeling.   **c.** observing.   **d.** inferring.

_____ 2. Constructing a graph is an example of

  a. measuring.   **b.** organizing data.   **c.** observing.   **d.** predicting.

_____ 3. Of the following steps in a scientific investigation, the last to be done is usually

  a. experimenting.   **c.** producing a model.
  b. observing.   **d.** hypothesizing.

_____ 4. A statement that explains observations and can be tested is called

  a. a hypothesis.   **b.** an inference.   **c.** a theory.   **d.** a model.

_____ 5. A visual, verbal, or mathematical explanation that is supported by data is called

  a. a hypothesis.   **b.** an inference.   **c.** a theory.   **d.** a model.

SHORT ANSWER Answer the questions in the space provided.

1. What are quantitative data? Give two examples of quantitative data. _____

   _____

   _____

2. What is an advantage of a peer review of a scientific paper? _____

   _____

3. How are a hypothesis, a prediction, and an experiment related? _____

   _____

   _____

4. What are some of the things scientists might do to analyze data? _____

   _____

   _____

5. **Critical Thinking** A scientist wanted to study the effect of a drug on the blood pressure of rats. She set up an experiment in which the experimental group consisted of rats that were injected with a salt solution containing the drug. What should the control group have consisted of?

   _____

   What were the dependent and independent variables in her experiment? _____

   _____

   _____

STRUCTURES AND FUNCTIONS Examine the drawing of the owl. In each space below, provide an observation that would support the inference given or provide an inference that could be derived from the observation given.

Observations	Inferences
_____	Owls live in trees.
_____	Owls feed on mice.
_____	Owls kill prey with their talons.
The owl has wings.	_____
Both of the owl's eyes face forward.	_____
It is night.	

SECTION 1-4 REVIEW

TOOLS AND TECHNIQUES

VOCABULARY REVIEW Circle the term that does not belong in each of the following groups, and briefly explain why it does not belong.

1. compound light, transmission electron, light electron, scanning electron _____

   _____

2. base unit, stage, nosepiece, objective lens _____

   _____

3. magnification, power of magnification, resolution, mass density _____

   _____

4. second, minute, meter, kilogram _____

   _____

5. meter, square meter, cubic meter, kilogram per cubic meter _____

   _____

MULTIPLE CHOICE Write the correct letter in the blank.

_____ 1. The ability of a microscope to show details clearly is called

   a. enlargement.   **b.** magnification.   **c.** reduction.   **d.** resolution.

_____ 2. One limitation of the scanning electron microscope is that it cannot be used to

   a. examine specimens smaller than cells.
   b. view living specimens.
   c. produce an enlarged image of a specimen.
   d. produce an image of the surface of a specimen.

_____ 3. A microscope with a 10× ocular lens and a 25× objective lens has a total power of magnification equal to

   a. 2.5×.   **b.** 35×.   **c.** 250×.   **d.** 2,500×.

_____ 4. The SI base unit for time is the

   a. second.   **b.** minute.   **c.** hour.   **d.** day.

_____ 5. The SI prefix that represents 1,000 times the base unit is

   a. deci.   **b.** centi.   **c.** kilo.   **d.** micro.

Name _____ Class _____ Date _____

SHORT ANSWER Answer the questions in the space provided.

1. Arrange the following parts in the order that matches the light path through a light microscope: specimen, ocular lens, objective lens, light source. _____

_____

2. What are the maximum magnifications of the LM, TEM, and SEM? _____

_____

3. Write the abbreviation for each of the following units: meter, kilometer, centimeter, millimeter, micrometer. What is the mathematical relationship between these units? _____

_____

_____

4. **Critical Thinking** A group of scientists want to determine whether the bacteria they are studying have viruses inside them. Which type of microscope should they use? Explain your answer.

_____

_____

_____

STRUCTURES AND FUNCTIONS Label each part of the figure in the spaces provided.

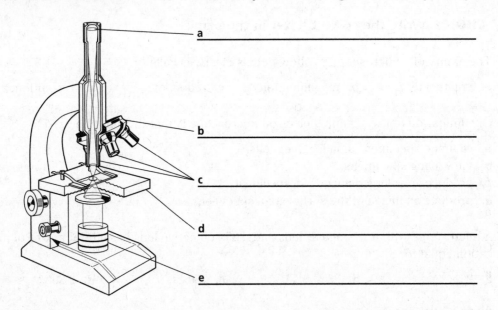

a _____

b _____

c _____

d _____

e _____

SECTION 2-1 REVIEW

COMPOSITION OF MATTER

VOCABULARY REVIEW Define the following terms.

1. atom _____

_____

2. neutron _____

_____

3. compound _____

_____

4. covalent bond _____

_____

5. ion _____

_____

MULTIPLE CHOICE Write the correct letter in the blank.

_____ 1. The atomic number of carbon is 6. Therefore, the number of protons in a carbon atom equals

    a. 3.   **b.** 6.   **c.** 7.   **d.** 12.

_____ 2. One of the kinds of particles found in the nucleus of an atom is the

    a. proton.   **b.** electron.   **c.** ion.   **d.** boron.

_____ 3. The maximum number of electrons that can be held in the orbitals in an atom's second energy level is

    a. 2.   **b.** 4.   **c.** 6.   **d.** 8.

_____ 4. Of the following elements, the one that is most likely to form ionic bonds is

    a. hydrogen.   **b.** carbon.   **c.** sodium.   **d.** oxygen.

_____ 5. An example of a compound is

    a. water.   **b.** hydrogen gas.   **c.** oxygen gas.   **d.** chloride ion.

SHORT ANSWER Answer the questions in the space provided.

1. What is the difference between mass and weight? _____

_____

_____

2. Identify the elements and the number of atoms of each element in each of the following compounds:

BO_2 _____   KCl _____

$C_6H_{12}O_6$ _____ NH_3 _____

3. How many pairs of electrons do the two oxygen atoms in an oxygen molecule share with each

other? Explain your answer. _____

_____

_____

4. **Critical Thinking** The atomic number of argon is 18. Will argon tend to form bonds with other

elements? Explain your answer. _____

_____

_____

_____

STRUCTURES AND FUNCTIONS Use the figure to answer the following questions.

The diagram below shows bonding of a hydrogen atom with a chlorine atom. The atomic number of hydrogen is 1. The atomic number of chlorine is 17. The orbitals corresponding to the third energy level can hold up to 8 electrons.

Cl   H   HCl

1. What kind of bond is formed between hydrogen and chlorine atoms?

_____

2. Describe the formation of this bond and the total number of electrons in the orbitals of each energy level.

_____

_____

SECTION 2-2 REVIEW

ENERGY

VOCABULARY REVIEW Distinguish between the terms in each of the following pairs of terms.

1. reactant, product _____

_____

2. catalyst, enzyme _____

_____

3. oxidation reaction, reduction reaction _____

_____

MULTIPLE CHOICE Write the correct letter in the blank.

_____ 1. The state of matter in which particles move most rapidly is

    a. liquid.   **b.** gas.   **c.** solid.   **d.** heat.

_____ 2. Every chemical reaction involves a

    a. change in the state of the matter in the reactants.
    b. net release of energy.
    c. transfer of energy.
    d. transfer of electrons between atoms.

_____ 3. Enzymes

    a. increase the amount of energy released in a reaction.
    b. decrease the amount of energy released in a reaction.
    c. catalyze only redox reactions.
    d. reduce the activation energy needed for a reaction.

_____ 4. In chemical reactions, the number of each kind of atom in the reactants is

    a. the same as in the products.
    b. less than in the products.
    c. more than in the products.
    d. b or c, depending on the kind of chemical reaction.

_____ 5. Redox reactions

    a. involve either reduction or oxidation, but not both.
    b. involve the transfer of electrons between atoms.
    c. do not occur in living things.
    d. always involve oxygen.

Name _____ Class _____ Date _____

SHORT ANSWER Answer the questions in the space provided.

1. In the chemical reaction shown below, write *R* over the reactants and *P* over the products:

$$C_{12}H_{22}O_{11} + H_2O \longrightarrow C_6H_{12}O_6 + C_6H_{12}O_6$$

2. What role do catalysts play in chemical reactions? _____

_____

_____

3. What does a two-direction arrow indicate in a chemical equation? _____

_____

4. In the chemical reaction shown below, write *R* over the substance that is reduced and *O* over the substance that is oxidized:

$$Na + Cl \longrightarrow Na^+ + Cl^-$$

5. Critical Thinking Sucrose, or table sugar, can react with water to form two other compounds, glucose and fructose. However, when you add sugar to a glass of water, this reaction proceeds extremely slowly. Why does it proceed slowly, and what else is needed to speed up the reaction?

_____

_____

_____

STRUCTURES AND FUNCTIONS Use the figure to answer the following questions.

The graph below represents the energy changes that occur as a chemical reaction progresses.

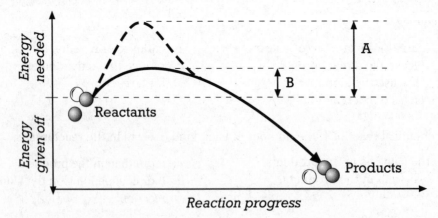

1. What is represented by arrow *A?* _____

2. What is represented by arrow *B?* _____

3. Is energy absorbed or released in this reaction? Explain your answer. _____

_____

SECTION 2-3 REVIEW

WATER AND SOLUTIONS

VOCABULARY REVIEW Define the following terms.

1. solvent _____

_____

2. aqueous solution _____

_____

3. hydroxide ion _____

_____

4. base _____

_____

5. buffer _____

_____

MULTIPLE CHOICE Write the correct letter in the blank.

_____ 1. The concentration of a solution is the measurement of the amount of

    a. acid dissolved in a fixed amount of base.

    b. solvent dissolved in a fixed amount of the solution.

    c. solute dissolved in a fixed amount of the solution.

    d. solvent dissolved in a fixed amount of the solute.

_____ 2. When water dissociates, it forms

    a. H^+ ions and H_2O.

    b. H^+ ions and OH^- ions.

    c. H^+ ions and H_3O^+ ions.

    d. OH^+ ions and H_3O^- ions.

_____ 3. An acid is a solution with more

    a. hydronium ions than hydroxide ions.

    b. hydroxide ions than hydronium ions.

    c. sodium ions than hydroxide ions.

    d. hydroxide ions than sodium ions.

_____ 4. An example of a base is

    a. pure water.   **b.** vinegar.   **c.** ammonia.   **d.** urine.

_____ 5. A solution with a pH above 7 is

    a. logarithmic.   **b.** neutral.   **c.** acidic.   **d.** alkaline.

SHORT ANSWER Answer the questions in the space provided.

1. What property of water allows it to stick to the sides of a vertical glass tube?

   _____

   _____

2. What states of matter can solutions be composed of? _____

3. How much sugar is there in 100 mL of a 10 percent aqueous sugar solution? _____

   What is the solvent in this solution? _____

4. What are the relative numbers of H_3O^+ and OH^- ions in an acidic, an alkaline, and a neutral solution?

   _____

   _____

   _____

5. How many times more hydroxide ions are there in a solution with a pH of 9 than in a solution

   with a pH of 3? _____

6. How are buffers important to the functioning of living systems? _____

   _____

   _____

7. **Critical Thinking** If a solution has a pH of 7.5, what would its new pH be if the concentration

   of H_3O^+ ions in the solution were increased by 100 times? Explain your reasoning. _____

   _____

   _____

STRUCTURES AND FUNCTIONS The diagram below represents a single water molecule. Draw three other water molecules near it, and use dashed lines to indicate where hydrogen bonds would form between the molecule shown below and the ones you drew.

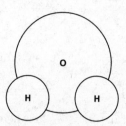

SECTION 3-1 REVIEW

CARBON COMPOUNDS

VOCABULARY REVIEW Define the following terms and provide one example for each.

1. organic compound _____

   _____

2. functional group _____

   _____

3. alcohol _____

   _____

4. monomer _____

   _____

5. polymer _____

   _____

MULTIPLE CHOICE Write the correct letter in the blank.

_____ 1. Organic compounds contain

     a. carbon and usually other elements.   **c.** only carbon.
     b. many kinds of elements except carbon.   **d.** only carbon and hydrogen.

_____ 2. The number of covalent bonds a carbon atom can form with other atoms is

     a. 1.   **b.** 2.   **c.** 4.   **d.** 8.

_____ 3. A covalent bond formed when two atoms share two pairs of electrons is called a

     a. single bond.   **b.** double bond.   **c.** triple bond.   **d.** quadruple bond.

_____ 4. The breakdown of a polymer involves

     a. hydrolysis.   **c.** the breaking of hydrogen bonds.
     b. a condensation reaction.   **d.** the breaking of ionic bonds.

_____ 5. ATP releases energy when

     a. it undergoes a condensation reaction.   **c.** a phosphate group is added to it.
     b. a hydroxyl group is added to it.   **d.** a phosphate group is removed from it.

SHORT ANSWER Answer the questions in the space provided.

1. Give an example of how a functional group can affect the properties of an organic compound.

   _____

   _____

2. Arrange the following in order of size, from smallest to largest: polymer, monomer, carbon atom, macromolecule. _____

3. Explain how a water molecule is produced when glucose and fructose undergo a condensation reaction. _____

   _____

   _____

4. What are the products of the hydrolysis of ATP? What else is released during this reaction?

   _____

   _____

5. **Critical Thinking** How would the variety of organic compounds be different if carbon had seven electrons in its outermost energy level instead of four? _____

   _____

   _____

STRUCTURES AND FUNCTIONS Use the figure to answer the following questions.

The formation of sucrose from glucose and fructose is represented by the chemical reaction shown below. Notice that this reaction can proceed in either direction.

GLUCOSE   FRUCTOSE   SUCROSE

1. What are the reactants and products of the forward (left-to-right) reaction? _____

   _____

2. Is the forward reaction a condensation reaction or hydrolysis? _____

3. What are the reactants and products of the reverse (right-to-left) reaction? _____

   _____

4. Is the reverse reaction a condensation reaction or hydrolysis? _____

SECTION 3-2 REVIEW

MOLECULES OF LIFE

VOCABULARY REVIEW Distinguish between the terms in each of the following pairs of terms.

1. monosaccharide, polysaccharide _____

_____

2. amino acid, protein _____

_____

3. nucleotide, nucleic acid _____

_____

MULTIPLE CHOICE Write the correct letter in the blank.

_____ 1. Glycogen, starch, and cellulose are

    a. monosaccharides. **b.** disaccharides. **c.** polysaccharides. **d.** simple sugars.

_____ 2. The different shapes and functions of different proteins are determined by

    a. the R groups of the amino acids they contain.

    b. the amino groups of the amino acids they contain.

    c. the carboxyl groups of the amino acids they contain.

    d. whether or not they contain any amino acids.

_____ 3. Most enzymes

    a. are changed by the reactions they catalyze.

    b. increase the activation energy of the reactions they catalyze.

    c. strengthen the chemical bonds in their substrate.

    d. are sensitive to changes in temperature or pH.

_____ 4. The large numbers of carbon-hydrogen bonds in lipids

    a. make lipids polar.

    b. store more energy than the carbon-oxygen bonds in other organic compounds.

    c. allow lipids to dissolve in water.

    d. are found in the carboxyl group at the end of the lipid.

_____ 5. The most important function of nucleic acids is

    a. catalyzing chemical reactions.

    b. forming a barrier between the inside and outside of a cell.

    c. storing energy.

    d. storing information related to heredity and protein synthesis.

Name _____ Class _____ Date _____

SHORT ANSWER Answer the questions in the space provided.

1. What are the storage and quick-energy forms of carbohydrates found in animals, and how are these forms structurally related to each other? _____

_____

_____

2. How many different kinds of monomers are there in starch? _____

How many different kinds of monomers are there in proteins? _____

3. What compound composes most of the cell membrane? _____

How is this compound suited to the function of the membrane? _____

_____

_____

4. Steroids are made up of what type of molecule? _____

Give two examples of steroids. _____

5. **Critical Thinking** Insects that live on land have a coating of wax on the outer surface of their

body. What function might the wax serve for these animals? _____

_____

STRUCTURES AND FUNCTIONS Label each part of the figure in the spaces provided.

The diagram below shows the interaction of an enzyme and its substrate during a chemical reaction.

a _____

c _____

b _____

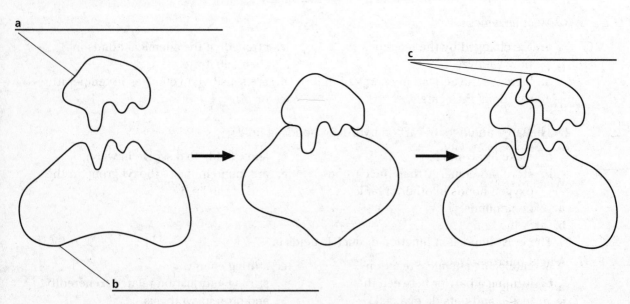

SECTION 4-1 REVIEW

THE HISTORY OF CELL BIOLOGY

VOCABULARY REVIEW Define the following terms.

1. cell _____

_____

2. cell theory _____

_____

MULTIPLE CHOICE Write the correct letter in the blank.

_____ 1. One early piece of evidence supporting the cell theory was the observation that

   a. only plants are composed of cells.   **c.** cells come from other cells.
   b. only animals are composed of cells.   **d.** animal cells come from plant cells.

_____ 2. The scientist who described cells as "many little boxes" was

   a. Robert Hooke.   **c.** Theodor Schwann.
   b. Anton van Leeuwenhoek.   **d.** Rudolf Virchow.

_____ 3. Living and nonliving things are different in that only

   a. nonliving things are made of cells.   **c.** living things are made of cells.
   b. nonliving things are made of atoms.   **d.** living things are made of atoms.

_____ 4. Microscopes were used to study cells beginning in the

   a. 16th century.   **c.** 18th century.
   b. 17th century.   **d.** 19th century.

_____ 5. The advantage of van Leeuwenhoek's microscopes was that

   a. they were simple.   **c.** the lenses could be moved.
   b. they had two lenses.   **d.** the lenses were ground very precisely.

_____ 6. Which of the following was a major event in the history of cell biology?

   a. cloning animals   **c.** discovery of cell parts
   b. growing bone tissue for transplant   **d.** All of the above

_____ 7. A light microscope uses optical lenses to magnify objects by

   a. bending light rays.   **c.** reflecting beams of light.
   b. bending electron beams.   **d.** reflecting beams of electrons.

SHORT ANSWER Answer the questions in the space provided.

1. State the three parts of the cell theory._____

_____

_____

_____

2. Why did it take 150 years for the cell theory to be developed after microscopes were invented?

_____

_____

_____

_____

3. Why did Hooke's cork cells appear to be empty? _____

_____

_____

4. **Critical Thinking** If you read that a new organism had been discovered, what would you know about the organism without examining it in terms of cells?

_____

_____

_____

STRUCTURES AND FUNCTIONS Use the figure to answer the following questions.

Timeline—History of Cell Biology

| Robert Hooke observes cork cells. | Rudolf Virchow adds to the cell theory. | Camillo Golgi discovers the Golgi apparatus in cells. | Tissue engineering used to grow new skin and bone for transplant. |

1827   1857   1996

1665   1855   1897   2004

| Karl Von Baer discovers the mammalian egg. | Kolliker describes mitochondria in muscle. | Researchers in Scotland clone a sheep from an adult sheep cell. |

1. Approximately how many years elapsed between the time cells were discovered and the observation of cell parts in muscle cells?

_____

2. When was the third part of the cell theory added? What was the time interval between this event and the discovery of cells?

_____

SECTION 4-2 REVIEW

INTRODUCTION TO CELLS

VOCABULARY REVIEW Define the following terms.

1. organelle _____

_____

2. nucleus _____

_____

3. eukaryote _____

_____

4. prokaryote _____

_____

MULTIPLE CHOICE Write the correct letter in the blank.

_____ 1. Cells are limited in size by the

    a. rate at which substances needed by the cell can enter the cell through its surface.

    b. rate at which the cell can manufacture genetic information.

    c. amount of material the cell can collect to fill itself.

    d. amount of cell membrane the cell can produce.

_____ 2. The diameter of most plant and animal cells is about

    a. 0.1 to 0.2 μm.   **b.** 10 to 50 μm.   **c.** 1 to 2 mm.   **d.** 10 to 50 mm.

_____ 3. The characteristic of a nerve cell that relates directly to its function in receiving and transmitting nerve impulses is its

    a. long extensions.

    b. flat shape.

    c. ability to change shape.

    d. ability to engulf and destroy bacteria.

_____ 4. One difference between eukaryotic and prokaryotic cells is that only

    a. prokaryotic cells are surrounded by a cell membrane.

    b. prokaryotic cells have a nucleus.

    c. eukaryotic cells have genetic information.

    d. eukaryotic cells have membrane-bound organelles.

SHORT ANSWER Answer the questions in the space provided.

1. How is the shape of a skin cell suited to its function? _____

_____

_____

2. How are the organelles of a single cell like the organs of a multicellular organism? _____

_____

3. Name two features of eukaryotic cells that prokaryotic cells lack. _____

_____

4. **Critical Thinking** When a spherical cell increases in diameter from 2 μm to 20 μm, by what factor does its surface area change? By what factor does its volume change? (The surface area of a sphere $= 4\pi \text{ radius}^2$, and the volume of a sphere $= 4/3\pi \text{ radius}^3$. Remember that diameter $= 2 \times \text{radius}$.)

_____

_____

STRUCTURES AND FUNCTIONS

1. These figures represent a eukaryotic cell and a prokaryotic cell. In the spaces below the diagrams, indicate which type of cell each diagram represents.

X _____

Y _____

a _____   b _____

2. List two features that formed the basis for your identification of these cells.

_____

_____

3. Identify the structures labeled X and Y. _____

CELL ORGANELLES AND FEATURES

VOCABULARY REVIEW Distinguish between the terms in each of the following pairs of terms.

1. nucleoplasm, nuclear envelope _____

_____

2. cytoskeleton, microtubule _____

_____

_____

3. cilia, flagella _____

_____

MULTIPLE CHOICE Write the correct letter in the blank.

_____ 1. The plasma membrane

    a. allows all substances to pass into and out of the cell.

    b. prevents all substances from passing into and out of the cell.

    c. is composed mainly of a protein bilayer.

    d. is composed mainly of a lipid bilayer.

_____ 2. Substances produced in a cell and exported outside of the cell would pass through the

    a. endoplasmic reticulum and Golgi apparatus.

    b. mitochondria and Golgi apparatus.

    c. nucleus and lysosomes.

    d. vacuoles and lysosomes.

_____ 3. Cells that have a high energy requirement generally have many

    a. nuclei.   **b.** flagella.   **c.** mitochondria.   **d.** microfilaments.

_____ 4. Viruses, bacteria, and old organelles that a cell ingests are broken down in

    a. ribosomes.

    b. lysosomes.

    c. the rough endoplasmic reticulum.

    d. the smooth endoplasmic reticulum.

_____ 5. Organelles that are surrounded by two membranes and contain DNA are the

    a. nucleus, the endoplasmic reticulum, and lysosomes.

    b. nucleus, the endoplasmic reticulum, and chloroplasts.

    c. nucleus and mitochondria.

    d. endoplasmic reticulum and the Golgi apparatus.

Name _____ Class _____ Date _____

SHORT ANSWER Answer the questions in the space provided.

1. What roles do membrane proteins play in transporting only certain substances into a cell?

_____

_____

2. What are ribosomes made of? _____

_____

What cellular function are they involved in? _____

_____

3. What is the cytoskeleton, and what are three of its major components? _____

_____

4. Describe the structural organization shared by cilia and flagella. _____

_____

5. **Critical Thinking** When lipid is added to a solution of a detergent in water, the detergent breaks up large globules of the lipid into much smaller globules. What effect do you think a detergent would

have on the integrity of cells? Explain your answer. _____

_____

_____

STRUCTURES AND FUNCTIONS This diagram represents a typical animal cell. Label each part of the figure in the spaces provided.

a. _____

b. _____

c. _____

d. _____

e. _____

f. _____

SECTION 4-4 REVIEW

UNIQUE FEATURES OF PLANT CELLS

VOCABULARY REVIEW Define the following terms.

1. cell wall _____

_____

2. plastid _____

_____

3. thylakoids _____

_____

4. chlorophyll _____

_____

5. central vacuole _____

_____

MULTIPLE CHOICE Write the correct letter in the blank.

_____ 1. Which of the following organelles is found in plant cells but not in animal cells?

    a. nucleus   **c.** mitochondrion
    b. chloroplast   **d.** Golgi apparatus

_____ 2. The end products of photosynthesis include

    a. carbon dioxide and water.   **c.** carbon dioxide and oxygen.
    b. sugars.   **d.** oxygen and water.

_____ 3. A cell that contains a cell wall, chloroplasts, and a central vacuole is a

    a. plant cell.   **b.** animal cell.   **c.** prokaryotic cell.   **d.** bacterial cell.

_____ 4. A central vacuole forms from

    a. chloroplasts.   **c.** the fusion of smaller vacuoles.
    b. fusion of amyloplasts.   **d.** the products of photosynthesis.

_____ 5. Thylakoids are located

    a. between the two membranes of a chloroplast.
    b. outside the outer membrane of a chloroplast.
    c. inside the inner membrane of a chloroplast.
    d. in chromoplasts.

SHORT ANSWER Answer the questions in the space provided.

1. How are secondary cell walls different from primary cell walls? _____

_____

_____

_____

2. What are plant cell walls made of? _____

_____

What is the function of cell walls? _____

_____

3. What is the appearance of a plant cell when water is plentiful? _____

_____

4. **Critical Thinking** Bacteria have a region called a nucleoid, in which their genetic material is located. Why, then, are bacteria classified as prokaryotes?

_____

_____

STRUCTURES AND FUNCTIONS Label each part of the figure in the spaces provided.

This diagram represents a typical plant cell.

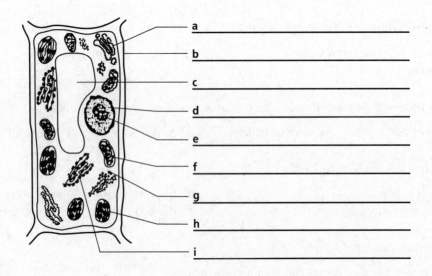

a _____

b _____

c _____

d _____

e _____

f _____

g _____

h _____

i _____

SECTION 5-1 REVIEW

PASSIVE TRANSPORT

VOCABULARY REVIEW Explain the relationship between the terms in each of the following pairs of terms.

1. concentration gradient, diffusion _____

_____

_____

2. osmosis, turgor pressure _____

_____

_____

3. hypertonic, plasmolysis _____

_____

_____

MULTIPLE CHOICE Write the correct letter in the blank.

_____ 1. Substances that can pass through cell membranes by diffusion include

    a. Na^+ ions.   **b.** Cl^- ions.   **c.** glucose.   **d.** oxygen.

_____ 2. The contractile vacuole of a paramecium should be active when the paramecium is in

    a. an isotonic environment.   **c.** a hypertonic environment.
    b. a hypotonic environment.   **d.** any environment.

_____ 3. When a human red blood cell is placed in a hypotonic environment, it will

    a. undergo cytolysis.   **c.** experience a decrease in turgor pressure.
    b. undergo plasmolysis.   **d.** be at equilibrium.

_____ 4. Facilitated diffusion is often used to transport

    a. ions.   **c.** molecules that are not soluble in lipids.
    b. water.   **d.** molecules that are too small to diffuse
                                  across the membrane.

_____ 5. Na^+ ions enter cells by

    a. diffusing across the lipid bilayer   **c.** binding to Na^+ carrier proteins.
        without assistance.   **d.** binding to Cl^- ions.
    b. diffusing through Na^+ ion channels.

Name _____ Class _____ Date _____

SHORT ANSWER Answer the questions in the space provided.

1. What happens to the movement of molecules at equilibrium? _____

_____

_____

2. How do carrier proteins transport substances across cell membranes? _____

_____

_____

3. What types of stimuli can cause the gates on ion channels to open or close? _____

_____

_____

4. Critical Thinking How does the interaction between a carrier protein and the substance it

transports resemble the interaction between an enzyme and its substrate? _____

_____

_____

_____

STRUCTURES AND FUNCTIONS The drawings below show the appearance of a red blood cell and a plant cell in isotonic, hypotonic, and hypertonic environments. Label each environment in the spaces provided.

RED BLOOD CELL

a _____   b _____   c _____

PLANT CELL

d _____   e _____   f _____

SECTION 5-2 REVIEW

ACTIVE TRANSPORT

VOCABULARY REVIEW Define the following terms.

1. active transport _____

_____

2. endocytosis _____

_____

3. vesicle _____

_____

4. phagocytosis _____

_____

MULTIPLE CHOICE Write the correct letter in the blank.

_____ 1. Facilitated-diffusion carrier proteins and cell-membrane pumps both

    a. require an input of energy.
    b. are specific for the kinds of substances they transport.
    c. transport substances up their concentration gradients.
    d. carry out active transport.

_____ 2. The sodium-potassium pump transports

    a. Na^+ out of the cell and K^+ into the cell.
    b. Na^+ and K^+ in both directions across the cell membrane.
    c. K^+ out of the cell and Na^+ into the cell.
    d. Na^+ during some cycles and K^+ during other cycles.

_____ 3. The energy needed to power the sodium-potassium pump is provided by the

    a. binding of ATP to the pump.
    b. transport of ATP by the pump.
    c. removal of a phosphate group from ATP.
    d. formation of ATP.

_____ 4. Pinocytosis involves the transport of

    a. large particles out of a cell.
    b. fluids into a cell.
    c. whole cells into another cell.
    d. lysosomes out of a cell.

_____ 5. Exocytosis is a

    a. type of passive transport.
    b. mechanism by which cells ingest other cells.
    c. transport process in which vesicles are formed from pouches in the cell membrane.
    d. way for cells to release large molecules, such as proteins.

Name _____ Class _____ Date _____

SHORT ANSWER Answer the questions in the space provided.

1. Why is the sodium-potassium transport mechanism called a "pump"? _____
   _____

2. Explain how a phagocyte destroys bacteria. _____
   _____
   _____

3. Describe how a cell produces and releases proteins. _____
   _____
   _____

4. **Critical Thinking** Why is it important that ions being transported across a cell membrane be
   shielded from the interior of the lipid bilayer? _____
   _____
   _____

STRUCTURES AND FUNCTIONS Use the figure to answer the following questions.

1. The diagrams below represent the six steps in one cycle of the sodium-potassium pump. The order
   of the steps has been scrambled. Beginning with diagram *d* (numbered *1*), sequence the remaining
   diagrams by writing the appropriate numeral in each blank.

2. On which side of the membrane are Na^+ ions released from the pump? _____

3. On which side of the membrane are K^+ ions released from the pump? _____

SECTION 6-1 REVIEW

THE LIGHT REACTIONS

VOCABULARY REVIEW Explain the relationship between the terms in each of the following pairs of terms.

1. granum, stroma _____

_____

2. chlorophyll *a*, carotenoids _____

_____

3. chemiosmosis, ATP synthase _____

_____

MULTIPLE CHOICE Write the correct letter in the blank.

_____ **1.** Chlorophyll *a*

    a. absorbs mostly orange-red and blue-violet light.

    b. absorbs mostly green light.

    c. is an accessory pigment.

    d. is responsible for the red color of many autumn leaves.

_____ **2.** The photosystems and electron transport chains are located in the

    a. outer chloroplast membrane.

    b. inner chloroplast membrane.

    c. thylakoid membrane.

    d. stroma.

_____ **3.** Both photosystem I and photosystem II

    a. receive electrons from other photosystems.

    b. donate electrons to a transport chain that generates NADPH.

    c. donate protons to each other.

    d. contain chlorophyll *a* molecules.

_____ **4.** Water participates directly in the light reactions of photosynthesis by

    a. donating electrons to NADPH.

    b. donating electrons to photosystem II.

    c. accepting electrons from the electron transport chains.

    d. accepting electrons from ADP.

_____ **5.** The energy that is used to establish the proton gradient across the thylakoid membrane comes from the

    a. synthesis of ATP.

    b. synthesis of NADPH.

    c. passage of electrons along the electron transport chain of photosystem II.

    d. splitting of water.

Name _____ Class _____ Date _____

SHORT ANSWER Answer the questions in the space provided.

1. Why is photosynthesis referred to as a biochemical pathway? _____

_____

2. How does the structure of a chloroplast enable it to build up a concentration gradient of protons?

_____

_____

_____

3. What are the energy-carrying end products of the light harvesting reactions? _____

4. Explain the function of accessory pigments. _____

_____

_____

5. **Critical Thinking** Which photosystem—I or II—most likely evolved first? Explain your reasoning.

_____

_____

_____

STRUCTURES AND FUNCTIONS Label the substances represented by the letters *a–d* below.

The diagram below summarizes the light reactions of photosynthesis.

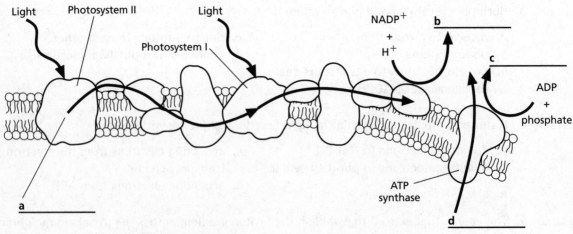

SECTION 6-2 REVIEW

THE CALVIN CYCLE

VOCABULARY REVIEW Define the following terms.

1. Calvin cycle ——————————————————————————————————

——

2. carbon fixation ——————————————————————————————————

——

3. stoma ——————————————————————————————————————

——

4. C$_4$ pathway ————————————————————————————————————

——

5. CAM pathway ——————————————————————————————————

——

MULTIPLE CHOICE Write the correct letter in the blank.

—————— 1. The Calvin cycle begins when CO_2 combines with a five-carbon carbohydrate called

   a. RuBP.   **b.** PGA.   **c.** 3-G3P.   **d.** NADPH.

—————— 2. For every three molecules of CO_2 that enter the Calvin cycle, the cycle produces six molecules of

   a. RuBP.   **b.** ATP.   **c.** 3-PGA.   **d.** NADPH.

—————— 3. Organic compounds that can be made from the products of the Calvin cycle include

   a. only carbohydrates.   **c.** only lipids.
   b. only amino acids.   **d.** carbohydrates, amino acids, and lipids.

—————— 4. C$_3$ and C$_4$ plants differ in terms of the number of

   a. steps in the Calvin cycle.   **c.** carbon atoms in the end product of the
   b. carbon atoms in the compound that   Calvin cycle.
       CO_2 is initially incorporated into.   **d.** ATP molecules used in the Calvin cycle.

—————— 5. As light intensity increases, the rate of photosynthesis

   a. continues to decrease.   **c.** initially decreases and then levels off.
   b. continues to increase.   **d.** initially increases and then levels off.

SHORT ANSWER Answer the questions in the space provided.

1. How many molecules of ATP and NADPH are used in a single turn of the Calvin cycle?

_____

2. Using (CH_2O) as the general formula for a carbohydrate, write the simplest overall equation for

photosynthesis. _____

3. How do CAM plants differ from both C_3 and C_4 plants? _____

_____

4. Why does the rate of photosynthesis increase, peak, and then decrease as temperature increases?

_____

_____

_____

5. **Critical Thinking** Stomata can open and close in response to changes in the CO_2 concentration inside the leaf. Would you expect stomata to open or close if the CO_2 concentration decreased?

Explain. _____

_____

_____

STRUCTURES AND FUNCTIONS In the blank spaces provided in the diagram, indicate the number of molecules of each substance that are involved when three CO_2 molecules enter the cycle.

The diagram below summarizes the Calvin cycle.

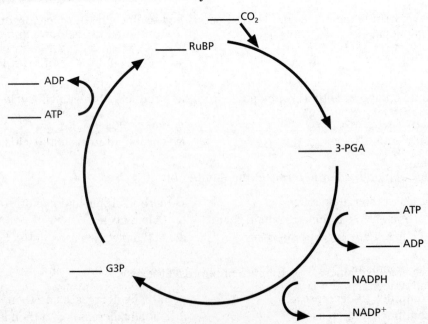

SECTION 7-1 REVIEW

GLYCOLYSIS AND FERMENTATION

VOCABULARY REVIEW Define the following terms.

1. cellular respiration _____

_____

2. glycolysis _____

_____

3. lactic acid fermentation _____

_____

4. alcoholic fermentation _____

_____

MULTIPLE CHOICE Write the correct letter in the blank.

_____ **1.** Glycolysis takes place

    a. in the cytosol.

    b. in the mitochondria.

    c. only if oxygen is present.

    d. only if oxygen is absent.

_____ **2.** During glycolysis, glucose is

    a. produced from two molecules of pyruvic acid.

    b. converted into two molecules of ATP.

    c. partially broken down and some of its stored energy is released.

    d. partially broken down and its stored energy is increased.

_____ **3.** Both lactic acid fermentation and alcoholic fermentation produce

    a. a two-carbon molecule from a six-carbon molecule.

    b. CO_2 from a three-carbon molecule.

    c. ATP from ADP and phosphate.

    d. NAD^+ from NADH and H^+.

_____ **4.** The efficiency of glycolysis is approximately

    a. 0.2%.   **b.** 2%.   **c.** 20%.   **d.** 200%.

_____ **5.** The anaerobic pathways provide enough energy to meet all of the energy needs of

    a. all organisms.

    b. all unicellular and most multicellular organisms.

    c. many unicellular and some multicellular organisms.

    d. no organisms.

Name _____ Class _____ Date _____

SHORT ANSWER Answer the questions in the space provided.

1. Why are the fermentation pathways referred to as "anaerobic" pathways? _____

_____

2. What are the energy-containing products of glycolysis? _____

_____

3. Of what importance are lactic acid fermentation and alcoholic fermentation to the cells that use

these pathways? _____

_____

4. **Critical Thinking** The vitamin niacin is an essential component of NAD^+. Niacin can be consumed
in food or manufactured in the body from tryptophan, an amino acid. How would a person's ability
to break down glucose through glycolysis be affected if the person's diet were deficient in both

niacin and tryptophan? Explain your answer. _____

_____

_____

STRUCTURES AND FUNCTIONS The diagram below depicts the stages of fermentation. Complete the diagram by writing the names of the pathways in the ovals and the names of the molecules in the boxes.

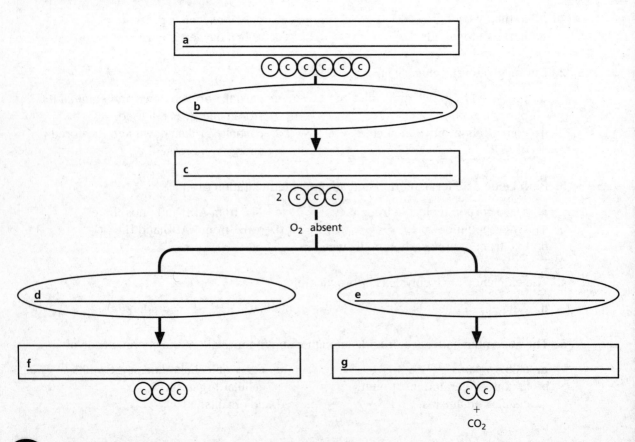

SECTION 7-2 REVIEW

AEROBIC RESPIRATION

VOCABULARY REVIEW Define the following terms.

1. aerobic respiration _____

_____

2. mitochondrial matrix _____

_____

3. Krebs cycle _____

_____

4. FAD _____

_____

MULTIPLE CHOICE Write the correct letter in the blank.

_____ 1. The breakdown product of glucose that diffuses into the mitochondrial matrix for further breakdown is

    a. acetyl CoA.   **b.** pyruvic acid.   **c.** oxaloacetic acid.   **d.** citric acid.

_____ 2. The starting substance of the Krebs cycle, which is regenerated at the end of the cycle, is

    a. acetyl CoA.   **b.** pyruvic acid.   **c.** oxaloacetic acid.   **d.** citric acid.

_____ 3. The Krebs cycle

    a. produces two molecules of CO_2.   **c.** produces NAD^+ from NADH and H^+.
    b. produces a six-carbon molecule from   **d.** generates most of the ATP produced
       six molecules of CO_2.   in aerobic respiration.

_____ 4. The electron transport chain of aerobic respiration

    a. generates O_2 from H_2O.
    b. produces NADH by chemiosmosis.
    c. pumps electrons into the mitochondrial matrix.
    d. pumps protons into the space between the inner and outer mitochondrial membranes.

_____ 5. The maximum efficiency of aerobic respiration is approximately

    a. 0.39%.   **b.** 3.9%.   **c.** 39%.   **d.** 390%.

SHORT ANSWER Answer the questions in the space provided.

1. In the Krebs cycle, what molecule acquires most of the energy that is released by the oxidation of acetyl CoA, and how many of these molecules are produced during each turn of the cycle?

_____

2. Which reactions of aerobic respiration occur in the inner mitochondrial membrane?

_____

3. Write the equation for the complete oxidation of glucose in aerobic respiration.

_____

4. **Critical Thinking** How is the structure of a mitochondrion well adapted for the activities it

carries out? _____

_____

_____

_____

_____

STRUCTURES AND FUNCTIONS Use the diagram to answer the following questions.

The diagram below summarizes the electron transport chain and chemiosmosis in aerobic respiration. Label the substances that are transported along the arrows labeled *a–d* in the spaces provided. Label the reactants or products that are represented by *e–g* in the spaces provided.

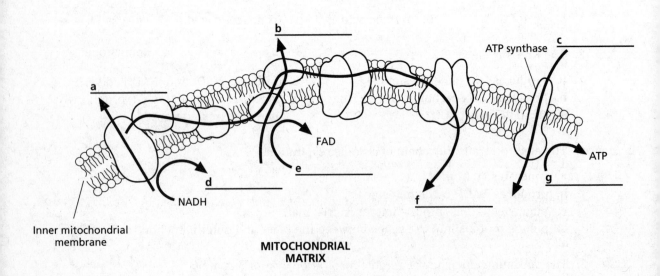

SECTION 8-1 REVIEW

CHROMOSOMES

VOCABULARY REVIEW Distinguish between the terms in each of the following pairs of terms.

1. histone, nonhistone protein _____

_____

2. chromatid, centromere _____

_____

3. sex chromosome, autosome _____

_____

4. diploid cell, haploid cell _____

_____

MULTIPLE CHOICE Write the correct letter in the blank.

_____ 1. During cell division, the DNA in a eukaryotic cell is tightly packed and coiled into structures called

    a. centromeres.   **b.** histones.   **c.** haploids.   **d.** chromosomes.

_____ 2. Between cell divisions, the DNA in a eukaryotic cell is uncoiled and spread out; in this form it is called

    a. chromatid.   **b.** chromatin.   **c.** histone.   **d.** nonhistone.

_____ 3. The chromosomes of most prokaryotes consist of proteins and

    a. a single circular DNA molecule.
    b. a single linear DNA molecule.
    c. a pair of linear DNA molecules joined in the center.
    d. a pair of homologous, circular DNA molecules.

_____ 4. Humans have 46 chromosomes in all cells except sperm and egg cells. How many of these chromosomes are autosomes?

    a. 2   **b.** 23   **c.** 44   **d.** 46

_____ 5. If an organism has a diploid, or $2n$, number of 16, how many chromosomes do its sperm cells or eggs cells contain?

    a. 8   **b.** 16   **c.** 32   **d.** 64

Name _____ Class _____ Date _____

SHORT ANSWER Answer the questions in the space provided.

1. What role do proteins play in enabling the enormous amount of DNA in a eukaryotic cell to fit

   into the nucleus, and what are those proteins called? _____

   _____

2. In what ways are homologous chromosomes similar? _____

   _____

3. What is the picture below called, and how is it used to determine the sex of a person?

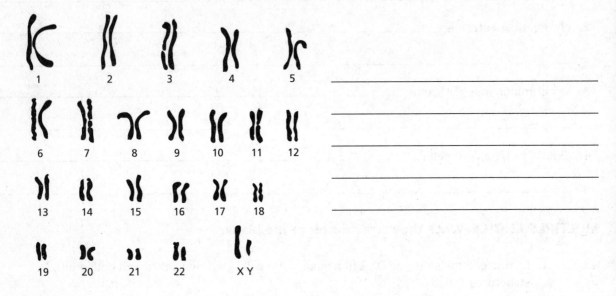

   _____

   _____

   _____

   _____

   _____

4. **Critical Thinking** Some relatively simple eukaryotes, such as the adder's tongue fern, may have many more chromosomes than a more complex eukaryote, such as a mammal. What might this suggest about the size and organization of chromosomes in different species?

   _____

   _____

   _____

STRUCTURES AND FUNCTIONS The diagram below shows structures isolated from the nucleus of a dividing eukaryotic cell. Label each structure or pair of structures in the space provided.

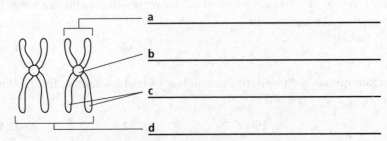

a _____

b _____

c _____

d _____

SECTION 8-2 REVIEW

CELL DIVISION

VOCABULARY REVIEW Circle the term that does not belong in each of the following groups, and briefly explain why it does not belong.

1. G_1 phase, G_2 phase, S phase, telophase _____

_____

2. anaphase, interphase, metaphase, prophase _____

_____

3. binary fission, mitosis, meiosis, cytokinesis _____

_____

4. cleavage furrow, cytokinesis, spindle fiber, cell plate _____

_____

5. centrioles, vesicles, kinetochore fibers, polar fibers _____

_____

MULTIPLE CHOICE Write the correct letter in the blank.

_____ 1. Prokaryotic cells reproduce by a process called

    a. mitosis.   **b.** meiosis.   **c.** binary fission.   **d.** binary fusion.

_____ 2. In eukaryotic cells, DNA is copied during a phase of the cell cycle called

    a. M phase.   **b.** S phase.   **c.** G_1 phase.   **d.** G_2 phase.

_____ 3. The cytoplasm of a eukaryotic cell divides by a process called

    a. mitosis.   **b.** meiosis.   **c.** replication.   **d.** cytokinesis.

_____ 4. The fibers that extend from centrosome to centrosome during mitosis are

    a. polar fibers.   **b.** spindle fibers.   **c.** kinetochore fibers.   **d.** binary fibers.

_____ 5. In the G_0 phase, cells

    a. synthesize DNA.   **c.** exit from the cell cycle.
    b. prepare for cell division.   **d.** move their chromosomes to the
                                     cell equator.

SHORT ANSWER Answer the questions in the space provided.

1. List the five main phases of the cell cycle, and briefly explain what occurs during each phase.

   _____

   _____

   _____

   _____

   _____

2. List the four phases of mitosis, and briefly explain what occurs during each phase.

   _____

   _____

   _____

   _____

   _____

3. Describe cytokinesis in a plant cell. _____

   _____

   _____

4. **Critical Thinking** What would happen to a cell and its offspring if the cells did not go through a

   G_1 phase during their cell cycle? Explain. _____

   _____

   _____

STRUCTURES AND FUNCTIONS In the spaces provided below, label each figure with the phase of mitosis that it represents.

 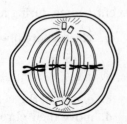  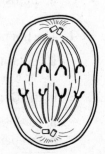

a _____ b _____ c _____ d _____

SECTION 8-3 REVIEW

MEIOSIS

VOCABULARY REVIEW Define the following terms.

1. oogenesis _____

_____

2. tetrad _____

_____

3. independent assortment _____

_____

4. polar bodies _____

_____

MULTIPLE CHOICE Write the correct letter in the blank.

_____ 1. During synapsis, the

  a. DNA in each chromosome is copied.
  b. spindle fibers disappear.
  c. cytoplasm divides.
  d. chromosomes line up next to their homologues.

_____ 2. During crossing-over, portions of chromatids

  a. double the amount of DNA in each chromosome.
  b. move from autosomes to sex chromosomes.
  c. break off and attach to adjacent chromatids on the homologous chromosome.
  d. separate from each other and move to opposite poles of the cell.

_____ 3. In which phase of meiosis do tetrads form?

  a. prophase I   **b.** telophase I   **c.** metaphase II   **d.** anaphase II

_____ 4. Meiosis II

  a. is preceded by the copying of DNA.
  b. separates chromatids into opposite poles of the cell.
  c. separates homologous chromosomes into opposite poles of the cell.
  d. produces diploid offspring cells.

_____ 5. In oogenesis, a diploid reproductive cell divides meiotically to produce

  a. one diploid gamete.
  b. four diploid gametes.
  c. one haploid gamete.
  d. four haploid gametes.

Name _____ Class _____ Date _____

SHORT ANSWER Answer the questions in the space provided.

1. Describe two ways in which genetic recombination occurs during meiosis. _____

_____

_____

_____

2. List the four phases of meiosis I, and briefly explain what occurs during each phase.

_____

_____

_____

_____

_____

_____

3. How do the products of meiosis I differ from those of meiosis II? _____

_____

_____

_____

4. **Critical Thinking** What are one advantage and one disadvantage of asexual reproduction

compared with sexual reproduction? _____

_____

_____

_____

STRUCTURES AND FUNCTIONS In the spaces provided below, label each figure with the phase of meiosis that it represents.

a _____   b _____   c _____   d _____

SECTION 9-1 REVIEW

MENDEL'S LEGACY

VOCABULARY REVIEW Distinguish between the terms in each of the following pairs of terms.

1. F_1 generation, F_2 generation _____

_____

2. dominant, recessive _____

_____

3. self-pollination, cross-pollination _____

_____

MULTIPLE CHOICE Write the correct letter in the blank.

_____ 1. Mendel obtained plants that were true-breeding for particular traits by

    a. growing plants from the seeds of other plants that showed that trait.

    b. discarding plants that showed other traits.

    c. allowing plants to self-pollinate for several generations.

    d. allowing plants to cross-pollinate for one generation.

_____ 2. When Mendel crossed a strain of tall pea plants with a strain of short pea plants, he observed that all of the plants in the F_1 generation were tall. This suggests that

    a. the tall trait was controlled by a dominant factor.

    b. the short trait was controlled by a dominant factor.

    c. both traits were controlled by a recessive factor.

    d. the strain of short plants was not capable of pollinating the strain of tall plants.

_____ 3. A cross between true-breeding green-podded pea plants and true-breeding yellow-podded pea plants produces only green-podded plants. When the F_1 generation is allowed to self-pollinate, the F_2 generation consists of

    a. only green-podded plants.

    b. only yellow-podded plants.

    c. about three-quarters yellow-podded plants and one-quarter green-podded plants.

    d. about three-quarters green-podded plants and one-quarter yellow-podded plants.

_____ 4. When alleles for different characteristics are on separate chromosomes, they are distributed to gametes independently. This observation is summarized by the law of

    a. cross-pollination.

    b. independent assortment.

    c. segregation.

    d. molecular genetics.

Name _____ Class _____ Date _____

SHORT ANSWER Answer the questions in the space provided.

1. What does the term *allele* mean as it is used in genetic crosses? _____

_____

2. Explain how the events of meiosis account for the law of segregation and the law of independent

assortment. _____

_____

_____

_____

3. If orange flower color in a plant is controlled by an allele *F* and red flower color is controlled by

an allele *f,* which flower color is dominant? _____

If true-breeding orange-flowered plants are crossed with true-breeding red-flowered plants, what

will be the flower color(s) of the F_1 plants? _____

4. **Critical Thinking** How would Mendel's observations and conclusions have been different if
   many of the characteristics he studied, such as seed color and seed texture, had been controlled

   by genes located close together on the same chromosome? _____

_____

_____

STRUCTURES AND FUNCTIONS In the spaces inside each gamete, indicate the four possible combinations of alleles the gametes could receive.

The diagram below shows the assortment of two pairs of homologous chromosomes during
meiosis. One pair has a gene for flower color (*R* allele = red, *r* allele = white). The other pair has a
gene for seed color (*B* allele = brown, *b* allele = gray).

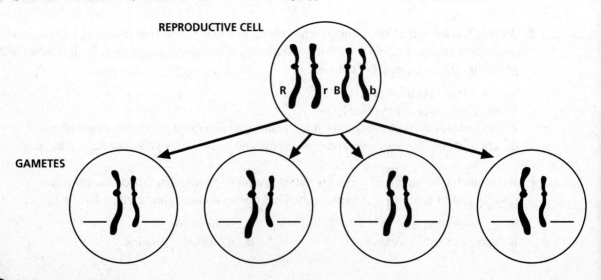

REPRODUCTIVE CELL

GAMETES

SECTION 9-2 REVIEW

GENETIC CROSSES

VOCABULARY REVIEW Define the following terms, and provide one example for each.

1. complete dominance _____

_____

_____

2. incomplete dominance _____

_____

_____

3. codominance _____

_____

_____

MULTIPLE CHOICE Write the correct letter in the blank.

_____ **1.** The appearance of an organism is its

    a. genotype.   **b.** phenotype.   **c.** genotypic ratio.   **d.** phenotypic ratio.

_____ **2.** A genetic cross performed many times produces 798 long-stemmed plants and 266 short-stemmed plants. The probability of obtaining a short-stemmed plant in a similar cross is

    a. 266/1,064.   **b.** 266/798.   **c.** 798/266.   **d.** 798/1,064.

_____ **3.** A monohybrid cross of two individuals that are heterozygous for a trait exhibiting complete dominance would probably result in a phenotypic ratio of

    a. 4 dominant:0 recessive.   **c.** 3 dominant:1 recessive.
    b. 1 dominant:3 recessive.   **d.** 1 dominant:1 recessive.

_____ **4.** To determine the genotype of an individual that shows the dominant phenotype, you would cross that individual with one that is

    a. heterozygous dominant.   **c.** homozygous dominant.
    b. heterozygous recessive.   **d.** homozygous recessive.

_____ **5.** In a dihybrid cross between an individual with the genotype *RRYY* and an individual with the genotype *rryy*, all of the offspring will have the genotype

    a. *RRYY.*   **b.** *RrYY.*   **c.** *RrYy.*   **d.** *rryy.*

Name _____ Class _____ Date _____

SHORT ANSWER Answer the questions in the space provided.

1. What is the difference between a homozygous individual and a heterozygous individual?

   _____

   _____

2. If the probability that a specific trait will appear in the F_2 generation is 0.25, how many individuals would be expected to show that trait in an F_2 generation consisting of 80 individuals?

   _____

3. A homozygous dominant individual (*AA*) is crossed with an individual that is heterozygous for the same trait (*Aa*). What are the possible genotypes of the offspring, and what percentage of the

   offspring is likely to show the dominant phenotype? _____

4. **Critical Thinking** Some animals, such as cows, normally produce only one offspring from each mating. If a cow showed a dominant phenotype, why would a typical testcross be a difficult way

   to determine the genotype of that animal? _____

   _____

   _____

   _____

STRUCTURES AND FUNCTIONS Write the possible genotypes of the offspring in the Punnett square below. Then answer the questions in the spaces provided.

A plant with the genotype *WwRr* is crossed with another plant with the same genotype.

WwRr

WwRr

1. What proportion of the offspring will be dominant for both traits?

   _____

2. What proportion of the offspring will have the same genotype as their parents?

   _____

3. What proportion of the offspring will be homozygous dominant for both traits?

   _____

4. What proportion of the offspring will be homozygous recessive for both traits?

   _____

SECTION 10-1 REVIEW

DISCOVERY OF DNA

VOCABULARY REVIEW Define the following terms.

1. virulent _____

   _____

2. transformation _____

   _____

3. bacteriophage _____

   _____

MULTIPLE CHOICE Write the correct letter in the blank.

_____ 1. The virulent strain of the bacterium *S. pneumoniae* causes disease because it
   a. has a capsule.   **c.** undergoes transformation.
   b. lacks a capsule.   **d.** does not undergo transformation.

_____ 2. Oswald Avery and his colleagues showed that the transforming agent in Griffith's experiments was

   a. RNA.   **b.** protein.   **c.** DNA.   **d.** an enzyme.

_____ 3. Hershey's and Chase's experiment led to the conclusion that
   a. protein is the hereditary molecule in viruses.
   b. DNA is responsible for transformation in bacteria.
   c. hereditary material can pass from cell to cell.
   d. DNA is the hereditary molecule in viruses.

_____ 4. Hershey and Chase used what organism in their experiments?

   a. *E. coli*   **b.** *S. pneumoniae*   **c.** *S. aureus*   **d.** *B. transformis*

_____ 5. The *S* strain and the *R* strain of *S. pneumoniae* are different in that
   a. the *R* strain produces a capsule but the *S* strain does not.
   b. the *S* strain produces a capsule but the *R* strain does not.
   c. the *R* strain is virulent but the *S* strain is not.
   d. the *R* strain contains protein but the *S* strain does not.

SHORT ANSWER Answer the questions in the space provided.

1. What was the purpose of Griffith's experiment 1, in which he injected a mouse with live *R* cells?

_____

_____

2. What was the purpose of Griffith's experiment 2, in which he injected a mouse with live *S* cells?

_____

_____

3. What was the purpose of Griffith's experiment 3, in which he injected a mouse with heat-killed *S* cells?

_____

_____

_____

4. What was the purpose of Griffith's experiment 4, in which he injected a mouse with a mixture of heat-killed *S* cells and live *R* cells?

_____

_____

_____

5. **Critical Thinking** Why is an *S* strain of bacteria able to cause disease in mammals but a *R* strain is not?

_____

_____

_____

STRUCTURES AND FUNCTIONS In the spaces provided, write the number of the experiment that resulted in the following conclusions.

Hershey-Chase's Experiments

Experiment Number	Preparation	Action	Result
Experiment 1	radioactive sulfur used to label protein in phage	infect *E. Coli* with sulfur-labeled phage	radioactive sulfur did not enter bacterial cell
Experiment 2	radioactive phosphorous used to label DNA in phage	infect *E. Coli* with phosphorous-labeled phage	radioactive phosporous entered bacterial cell

_____ 1. DNA is the hereditary material.

_____ 2. Protein is not the hereditary material.

SECTION 10-2 REVIEW

DNA STRUCTURE

VOCABULARY REVIEW Define the following terms and provide one example for each.

1. purine _____

_____

2. pyrimidine _____

_____

3. complementary base pair _____

_____

4. nitrogenous base _____

_____

MULTIPLE CHOICE Write the correct letter in the blank.

_____ 1. The primary function of DNA in cells is to

    a. serve as a storage form for unused nucleotides.

    b. occupy space in the nucleus to keep the nucleus from collapsing.

    c. store information that tells the cells which proteins to make.

    d. serve as a template for making long, spiral carbohydrates.

_____ 2. The two strands of a DNA molecule are held together by

    a. ionic bonds.   **b.** covalent bonds.   **c.** peptide bonds.   **d.** hydrogen bonds.

_____ 3. According to the base-pairing rules, guanine binds with

    a. cytosine.   **b.** adenine.   **c.** thymine.   **d.** guanine.

_____ 4. Which of the following is NOT a correct structure of a nucleotide?

    a. adenine—deoxyribose—phosphate   **c.** cytosine—deoxyribose—phosphate

    b. adenine—ribose—phosphate   **d.** guanine—deoxyribose—phosphate

_____ 5. The percentage of adenine in DNA is

    a. equal to the percentage of cytosine.

    b. equal to the percentage of thymine.

    c. not related to the percentage of thymine.

    d. equal to the percentage of guanine.

Name _____ Class _____ Date _____

SHORT ANSWER Answer the questions in the space provided.

1. What are the three parts of a DNA nucleotide, and how are they connected to each other?

_____

_____

2. If 15% of the nucleotides in a DNA molecule contain guanine, what percentage of the nucleotides

contain each of the other three bases? Explain your reasoning. _____

_____

_____

3. Why is complementary base pairing important in DNA structure?

_____

_____

_____

4. **Critical Thinking** How did X-ray diffraction photographs help Watson and Crick determine the structure of DNA?

_____

_____

STRUCTURES AND FUNCTIONS Label each part of the figure in the spaces provided.

The diagram below shows two nucleotide base pairs in a segment of a DNA molecule.

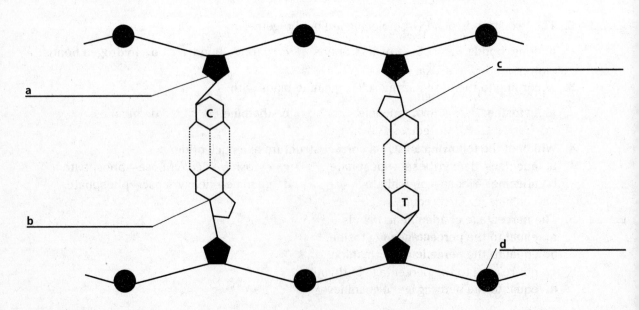

a _____

b _____

c _____

d _____

SECTION 10-3 REVIEW

DNA REPLICATION

VOCABULARY REVIEW Define the following terms.

1. replication fork _____

_____

2. helicase _____

_____

3. semi-conservative replication _____

_____

MULTIPLE CHOICE Write the correct letter in the blank.

_____ **1.** Before replication can take place,

    a. DNA polymerases must add complementary nucleotides to the DNA.
    b. the two strands of DNA must separate.
    c. the covalent bonds in DNA must break.
    d. helicases must break the bonds in the nucleotides.

_____ **2.** Replication of the two DNA strands takes place

    a. in two different directions.
    b. in the same direction of the replication fork.
    c. in a direction opposite to that of the replication fork.
    d. at right angles to the direction of the replication fork.

_____ **3.** In replication in prokaryotes,

    a. there are two origins.
    b. two replication forks move in opposite directions.
    c. replication proceeds in one direction.
    d. there are no replication forks.

_____ **4.** A mutation is a
    a. change in the direction of a replication fork.
    b. form of cancer.
    c. kind of DNA replication.
    d. change in the nucleotide sequence of DNA.

_____ **5.** Which of the following enzymes is involved with breaking hydrogen bonds?

    a. DNA polymerase   **c.** DNA helicase
    b. DNA ligase   **d.** Both a and b

SHORT ANSWER Answer the questions in the space provided.

1. How does replication occur so quickly in eukaryotes?

   _____

   _____

2. Why is it important that exact copies of DNA are produced during replication?

   _____

   _____

3. How is DNA replication related to cancer?

   _____

   _____

4. **Critical Thinking** Why is it advantageous to have weak hydrogen bonds between complementary bases and strong covalent bonds between phosphate and deoxyribose groups in a DNA molecule?

   _____

   _____

STRUCTURES AND FUNCTIONS The figure below shows DNA replicating. In the space provided, describe what is occurring at each lettered section of the figure.

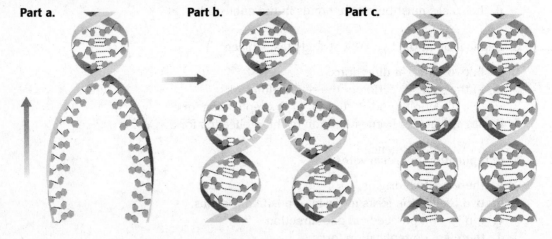

Part a.   **Part b.**   **Part c.**

Part a. _____

   _____

Part b. _____

   _____

Part c. _____

   _____

SECTION 10-4 REVIEW

PROTEIN SYNTHESIS

VOCABULARY REVIEW Define the following terms.

1. codon _____

_____

2. translation _____

_____

3. anticodon _____

_____

MULTIPLE CHOICE Write the correct letter in the blank.

_____ 1. A protein is a polymer consisting of a specific sequence of

    a. amino acids.   **c.** RNA nucleotides.
    b. fatty acids.   **d.** DNA nucleotides.

_____ 2. The genetic code specifies the correlation between

    a. a DNA-nucleotide sequence and an RNA-nucleotide sequence.
    b. an mRNA-nucleotide sequence and a tRNA-nucleotide sequence.
    c. an mRNA-nucleotide sequence and an rRNA-nucleotide sequence.
    d. an RNA-nucleotide sequence and an amino-acid sequence.

_____ 3. During translation, one end of a tRNA molecule pairs with a complementary

    a. nucleotide sequence in DNA.   **c.** tRNA molecule.
    b. mRNA codon.   **d.** protein molecule.

_____ 4. In eukaryotic cells, RNA is copied from DNA in the

    a. ribosomes.   **c.** nuclear membrane.
    b. nucleus.   **d.** cytosol.

_____ 5. Two amino acids are linked by a peptide bond when

    a. two ribosomes attach simultaneously to the same mRNA transcript.
    b. two tRNAs pair with neighboring codons on an mRNA transcript.
    c. two codons on an mRNA transcript bind to each other.
    d. a ribosome attaches to two codons on an mRNA transcript.

SHORT ANSWER Answer the questions in the space provided.

1. List, in order, the tRNA anticodons that are complementary to the mRNA sequence

   AUGCAUGCAAGUUAG. _____

   How many amino acids will be in the polypeptide that is initially formed when this mRNA

   sequence is translated? _____

2. Explain why methionine is the first amino acid in every growing polypeptide. _____

   _____

3. Describe three ways that RNA differs from DNA. _____

   _____

   _____

4. **Critical Thinking** How would a deletion of one nucleotide in the middle of an mRNA transcript

   affect the polypeptide specified by that transcript? _____

   _____

   _____

   _____

STRUCTURES AND FUNCTIONS Label each part of the figure in the spaces provided.

The diagram below summarizes the events that occur during translation.

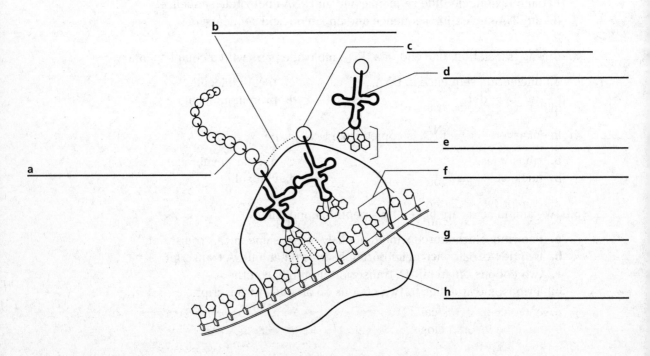

CONTROL OF GENE EXPRESSION

VOCABULARY REVIEW Explain the relationship between the terms in each of the following pairs of terms.

1. regulator gene, repressor protein _____

_____

2. operator, operon _____

_____

3. intron, exon _____

_____

4. transcription factor, enhancer _____

_____

MULTIPLE CHOICE Write the correct letter in the blank.

_____ **1.** A gene is expressed when it is

    a. present in the genome of an individual.
    b. prevented from interacting with RNA polymerase.
    c. transcribed into mRNA.
    d. duplicated during the replication of DNA.

_____ **2.** In the *lac* operon of *E. coli,* lactose functions as

    a. a promoter.   **b.** an operator.   **c.** a repressor protein   **d.** an inducer.

_____ **3.** In eukaryotic cells, transcription occurs

    a. on parts of the DNA that are uncoiled.   **c.** only on exons.
    b. only on introns.   **d.** on all parts of the DNA.

_____ **4.** Unlike gene expression in prokaryotes, gene expression in eukaryotes

    a. cannot be regulated before transcription has occurred.
    b. can be regulated after transcription has occurred.
    c. does not involve promoters.
    d. involves the transcription of groups of genes called operons.

_____ **5.** Enhancers

    a. code for proteins called inducers.   **c.** are found only in prokaryotic genomes.
    b. must be located close to the genes   **d.** facilitate transcription by binding to
        they activate.   transcription factors.

SHORT ANSWER Answer the questions in the space provided.

1. What is an operon, and in what type of organism are operons found? _____

_____

2. Describe what occurs during activation of the *lac* operon. _____

_____

_____

3. Describe what occurs during repression of the *lac* operon. _____

_____

4. **Critical Thinking** How does the absence of a nuclear envelope in prokaryotes prevent prokaryotes from controlling gene expression by modifying RNA after transcription?

_____

_____

STRUCTURES AND FUNCTIONS Use the figure to answer the following questions.

1. The diagram below represents the *lac* operon in the presence of lactose. Label each part of the diagram in the space provided.

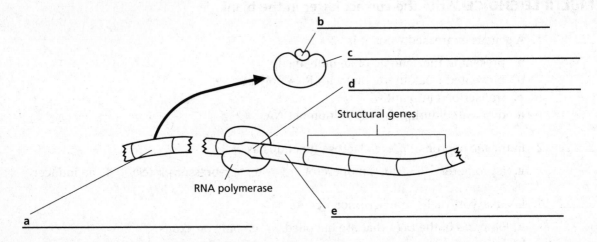

2. If the regulator gene were deleted, how would this affect expression of the structural genes?

Explain your answer. _____

_____

3. Is transcription of the structural genes activated or repressed under the conditions shown

above? Explain your answer. _____

_____

SECTION 11-2 REVIEW

GENE EXPRESSION IN DEVELOPMENT AND CELL DIVISION

VOCABULARY REVIEW Distinguish between the terms in each of the following pairs of terms.

1. homeobox, homeotic gene _____

_____

2. proto-oncogene, oncogene _____

_____

3. sarcoma, lymphoma _____

_____

4. oncogene, tumor-suppressor gene _____

_____

MULTIPLE CHOICE Write the correct letter in the blank.

_____ 1. The expression of different genes in different cells of a multicellular organism

    a. contributes to the development of form in an organism.
    b. causes the uncontrolled proliferation of cells.
    c. is caused by the transfer of cells from one organism to another.
    d. results from mutations that destroy normal gene functioning.

_____ 2. Homeoboxes are

    a. found only in prokaryotes.
    b. found only in *Drosophila.*
    c. mutations that can have devastating consequences on development.
    d. DNA sequences that regulate patterns of development.

_____ 3. The major distinguishing characteristic of cancer is

    a. uncontrolled cell division.
    b. production of viruses.
    c. metastasis.
    d. tumor formation.

_____ 4. More than 85 percent of all lung cancers are caused by

    a. asbestos.   **b.** tobacco smoke.   **c.** X rays.   **d.** ultraviolet light.

_____ **5.** A gene whose normal function is to prevent uncontrolled cell division is

    a. an oncogene.   **c.** a homeotic gene.

    b. a cancer gene.   **d.** a tumor-suppressor gene.

SHORT ANSWER Answer the questions in the space provided.

1. How do homeotic genes regulate development in *Drosophila?* _____

_____

_____

2. What factors influence whether a person will develop cancer? _____

_____

_____

3. How can viruses induce cancer? _____

_____

4. What are two key characteristics of cancer cells? _____

_____

5. **Critical Thinking** A great deal of research on the causes of and a possible cure for cancer focuses

on the genes that control the cell cycle. Why? _____

_____

_____

_____

STRUCTURES AND FUNCTIONS Complete the flowchart below by filling in the three boxes at the bottom.

```
  ┌──────────────────┐              ┌──────────────────┐
  │ Proto-oncogenes  │              │ Tumor-suppressor │
  │                  │              │     genes        │
  └──────────────────┘              └──────────────────┘

        Normal         ( Mutations )          Normal

  ┌──────────────┐   ┌──────────────┐   ┌──────────────┐
  │ Effect:      │   │ Effect:      │   │ Effect:      │
  │              │   │              │   │              │
  │              │   │              │   │              │
  │              │   │              │   │              │
  └──────────────┘   └──────────────┘   └──────────────┘
```

CHROMOSOMES AND INHERITANCE

VOCABULARY REVIEW Distinguish between the terms in each of the following pairs of terms.

1. sex chromosome, autosome _____

_____

2. germ-cell mutation, somatic-cell mutation _____

_____

3. translocation, nondisjunction _____

_____

_____

4. deletion, inversion _____

_____

5. substitution, frameshift mutation _____

_____

_____

MULTIPLE CHOICE Write the correct letter in the blank.

_____ 1. Genes that belong to the same linkage group tend to be

    a. located on different chromosomes.   **c.** found only in males.
    b. inherited together.   **d.** found only in somatic cells.

_____ 2. Two genes that are one map unit apart are separated by crossing-over

    a. 1% of the time.   **b.** 20% of the time.   **c.** 50% of the time.   **d.** 100% of the time.

_____ 3. Mutations that can be inherited arise in

    a. somatic cells.   **b.** body cells.   **c.** germ cells.   **d.** skin cells.

_____ 4. Which of the following sequences could result from an inversion of the sequence GAGACATT?

    a. GAGCATT   **b.** GTGACATT   **c.** CTCTGATT   **d.** GATACAGT

_____ 5. Which of the following is a point mutation that does not produce a frameshift?

    a. substitution   **b.** insertion   **c.** deletion   **d.** inversion

SHORT ANSWER Answer the questions in the space provided.

1. In humans and fruit flies, which parent determines the sex of the offspring? Explain why. _____

_____

_____

2. How did Morgan determine that red-eye color in *Drosophila* is an X-linked trait? _____

_____

_____

_____

3. Explain why traits that are controlled by genes on the same chromosome do not always appear

in the expected ratio in offspring. _____

_____

_____

4. **Critical Thinking** Would a frameshift mutation have a more serious effect if it occurred near

the beginning of a gene or the end of a gene? Explain your answer. _____

_____

_____

_____

STRUCTURES AND FUNCTIONS Use the data in the table below to indicate the position of these genes on the chromosome map shown below. Assuming that the gene for white eyes has a chromosome map unit number of 1, write the map unit numbers above each gene's position on the chromosome map.

The *Drosophila* genes for white eyes, vermilion eyes, and miniature wings are located on the same chromosome. The table shows how often these genes are separated by crossing-over.

Genes	Frequency of crossing-over
Vermilion eyes and miniature wings	3%
White eyes and vermilion eyes	30%
White eyes and miniature wings	33%

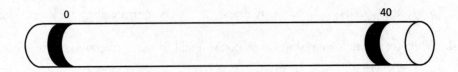

0   40

SECTION 12-2 REVIEW

HUMAN GENETICS

VOCABULARY REVIEW Name a trait or genetic disorder that is caused by each of the following patterns of inheritance.

1. polygenic inheritance _____

2. multiple alleles _____

3. autosomal dominant _____

4. sex-influenced trait _____

MULTIPLE CHOICE Write the correct letter in the blank.

_____ 1. Which individual(s) in the pedigree shown below must be a carrier?

   a. 1 only
   b. 4 only
   c. 3 only
   d. both 1 and 4

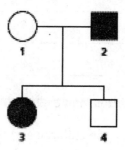

_____ 2. Since the ABO blood group alleles are codominant, an individual with the genotype $I^A I^B$ will have blood type

   a. A.   **b.** B.   **c.** AB.   **d.** O.

_____ 3. Which of the following human traits is not a polygenic trait?

   a. skin color   **b.** eye color   **c.** height   **d.** ABO blood type

_____ 4. A trait whose expression is affected by the presence of sex hormones is said to be

   a. sex-influenced.   **b.** sex-linked.   **c.** X-linked.   **d.** Y-linked.

_____ 5. In humans, PKU can be treated by

   a. insulin injections.   **c.** gene therapy.
   b. diet.   **d.** surgery.

SHORT ANSWER Answer the questions in the space provided.

1. Why is pattern baldness more common in men than in women? _____

_____

_____

_____

2. Briefly describe how amniocentesis and chorionic villi sampling are used in genetic screening.

_____

_____

_____

_____

3. Explain the difference between a sex-linked trait and a sex-influenced trait.

_____

_____

_____

_____

4. **Critical Thinking** A couple has four children, and each child has a different ABO blood type.

   What are the blood types and genotypes of the children and the parents? _____

_____

_____

STRUCTURES AND FUNCTIONS In the two pedigrees below, indicate all possible offspring in generation II by correctly filling in the male and female symbols for generation II. Use a completely filled symbol to represent an individual who displays the trait and a half-filled symbol to represent a carrier.

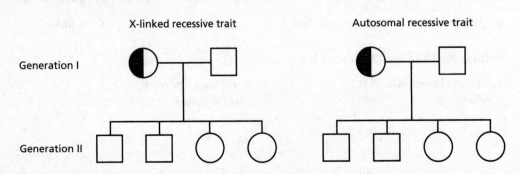

DNA TECHNOLOGY

VOCABULARY REVIEW Define the following terms.

1. DNA fingerprint _____

_____

2. gel electrophoresis _____

_____

3. probe _____

_____

4. primer _____

_____

MULTIPLE CHOICE Write the correct letter in the blank.

_____ 1. To cut DNA molecules into pieces at specific sequences of nucleotides, genetic engineers use
  a. cloning vectors.
  b. insulin.
  c. bacteria.
  d. restriction enzymes.

_____ 2. In gel electrophoresis, DNA fragments migrate toward one end of a gel because they are
  a. pulled toward that end by gravity.
  b. attracted to complementary DNA fragments at that end of the gel.
  c. attracted to the positively charged end of the gel.
  d. repelled by hydrophobic molecules at the other end of the gel.

_____ 3. The accuracy of DNA fingerprinting can be increased by comparing
  a. segments of DNA that tend to vary the least from person to person.
  b. noncoding segments from several loci.
  c. DNA from identical twins.
  d. repeat patterns at only one or two sites in the genome.

_____ 4. In addition to DNA polymerase and primers, the polymerase chain reaction also requires
  a. a large amount of DNA.
  b. restriction enzymes.
  c. a supply of the four DNA nucleotides.
  d. complementary sequences of RNA.

_____ 5. To obtain bacteria that produce insulin, genetic engineers
  a. remove repressor proteins that inhibit the expression of the bacterial insulin gene.
  b. insert a vector containing the human gene for insulin into bacteria.
  c. search for bacteria that can grow in a medium that lacks insulin.
  d. grow normal bacteria in a nutrient medium that contains a large amount of sugar.

Name _____ Class _____ Date _____

SHORT ANSWER Answer the questions in the space provided.

1. How are radioactive probes useful in DNA fingerprinting? _____

_____

_____

2. How is the polymerase chain reaction useful in DNA fingerprinting? _____

_____

_____

3. **Critical Thinking** Why is it necessary to use the same restriction enzyme to cut two pieces of

DNA that are to be joined together? _____

_____

4. List three ways that DNA technology could be used to improve the lives of humans. _____

_____

_____

STRUCTURES AND FUNCTIONS In the spaces provided, write the names for the objects labeled *a–f*.

The diagram below summarizes the procedure for transferring a human gene into a bacterium.

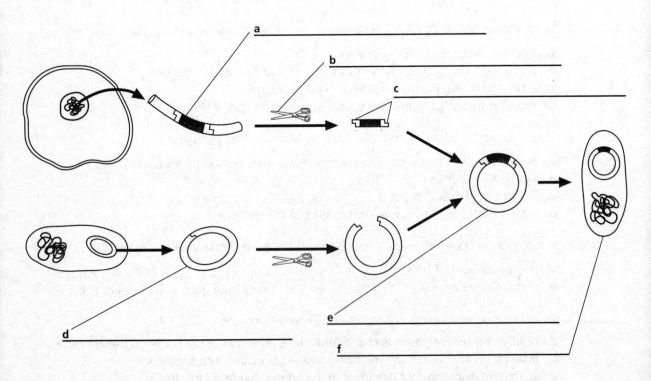

a _____

b _____

c _____

d _____

e _____

f _____

SECTION 13-2 REVIEW

THE HUMAN GENOME PROJECT

VOCABULARY REVIEW Define the following terms.

1. proteomics _____

_____

2. bioinformatics _____

_____

3. single nucleotide polymorphisms (SNP) _____

_____

4. Human Genome Project _____

_____

MULTIPLE CHOICE Write the correct letter in the blank.

_____ 1. One of the goals of the Human Genome Project is to
a. increase the number of genes in the human genome.
b. map the location of only the most important genes on each chromosome.
c. clone the entire human genome in bacteria.
d. determine the nucleotide sequence of the entire human genome.

_____ 2. One of the surprising discoveries of the Human Genome Project was that
a. the human genome consists of only about 30,000 to 40,000 genes.
b. 98 percent of the human genome codes for proteins.
c. each gene encodes only a single protein.
d. the human genome contains no transposons.

_____ 3. An understanding of the human genome is aided by an understanding of
a. mathematics.   c. DNA fingerprints.
b. computer science.   d. the genomes of model species.

_____ 4. What percentage of the human genome codes for proteins?
a. 98 percent
b. 10 percent
c. 25 percent
d. 2 percent

_____ 5. A DNA microarray is an important tool because it
a. can cure cancer.   c. identifies an individual.
b. shows which genes are active in a cell.   d. dyes tumor cells to kill them.

SHORT ANSWER Answer the questions in the space provided.

1. Why did scientists want to map the human genome? _____

_____

_____

2. List three important discoveries that resulted from the Human Genome Project. _____

_____

_____

_____

3. **Critical Thinking** Why is it more important to understand the human proteome than the

human genome? _____

_____

_____

STRUCTURES AND FUNCTIONS Use the table to answer the following questions in the spaces provided.

1. What is the relationship, if any, between the complexity of an organism and the size of its genome?

_____

_____

_____

_____

_____

Kingdom	Organism (common name)	Genome size (million bases)	Number of genes
Archaebacteria	Pyrococcus	1.9	2,065
Eubacteria	Chlamydia	1.0	894
	E. coli	4.6	4,289
Protista	Amoeba	34	~9,000
Fungi	Yeast	12	6,000
Plantae	Mustard	125	23,174
	Easter lily	100,000	~25,000
Animalia	Fruitfly	120	13,600
	Roundworm	97	19,049
	Frog	1,700	~30,000
	Human	3,300	35,000
	Mouse	3,630	~30,000
	Zebrafish	1,700	~3,000

2. What might explain why there is not a direct relationship between the size of an organism's genome and the number of genes it contains?

_____

_____

_____

SECTION 13-3 REVIEW

GENETIC ENGINEERING

VOCABULARY REVIEW Define the following terms.

1. DNA vaccine _____

_____

2. telomere _____

_____

3. bioethics _____

_____

4. gene therapy _____

_____

MULTIPLE CHOICE Write the correct letter in the blank.

_____ 1. Many of the pharmaceutical products being produced by DNA technology are

    a. carbohydrates.   **b.** lipids.   **c.** proteins.   **d.** polysaccharides.

_____ 2. When the human body mobilizes its defenses against a pathogen, the body recognizes the pathogen's

    a. surface proteins. **b.** DNA.   **c.** RNA.   **d.** genome.

_____ 3. DNA technology is being used to develop crop plants that are

    a. less toxic to the pests that normally feed on them.

    b. more susceptible to herbicides.

    c. unable to fix nitrogen in the atmosphere.

    d. resistant to some diseases.

_____ 4. Scientists have inserted genes into rice plants that

    a. code for enzymes that cause rice to ripen quickly.

    b. increase the iron and beta carotene levels.

    c. code for substances that cause allergies in people.

    d. increase the thickness of the seed coat.

_____ 5. Some people are concerned that genetically engineered crop plants could

    a. transmit their new genes to wild plant species, producing "superweeds."

    b. transmit their new genes to the animals that eat the plants, producing "superanimals."

    c. exchange genes with animals, producing plant-animal hybrids.

    d. be wiped out by native plant species.

SHORT ANSWER Answer the questions in the space provided.

1. How does a DNA vaccine prevent future disease? _____

   _____

   _____

   _____

2. If Dolly's cloning was successful, why was her lifespan shorter than normal? _____

   _____

   _____

3. Why doesn't gene therapy cure cystic fibrosis? _____

   _____

   _____

4. Describe a potential problem that could arise from genetic engineering. _____

   _____

5. **Critical Thinking** What is a possible beneficial change besides those mentioned in the text that

   could be made to crop plants using DNA technology? _____

   _____

   _____

STRUCTURES AND FUNCTIONS The flowchart below summarizes some of the successes of genetic engineering. Complete the chart by filling in the blanks.

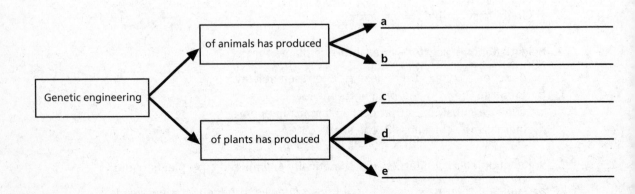

SECTION 14-1 REVIEW

BIOGENESIS

VOCABULARY REVIEW Define the following terms.

1. biogenesis _____

2. spontaneous generation _____

3. vital force _____

MULTIPLE CHOICE Write the correct letter in the blank.

_____ 1. One of the observations that led people to think that life could arise from nonliving things was that

    a. maggots turned into oval cases from which flies eventually emerged.
    b. fish appeared in ponds that had been dry the previous season.
    c. large fish developed from smaller fish, which hatched from fish eggs.
    d. fish grew larger by eating other living things, such as flies.

_____ 2. The purpose of the netting in Redi's experiment was to prevent

    a. maggots from leaving the jar.
    b. air from leaving the jar.
    c. adult flies from entering the jar.
    d. bacteria from entering the jar.

_____ 3. In the experimental group in Spallanzani's experiment, the

    a. broth remained clear.
    b. flask contained no broth.
    c. broth was not boiled.
    d. flask was not sealed.

_____ 4. Spallanzani's opponents disagreed with his conclusion that microorganisms from the air contaminated the boiled meat broth. They argued that Spallanzani

    a. heated the flasks too long, killing the microorganisms in the broth.
    b. heated the flasks too long, destroying the "vital force" in the air inside the flasks.
    c. waited too long before he sealed the flasks after heating them.
    d. accidentally contaminated the broth when he sealed the flasks.

_____ 5. In Pasteur's experiment, the function of the curved neck on the flask was to prevent

    a. air from entering the body of the flask.
    b. air from leaving the body of the flask.
    c. solid particles from entering the body of the flask.
    d. broth from spilling out of the flask.

Name _____ Class _____ Date _____

SHORT ANSWER Answer the questions in the space provided.

1. What observations made in the 1600s and 1700s led some people to believe that there was a "vital force" in the air? _____

_____

_____

2. Why did Spallanzani boil the broth in his experiment? _____

_____

_____

3. How did Pasteur's experiment differ from Spallanzani's experiment? _____

_____

_____

_____

4. How did Pasteur's experiment answer the objections raised by supporters of the "vital force" hypothesis? _____

_____

_____

5. **Critical Thinking** How might the believers in spontaneous generation have disputed Redi's conclusion if Redi had not used a control group? _____

_____

_____

STRUCTURES AND FUNCTIONS The diagrams below illustrate steps in the control and experimental groups of Spallanzani's experiment. In the spaces provided, list the steps in each group in their proper order. A step may be used in more than one group.

Broth becomes cloudy.	Flask is sealed.	Broth is boiled.	Broth remains clear.	Flask is open.
a	b	c	d	e

Control group _____

Experimental group _____

EARTH'S HISTORY

VOCABULARY REVIEW Explain the relationship between the terms in each of the following pairs of terms.

1. radioactive isotope, radioactive dating _____

_____

2. radioactive decay, half-life _____

_____

_____

3. microsphere, coacervate _____

_____

_____

MULTIPLE CHOICE Write the correct letter in the blank.

_____ 1. The age of Earth is estimated to be

    a. about 700,000 years.   **c.** about 400 million years.
    b. about 50 million years.   **d.** more than 4 billion years.

_____ 2. Sulfur has an atomic number of 16. Therefore, the isotope sulfur-35 has

    a. 19 protons and 16 neutrons.   **c.** 16 protons and 19 neutrons.
    b. 35 protons and 16 neutrons.   **d.** 16 protons and 35 neutrons.

_____ 3. When performing radioactive dating, scientists measure the

    a. number of protons and neutrons in the nucleus of a radioactive isotope.
    b. amount of a particular radioactive isotope contained in a material.
    c. age of a living organism that is exposed to radioactive isotopes.
    d. rate at which the mass of an object decreases over time.

_____ 4. Carbon-14 dating is useful for estimating the age of

    a. relatively young organic material.   **c.** Earth.
    b. old rocks.   **d.** the solar system.

_____ 5. Researchers using the technique of Miller and Urey have been able to produce

    a. amino acids and nucleotides.   **c.** ATP and mitochondria.
    b. proteins and DNA.   **d.** cell membranes and simple cells.

SHORT ANSWER Answer the questions in the space provided.

1. Explain how the half-life of a radioactive isotope affects the usefulness of that isotope in dating specific types of rocks. _____

_____

_____

2. Why do some scientists think that areas protected from the atmosphere might have favored the production of organic compounds on early Earth? _____

_____

_____

3. Why was the discovery of microspheres and coacervates an important contribution to the understanding of how life might have originated on Earth? _____

_____

_____

4. **Critical Thinking** Does radioactive dating with isotopes of uranium and thorium provide an estimate of the beginning, middle, or end of the period of Earth's formation? Explain your answer.

_____

_____

_____

_____

STRUCTURES AND FUNCTIONS Use the figure to answer the following question.

The graph below represents the radioactive decay of an isotope. If the half-life of thorium-230 is 75,000 years, how old is a rock that contains only 1/16th of its original thorium-230? Show your calculations in the space below.

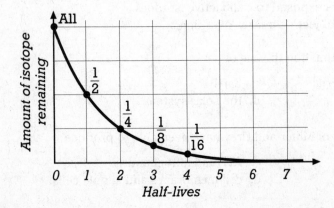

SECTION 14-3 REVIEW

THE FIRST LIFE-FORMS

VOCABULARY REVIEW Define the following terms.

1. ribozyme _____

2. chemosynthesis _____

_____

3. cyanobacteria _____

4. endosymbiosis _____

_____

_____

MULTIPLE CHOICE Write the correct letter in the blank.

_____ 1. The idea that life may have started with self-replicating molecules of RNA is based on the observation that RNA can

    a. take on a great variety of shapes and act as an enzyme.
    b. link nucleotides together to form proteins.
    c. create proteins that have the ability to replicate themselves.
    d. produce ribozymes that have the ability to produce other ribozymes.

_____ 2. The first organisms on Earth were probably

    a. autotrophic, aerobic eukaryotes.
    b. heterotrophic, aerobic eukaryotes.
    c. autotrophic, aerobic prokaryotes.
    d. heterotrophic, anaerobic prokaryotes.

_____ 3. The main difference between chemosynthetic autotrophs and photosynthetic autotrophs is that only

    a. photosynthetic autotrophs use CO_2 as a carbon source.
    b. chemosynthetic autotrophs use CO_2 as a carbon source.
    c. chemosynthetic autotrophs obtain energy from inorganic molecules.
    d. photosynthetic autotrophs synthesize organic compounds.

_____ 4. An early function of aerobic respiration may have been to

    a. increase the amount of oxygen in the upper atmosphere.
    b. prevent the destruction of essential organic compounds by oxygen.
    c. provide more oxygen for photosynthesis.
    d. enable land animals to breathe.

_____ 5. The eukaryotic organelle that is thought to have evolved from aerobic prokaryotes is the

    a. chloroplast.   **b.** nucleus.   **c.** ribosome.   **d.** mitochondrion.

SHORT ANSWER Answer the questions in the space provided.

1. Explain how early RNA molecules might have been able to respond to natural selection. _____

_____

_____

_____

2. What role did the appearance of the ozone layer play in the evolution of early life on Earth?

_____

_____

_____

3. Name three characteristics of mitochondria and chloroplasts that support the endosymbiotic

hypothesis of eukaryotic evolution. _____

_____

_____

4. **Critical Thinking** How would endosymbiosis have been mutually beneficial for pre-eukaryotic

cells and for the small prokaryotes that invaded them? _____

_____

_____

_____

_____

STRUCTURES AND FUNCTIONS Arrange the organisms listed below in the order in which
they are thought to have originated on Earth by writing their names in the spaces provided
in the figure.

photosynthetic prokaryotes
photosynthetic eukaryotes
chemosynthetic prokaryotes
aerobic eukaryotes
heterotrophic prokaryotes

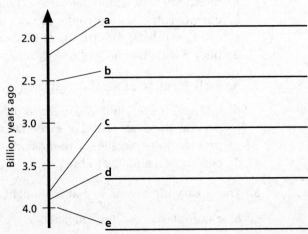

SECTION 15-1 REVIEW

HISTORY OF EVOLUTIONARY THOUGHT

VOCABULARY REVIEW Define the following terms.

1. evolution _____

_____

2. natural selection _____

_____

MULTIPLE CHOICE Write the correct letter in the blank.

_____ 1. If Lamarck's hypothesis of species modification were true, the children of a person who developed large muscles by lifting weights would be born with

    a. smaller-than-average muscles.
    b. normal-sized muscles.
    c. normal-sized muscles that would become larger only if the children also lifted weights.
    d. larger-than-average muscles.

_____ 2. What is the idea developed by Charles Lyell stating that the geologic processes that shaped Earth in the past continue to operate today?

    a. inheritance of acquired characteristics   **c.** uniformitarianism
    b. catastrophism   **d.** descent with modification

_____ 3. Darwin used the phrase "descent with modification" to mean that

    a. new species descended from preexisting species, and species must be able to change over time.
    b. organisms that descend from high elevations are modified as they acquire new traits.
    c. all living things descended from a recent common ancestor on the Galápagos Islands.
    d. individuals modify their behavior to survive and then pass those modifications on to their descendants.

_____ 4. According to Darwin's theory of natural selection,

    a. individuals are modified by adverse environmental conditions.
    b. the environment affects all organisms in a population in the same way.
    c. populations of all organisms grow unchecked under natural conditions.
    d. organisms that have more favorable traits tend to leave more offspring.

_____ 5. In an evolutionary sense, an individual organism has high fitness if it

    a. has a large number of acquired traits.
    b. can run long distances without becoming exhausted.
    c. reproduces more successfully than other individuals.
    d. evolves into another organism rather than becoming extinct.

SHORT ANSWER Answer the questions in the space provided.

1. Why are acquired traits not directly related to the process of evolution? _____
   _____
   _____

2. How did the ideas of Thomas Malthus influence Darwin's thinking about evolution? _____
   _____
   _____

3. What is the relationship between evolution and natural selection? _____
   _____
   _____

4. **Critical Thinking** If Lamarck and Darwin had debated why giraffes have such long necks, how
   would their explanations have differed? _____
   _____
   _____
   _____

STRUCTURES AND FUNCTIONS Use the figure to answer the following question.

Which of the parent birds shown below (*A* or *B*) appears to have greater fitness? Explain your answer.

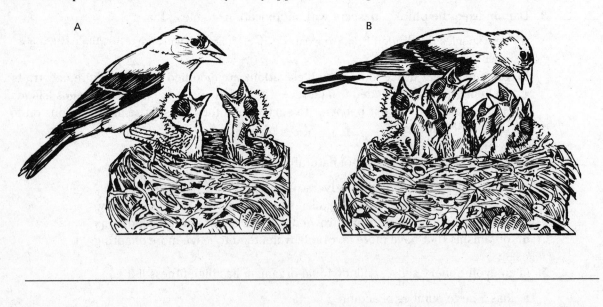

_____
_____
_____

SECTION 15-2 REVIEW

EVIDENCE OF EVOLUTION

VOCABULARY REVIEW Explain the relationship between the terms in each of the following pairs of terms.

1. homologous structure, analogous structure _____

_____

2. fossil, principle of superposition _____

_____

3. relative age, absolute age _____

_____

MULTIPLE CHOICE Write the correct letter in the blank.

_____ 1. The wing of a bat and the foreleg of an alligator are

    a. analogous features.   **c.** vestigial features.
    b. homologous features.   **d.** artificially selected features.

_____ 2. Features that were useful to an ancestral organism but are not useful to a modern organism that inherited them are said to be

    a. analogous.   **b.** homologous.   **c.** vestigial.   **d.** artificially selected.

_____ 3. According to the principle of superposition, the lowest layer in a cross section of a rock sequence

    a. is the most recent.   **c.** has the fewest fossils.
    b. is the oldest.   **d.** contains only the fossils of burrowing animals.

_____ 4. Embryological comparisons reveal that

    a. many vertebrate embryos look similar at early stages of development.
    b. embryos of different vertebrates look more similar as development proceeds.
    c. rabbit embryos look like adult fish.
    d. gorillas begin life as fish and then develop into gorillas during an embryonic stage.

_____ 5. Fossils are

    a. remains or traces of preexisting organisms.
    b. all extinct organisms.
    c. deeply buried sedimentary rock strata.
    d. from animals but not plants.

SHORT ANSWER Answer the questions in the space provided.

1. When trying to determine the evolutionary relationship between two species, would a biologist

   concentrate on homologous features or analogous features? Explain why. _____

   _____

2. If an animal has a vestigial structure, what might a biologist infer about the animal's evolutionary

   history? _____

   _____

3. How does biogeography contribute to an understanding of evolution? _____

   _____

   _____

   _____

4. Explain the evidence that indicates that species evolve over time.

   _____

   _____

   _____

5. **Critical Thinking** Why do vestigial structures persist in modern organisms? _____

   _____

   _____

STRUCTURES AND FUNCTIONS   Indicate the relative ages of the fossilized organisms
listed below by placing them in a strata on the diagram of a cross section of sedimentary
rock below.

   trilobites, mammal fossils, oldest fossil, youngest fossil, first land plants, first dinosaurs

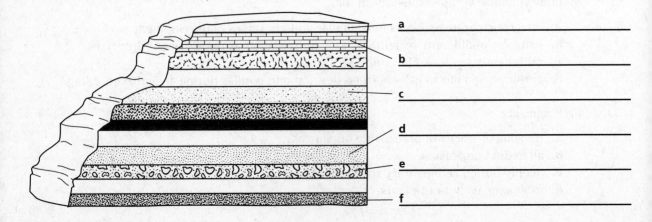

a _____

b _____

c _____

d _____

e _____

f _____

SECTION 15-3 REVIEW

EVOLUTION IN ACTION

VOCABULARY REVIEW Provide one example for each of the following terms.

1. adaptive radiation _____

2. artificial selection _____

3. coevolution _____

4. convergent evolution _____

5. divergent evolution _____

6. resistance _____

MULTIPLE CHOICE Write the correct letter in the blank.

_____ 1. What is the process called by which different species evolve similar traits?

   a. coevolution.
   b. convergent evolution.
   c. divergent evolution.
   d. adaptive radiation.

_____ 2. The evolutionary pattern illustrated by the finch species on the Galápagos Islands is an example of

   a. coevolution.
   b. convergent evolution.
   c. divergent evolution.
   d. artificial selection.

_____ 3. Divergent evolution would be most likely in which of the following situations?

   a. A group of organisms is isolated from the main population on three isolated islands with different environmental conditions.
   b. Individuals in a large population experience the same environmental conditions.
   c. Individuals in a small population experience the same environmental conditions.
   d. A group of organisms which are well adapted to the environment live on a remote island.

_____ 4. The corresponding changes of two or more species that are closely associated with each other, such as a plant and an animal that pollinates it, are called

   a. adaptive radiation.
   b. divergent evolution.
   c. convergent evolution.
   d. coevolution.

_____ 5. In artificial selection, humans select for

   a. a desirable trait.
   b. an undesirable trait.
   c. a vestigial trait.
   d. a trait that makes the organisms less fit.

Name _____ Class _____ Date _____

SHORT ANSWER Answer the questions in the space provided.

1. What is adaptive radiation?

_____

_____

_____

2. What could happen to a tree-dwelling species of lizard if all the trees in an area died?

_____

_____

_____

3. Give three examples of artificial selection. Include examples of both animals and plants.

_____

_____

_____

4. **Critical Thinking** Would a species that lives a long time, but has few offspring, be more or less likely to become extinct after a sudden change in its environment than a species that has a short life, but produces large numbers of offspring? Explain.

_____

_____

_____

STRUCTURES AND FUNCTIONS

The diagram shows several groups of primates and a hypothesis of how they are related based on differences in DNA. What pattern of evolution does the diagram represent? According to this hypothesis, when did the rhesus monkey and the green monkey diverge? Which group of primates existed before the others?

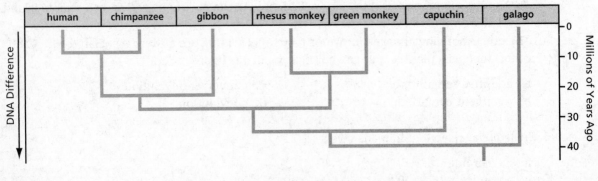

_____

_____

SECTION 16-1 REVIEW

GENETIC EQUILIBRIUM

VOCABULARY REVIEW Define the following terms.

1. population genetics _____

_____

2. gene pool _____

_____

3. allele frequency _____

_____

4. phenotype frequency _____

_____

5. Hardy-Weinberg genetic equilibrium _____

_____

MULTIPLE CHOICE Write the correct letter in the blank.

_____ 1. The smallest unit in which evolution occurs is

    a. an individual organism.   **c.** a species.
    b. a population.   **d.** a kingdom.

_____ 2. Length, weight, and many other quantitative traits in a population tend to show variation
that, when plotted on a graph, looks like

    a. a population wave.   **c.** a bell curve.
    b. a gene pool.   **d.** an equilibrium plot.

_____ 3. If a population of four o'clock flowers consists of five *RR* plants (red flowers), two *Rr*
plants (pink flowers), and one *rr* plant (white flowers), the phenotype frequency of plants
with pink flowers is

    a. 0.125.   **b.** 0.25.   **c.** 0.5.   **d.** 0.75.

_____ 4. In the population described in question 3, the frequency of the *R* allele is

    a. 0.125.   **b.** 0.25.   **c.** 0.5.   **d.** 0.75.

_____ 5. For a population to be in genetic equilibrium,

    a. individuals must not enter or leave   **c.** the population must be small.
       the population.   **d.** selection must occur.
    b. the population must be evolving.

SHORT ANSWER Answer the questions in the space provided.

1. What types of individuals in a population are represented by the two ends of a bell curve?

   _____

   _____

2. What are the three main ways that variations in genotype arise in a population? _____

   _____

   _____

3. What five assumptions must be made for the Hardy-Weinberg genetic equilibrium to apply to

   a population? _____

   _____

   _____

4. **Critical Thinking** Does a gene pool include the genes of individuals that cannot reproduce?

   Explain your answer. _____

   _____

   _____

STRUCTURES AND FUNCTIONS The drawing below shows a population of four o'clock flowers. Using the information given in the table below the drawing, predict the phenotype frequencies and allele frequencies in the offspring of this population. Write your answers in the table below. Show your calculations.

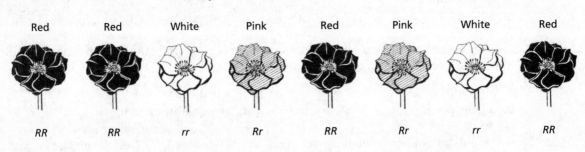

Red	Red	White	Pink	Red	Pink	White	Red
RR	RR	rr	Rr	RR	Rr	rr	RR

PARENTS		OFFSPRING	
Phenotype frequency	**Allele frequency**	**Phenotype frequency**	**Allele frequency**
Red: 0.5	R: 0.625	Red: _____	R: _____
White: 0.25	r: 0.375	White: _____	r: _____
Pink: 0.25		Pink: _____	

SECTION 16-2 REVIEW

DISRUPTION OF GENETIC EQUILIBRIUM

VOCABULARY REVIEW Distinguish between the terms in each of the following pairs of terms.

1. immigration, emigration _____

_____

2. gene flow, genetic drift _____

_____

3. random mating, assortative mating _____

_____

4. stabilizing selection, directional selection _____

_____

MULTIPLE CHOICE Write the correct letter in the blank.

_____ 1. Any violation of the conditions necessary for Hardy-Weinberg equilibrium can result in

    a. independent assortment.   **c.** evolution.
    b. disorganizing selection.   **d.** eventual extinction.

_____ 2. The movement of reproductive individuals from one population to another results in

    a. infertile offspring.   **c.** genetic drift.
    b. spontaneous mutation.   **d.** gene flow.

_____ 3. Genetic drift is most likely to occur in

    a. small populations.   **c.** populations that migrate.
    b. large populations.   **d.** populations that have a low frequency
                            of mutation.

_____ 4. Assortative mating occurs when

    a. one animal mates with a variety of other individuals during its lifetime.
    b. males choose to mate with females that are the most fertile.
    c. an individual chooses mates that are similar to itself.
    d. females choose to mate with males that are from other populations.

_____ 5. Starlings produce an average of five eggs in each clutch. If there are more than five, the parents cannot adequately feed the young. If there are fewer than five, predators may destroy the entire clutch. This is an example of

    a. disruptive selection.   **c.** directional selection.
    b. stabilizing selection.   **d.** sexual selection.

Name _____ Class _____ Date _____

SHORT ANSWER Answer the questions in the space provided.

1. List five conditions that can cause evolution to take place. _____

_____

2. Explain how a Hardy-Weinberg genetic equilibrium is affected by mutations. _____

_____

_____

3. What is one potential negative consequence of nonrandom mating based on geographic proximity?

_____

_____

4. How might being brightly colored increase the fitness of the males of some bird species? _____

_____

5. Why is genetic homozygosity dangerous to a nearly extinct species? _____

_____

6. Critical Thinking If a cow develops a preference for eating white four o'clock flowers and ignoring pink and red four o'clock flowers, what type of selection is being demonstrated? Would the cow eventually eliminate all white four o'clock flowers from the population on which it feeds?

_____

_____

_____

_____

STRUCTURES AND FUNCTIONS Label the three types of selection illustrated by the graphs below.

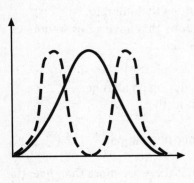

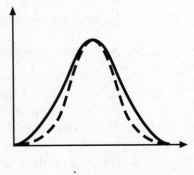

a _____   b _____   c _____

SECTION 16-3 REVIEW

FORMATION OF SPECIES

VOCABULARY REVIEW Define the following terms.

1. morphology _____

_____

2. geographic isolation _____

_____

3. punctuated equilibrium _____

_____

MULTIPLE CHOICE Write the correct letter in the blank.

_____ 1. One limitation of the morphological species concept is that

     a. morphological characteristics are not easy to observe.
     b. it cannot be applied to extinct organisms.
     c. members of different species often appear quite different.
     d. there can be morphological differences among individuals in a single population.

_____ 2. According to the biological species concept, a species is a population of organisms that

     a. can successfully interbreed but cannot breed with other groups.
     b. have a similar structure and appearance.
     c. are physically separated from other organisms with a similar appearance.
     d. can hybridize with each other to produce infertile offspring.

_____ 3. Fish populations that do not interbreed because they live in different ponds may evolve into separate species due to

     a. ecological isolation.   **c.** prezygotic isolation.
     b. geographic isolation.   **d.** postzygotic isolation.

_____ 4. Bird populations that do not interbreed because they cannot recognize each other's mating calls may evolve into separate species due to

     a. ecological isolation.   **c.** prezygotic isolation.
     b. geographic isolation.   **d.** postzygotic isolation.

_____ 5. A pattern of rapid evolutionary changes followed by long periods of no change is described as

     a. gradual evolution.   **c.** reproductive isolation.
     b. punctuated equilibrium.   **d.** continuous speciation.

SHORT ANSWER Answer the questions in the space provided.

1. What are two limitations of the biological species concept? _____

_____

2. What is one advantage of prezygotic isolation over postzygotic isolation? _____

_____

3. Describe two pieces of evidence indicating that speciation does not always occur at the same rate.

_____

_____

_____

_____

4. **Critical Thinking** Some scientists predict that if global warming continues over the next few centuries, melting of the polar ice caps will raise the level of the oceans, causing some peninsulas to become islands. How might this change eventually affect the species that live on these peninsulas?

_____

_____

_____

STRUCTURES AND FUNCTIONS The graph below shows the mating seasons of several species of frogs. On the basis of the information shown in the graph, do the peeper frog and the leopard frog likely have barriers to reproduction in addition to slightly different mating seasons? What other barriers might be in operation? Explain your answers.

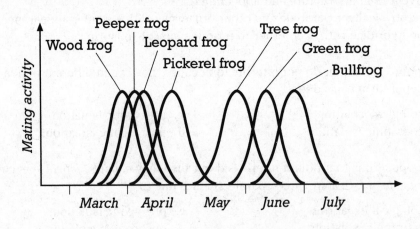

_____

_____

_____

SECTION 17-1 REVIEW

BIODIVERSITY

VOCABULARY REVIEW Distinguish between the terms in each of the following pairs of terms.

1. taxonomy, taxon _____

_____

2. kingdom, species _____

_____

3. phylum, division _____

_____

4. species name, species identifier _____

_____

5. species, subspecies _____

_____

MULTIPLE CHOICE Write the correct letter in the blank.

_____ **1.** Aristotle classified animals on the basis of

    a. their size.
    b. their evolutionary history.
    c. where they lived.
    d. what they ate.

_____ **2.** The main criterion used in Linnaeus's system of classification is an organism's

    a. evolutionary history.
    b. morphology.
    c. taxonomy.
    d. hierarchy.

_____ **3.** Each subset within a class of organisms is called a(n)

    a. order.
    b. family.
    c. genus.
    d. phylum.

_____ **4.** In the scientific name of an organism, the first part is the

    a. species identifier.
    b. variety.
    c. subspecies.
    d. genus.

_____ **5.** The species name of the pangolin is

    a. Manis temminckii.
    b. manis temminckii.
    c. *Manis temminckii.*
    d. *Manis Temminckii.*

Name _____ Class _____ Date _____

SHORT ANSWER Answer the questions in the space provided.

1. How were the classification systems of Aristotle and Linnaeus similar? _____

_____

_____

2. The word part *bi-* means "two," and the word part *nomen* means "name." Explain how these word

parts relate to the system scientists use to identify organisms. _____

_____

3. How does the classification process used by modern taxonomists differ from that used by Linnaeus?

_____

_____

4. **Critical Thinking** Explain why Aristotle's system of classifying animals is no longer used by

biologists. Use examples from the animal kingdom to support your answer. _____

_____

_____

_____

STRUCTURES AND FUNCTIONS Use the figure to fill in the names of the seven levels of organization in the modern Linnaean system of classifying organisms, with *a* representing the smallest category and *h* the largest category.

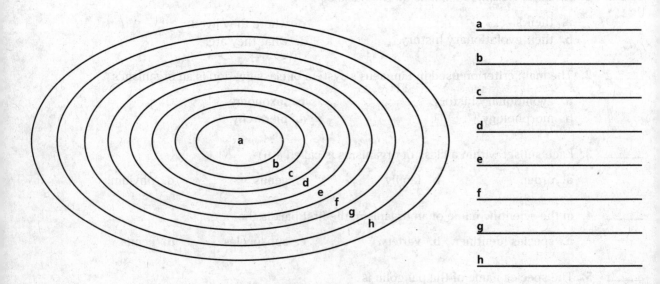

a _____

b _____

c _____

d _____

e _____

f _____

g _____

h _____

SECTION 17-2 REVIEW

SYSTEMATICS

VOCABULARY REVIEW Define the following terms.

1. systematics _____

_____

2. phylogenetic diagram _____

_____

3. cladistics _____

_____

MULTIPLE CHOICE Write the correct letter in the blank.

_____ 1. The scales of snakes and the scales of pangolins

    a. are shared derived characters.   **c.** suggest descent from a common ancestor.
    b. are homologous structures.   **d.** evolved independently in the two groups.

_____ 2. In cladistics, what term is used for a group of organisms that includes an ancestor and all of its descendants?

    a. class   **c.** phylum
    b. clade   **d.** species

_____ 3. The molecular-clock model of evolutionary relationships is based on the assumption that changes in macromolecule sequences

    a. are not random.
    b. are affected by natural selection.
    c. are greater in species with more-distant common ancestors.
    d. occur at different rates in different organisms.

_____ 4. One example of a derived character is provided by the

    a. feathers of birds.   **c.** scales of pangolins.
    b. scales of snakes.   **d.** chromosomes of chimpanzees.

_____ 5. Which of the following do cladistic taxonomists NOT compare when hypothesizing evolutionary relationships among organisms?

    a. morphological similarities   **c.** homologous chromosomes
    b. analogous structures   **d.** shared derived characters

SHORT ANSWER Answer the questions in the space provided.

1. List three types of evidence used by systematic taxonomists to construct phylogenetic diagrams.

_____

_____

_____

2. What is an out-group in cladistic analysis? _____

_____

_____

_____

3. How do derived characters help cladistic taxonomists determine phylogenetic relationships?

_____

_____

_____

4. **Critical Thinking** A paleontologist studying two modern species finds a 7-million-year-old fossil organism with a morphology similar to the modern species and concludes that it is an ancestor of both. A molecular biologist studying the amino acid sequence of a particular protein in both modern species concludes that the two species last shared a common ancestor 12.5 million years ago. Suggest possible reasons for the discrepancy in the two conclusions.

_____

_____

_____

STRUCTURES AND FUNCTIONS Use the figure to answer the following questions.

The phylogenetic diagram shown below indicates the evolutionary relationships for a hypothetical group of modern organisms, labeled 1–5, and their ancestors, labeled A–G.

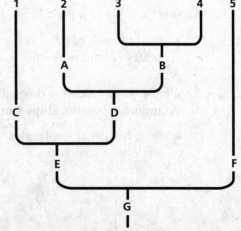

1. Which two modern organisms are likely to

   be most closely related? _____

2. What was the most recent common ancestor

   of organisms 2 and 3? _____

3. What was the most recent common ancestor

   of organisms 1 and 5? _____

MODERN CLASSIFICATION

VOCABULARY REVIEW For each of the kingdoms listed below, state the cell type (prokaryotic or eukaryotic), number of cells (unicellular, multicellular, or both), and form of nutrition (autotrophy, heterotrophy, or both).

1. Archaebacteria _____

2. Eubacteria _____

3. Protista _____

4. Fungi _____

5. Plantae _____

6. Animalia _____

MULTIPLE CHOICE Write the correct letter in the blank.

_____ 1. The organisms that live in hostile environments that cannot support other forms of life are members of the domain

    a. Bacteria.   **b.** Archaea.   **c.** Eukarya.   **d.** None of the above

_____ 2. Amoebas and paramecia belong to the kingdom

    a. Fungi.   **b.** Plantae.   **c.** Protista.   **d.** Archaea.

_____ 3. Mushrooms, puffballs, mildews, and some molds belong to the kingdom

    a. Fungi.   **b.** Plantae.   **c.** Protista.   **d.** Eukarya.

_____ 4. The domain that includes the oldest known fossil cells is called

    a. Eukarya.   **b.** Archaea.   **c.** Bacteria.   **d.** Eubacteria.

_____ 5. The domain that includes organisms with true nuclei and membrane-bound organelles is called

    a. Bacteria.   **b.** Archaea.   **c.** Animalia.   **d.** Eukarya.

_____ 6. The domain Eukarya includes

    a. archaea, protists, fungi, and plants.
    b. protists, fungi, plants, and animals.
    c. protists, fungi, eubacteria, and archaea.
    d. fungi, eubacteria, plants, and animals.

SHORT ANSWER Answer the questions in the space provided.

1. What characteristics distinguish archaea from bacteria? _____

_____

_____

2. What characteristics distinguish fungi from plants? _____

_____

_____

3. Which kingdoms include multicellular heterotrophic organisms? _____

_____

4. What evidence led scientists to develop the three-domain system of classification? _____

_____

_____

5. **Critical Thinking** Another possible way to classify organisms would be to separate them into unicellular and multicellular organisms. Explain why this is not a useful classification system.

_____

_____

_____

_____

STRUCTURES AND FUNCTIONS The diagram below represents the relationship between the three-domain system and the six-kingdom system of classifying organisms. Label each box in the diagram with the correct domain or kingdom name.

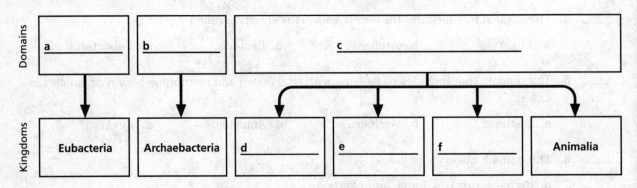

SECTION 18-1 REVIEW

INTRODUCTION TO ECOLOGY

VOCABULARY REVIEW Define the following terms.

1. ecology _____
_____

2. interdependence _____
_____

3. biosphere _____
_____

4. ecosystem _____
_____

5. community _____
_____

6. population _____
_____

MULTIPLE CHOICE Write the correct letter in the blank.

_____ 1. All the robins in an area would be an example of a(n)

    a. community.   **b.** population.   **c.** ecosystem.   **d.** biosphere.

_____ 2. The broadest, most inclusive level of ecological organization is the

    a. population.   **b.** community.   **c.** biosphere.   **d.** ecosystem.

_____ 3. A pond is an example of

    a. a population.   **b.** a community.   **c.** a biosphere.   **d.** an ecosystem.

_____ 4. Ecologists use models to

    a. make predictions about the future behavior of an ecosystem.
    b. substitute for observations from the natural world.
    c. increase the complexity of simple ecosystems.
    d. account for the influence of every variable in a real environment.

Name _____ Class _____ Date _____

SHORT ANSWER Answer the questions in the space provided.

1. How does the production of acorns by oak trees affect Lyme disease in humans? _____

_____

_____

2. Why do ecological models commonly have limited applications? _____

_____

_____

3. How does a population differ from a community? _____

_____

_____

4. **Critical Thinking** How might the destruction of large areas of tropical rain forest have world-

wide consequences? _____

_____

_____

STRUCTURES AND FUNCTIONS The drawings below represent five levels of ecological organization. In the spaces provided, label the levels and number them from 1 to 5, with 1 being the most inclusive.

_____   _____   _____

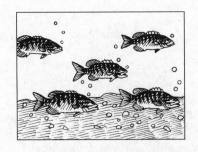 

_____   _____

Name _____ Class _____ Date _____

ECOLOGY OF ORGANISMS

VOCABULARY REVIEW Distinguish between the terms in each of the following pairs of terms.

1. habitat, resource _____

_____

2. biotic factor, abiotic factor _____

_____

3. conformer, regulator _____

_____

_____

4. dormancy, migration _____

_____

_____

5. generalist, specialist _____

MULTIPLE CHOICE Write the correct letter in the blank.

_____ 1. One biotic factor that could influence a plant might be

    a. the amount of sunlight.   **c.** carbon dioxide concentration.
    b. soil pH.   **d.** a pollinating insect.

_____ 2. People who spend time at high elevations develop more red blood cells, which helps them obtain oxygen from the "thin air." This phenomenon is an example of

    a. acclimation.   **b.** adaptation.   **c.** migration.   **d.** dormancy.

_____ 3. An animal that maintains its body temperature within a narrow range even when the environmental temperature varies is an example of a

    a. specialist.   **b.** generalist.   **c.** regulator.   **d.** conformer.

_____ 4. The role a species plays in its environment is called the species'

    a. habitat.   **b.** niche.   **c.** resources.   **d.** tolerance curve.

_____ 5. An animal that feeds on leaves from only a few species of plants is an example of a

    a. specialist.   **b.** generalist.   **c.** regulator.   **d.** conformer.

SHORT ANSWER Answer the questions in the space provided.

1. Give three examples of abiotic factors and explain how they interact. _____

_____

_____

_____

2. What are two ways that some organisms can escape from unfavorable environmental conditions?

_____

_____

3. Explain why the Virginia opossum is considered a generalist and the koala is considered a specialist.

_____

_____

4. Explain how a species' habitat differs from its niche. _____

_____

_____

5. **Critical Thinking** How could knowledge of a pest organism's tolerance limits be used in

pest control? _____

_____

_____

_____

STRUCTURES AND FUNCTIONS Label the curves in the graph below according to the type of organism they represent, and give a specific example of each type of organism.

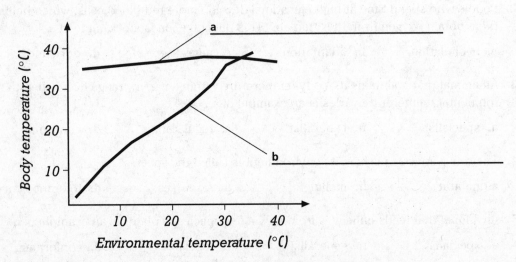

SECTION 18-3 REVIEW

ENERGY TRANSFER

VOCABULARY REVIEW Distinguish between the terms in each of the following groups of terms.

1. producer, consumer _____

_____

2. gross primary productivity, net primary productivity _____

_____

_____

3. food chain, food web _____

_____

MULTIPLE CHOICE Write the correct letter in the blank.

_____ 1. The term *biomass* refers to the

    a. weight of the biosphere.
    b. volume of plants in a community.
    c. organic material in an ecosystem.
    d. amount of energy produced through chemosynthesis.

_____ 2. A detritivore is an organism that

    a. feeds on both producers and consumers.
    b. feeds on the "garbage" of an ecosystem.
    c. converts biomass into "garbage" in an ecosystem.
    d. produces carbohydrates by using energy from inorganic molecules.

_____ 3. An organism's position in the sequence of energy transfers in an ecosystem is known as its

    a. trophic level.
    b. energy level.
    c. net productivity.
    d. feeding location.

_____ 4. The percentage of energy transferred from one level to another in a food chain is usually

    a. greater than 90 percent.
    b. about 75 percent.
    c. about 50 percent.
    d. less than 20 percent.

_____ 5. Compared to the lowest trophic level, the highest trophic level contains

    a. more individuals.
    b. less energy.
    c. more producers.
    d. fewer carnivores.

Name _____ Class _____ Date _____

SHORT ANSWER Answer the questions in the space provided.

1. Rank the following ecosystems in order of their net primary productivity, from lowest to highest: open ocean, tropical rain forest, desert, lake. _____

_____

2. Why are producers the first trophic level to benefit from the activity of decomposers? _____

_____

3. Give three reasons why energy transfer between trophic levels is not 100 percent. _____

_____

_____

4. Why are food chains short? _____

_____

5. **Critical Thinking** What would happen to the energy flow through an ecosystem if the

decomposers were eliminated? _____

_____

_____

STRUCTURES AND FUNCTIONS The diagram below shows part of a food web. Each arrow indicates energy passing from one member (the food) to another (the consumer). Only some of the indicated relationships are possible. Write yes in the spaces corresponding to the possible relationships and no in the spaces corresponding to the relationships that are not possible.

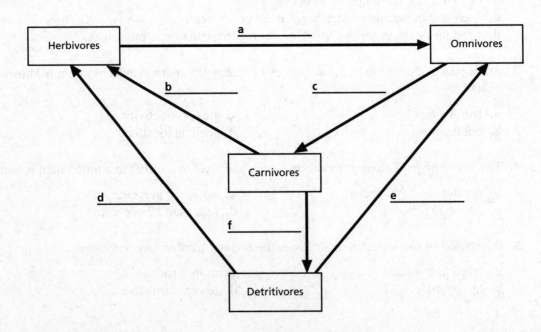

ECOSYSTEM RECYCLING

VOCABULARY REVIEW Explain the relationship between the terms in each of the following groups of terms.

1. water cycle, carbon cycle, nitrogen cycle _____

_____

_____

2. nitrogen fixation, nitrification, denitrification _____

_____

_____

_____

MULTIPLE CHOICE Write the correct letter in the blank.

_____ 1. The term *groundwater* refers to water that

    a. exists in lakes or ponds.
    b. is found in soil or in underground formations.
    c. has fallen to sea level.
    d. lies on the surface of the ground after a heavy rain.

_____ 2. At least 90 percent of the water that returns to the atmosphere from terrestrial ecosystems does so through

    a. transpiration in plants.
    b. excretion in animals.
    c. sweating in animals.
    d. precipitation.

_____ 3. Two sources of carbon dioxide released into the atmosphere in the carbon cycle are

    a. photosynthesis and decomposition.
    b. cellular respiration and photosynthesis.
    c. combustion and transpiration.
    d. cellular respiration and combustion.

_____ 4. Two components of the nitrogen cycle that produce ammonia are

    a. nitrification and denitrification.
    b. nitrogen fixation and nitrification.
    c. nitrogen fixation and ammonification.
    d. ammonification and denitrification.

_____ 5. Animals obtain nitrogen

    a. through a mutualistic relationship with nitrogen-fixing bacteria.
    b. from the proteins and nucleic acids in the organisms they consume.
    c. by absorbing nitrates and ammonia from the soil.
    d. by absorbing nitrogen gas from the atmosphere.

Name _____ Class _____ Date _____

SHORT ANSWER Answer the questions in the space provided.

1. Name three processes in the water cycle, and state whether each process removes water from

the atmosphere or returns it to the atmosphere. _____

_____

_____

2. Describe the cycling of carbon in the carbon cycle. _____

_____

_____

3. Where are nitrogen-fixing bacteria found? How do these bacteria benefit plants? _____

_____

_____

4. **Critical Thinking** If a crop, such as corn, is grown in the same field year after year, a nitrogen-
   containing fertilizer must be added to the soil each time a new crop is planted. Why isn't a single

   application of fertilizer sufficient? _____

_____

_____

STRUCTURES AND FUNCTIONS The diagram below represents the effect of the water, carbon, and nitrogen cycles on the life of a plant. Identify the process indicated in the three cycles.

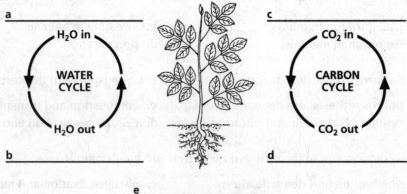

a _____
H_2O in
WATER CYCLE
H_2O out
b _____

c _____
CO_2 in
CARBON CYCLE
CO_2 out
d _____

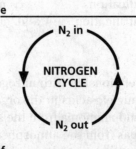

e _____
N_2 in
NITROGEN CYCLE
N_2 out
f _____

UNDERSTANDING POPULATIONS

VOCABULARY REVIEW Contrast the following terms.

1. population density, dispersion _____

_____

2. death rate, life expectancy _____

_____

MULTIPLE CHOICE Write the correct letter in the blank.

_____ 1. One can estimate a population's size by counting individuals in a sample of the population if the

    a. distribution of individuals in the sample is the same as that in the population.
    b. density in the sample is greater than the population density.
    c. dispersion in the sample is less than that in the population.
    d. sample size is larger than the population size.

_____ 2. A random distribution of individuals in a population would be most likely to result from

    a. clumped food resources.
    b. territorial behavior by the individuals in the population.
    c. herding behavior by the individuals in the population.
    d. the dispersal of seeds by the wind.

_____ 3. Although the United States has a larger total population than Japan, population density is greater in Japan because the

    a. people in the United States have less education and medical care.
    b. people in Japan all live in the cities.
    c. geographical area is greater in the United States.
    d. birth rate is lower than the death rate in Japan.

_____ 4. A population is likely to grow most rapidly if it has

    a. a high percentage of old individuals.
    b. a high percentage of young individuals.
    c. about the same percentage of individuals in each age range.
    d. individuals with a low birth rate.

_____ 5. In a population with a Type I survivorship curve, the likelihood of dying is

    a. low until late in life, when it increases rapidly.
    b. high early in life and much lower in older individuals.
    c. high early in life and late in life, but much lower in middle-aged individuals.
    d. fairly constant throughout life.

Name _____ Class _____ Date _____

SHORT ANSWER Answer the questions in the space provided.

1. How do the three main patterns of population dispersion differ from one another? _____
_____
_____

2. Give an example of a social behavior that can produce a clumped distribution. _____
_____

3. Give an example of a social behavior that can produce a uniform distribution. _____
_____

4. Critical Thinking What would the survivorship curve for humans look like if there were a worldwide epidemic of a fatal disease that affected only children under five years of age?
_____
_____

STRUCTURES AND FUNCTIONS Use the figure to answer the following questions.

The graph below shows three different types of survivorship curves.

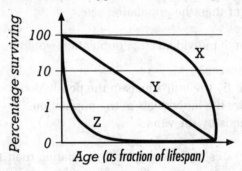

1. Which curve corresponds to a species in which 0.3% of the individuals are alive after one-quarter of their lifespan has passed and 0.1% are alive after one-half of their lifespan has passed?
_____

2. Which curve corresponds to a species in which 95% of the individuals are alive after one-quarter of their lifespan has passed and 90% are alive after one-half of their lifespan has passed?
_____

3. Which curve corresponds to a species in which 10% of the individuals are alive after one-third of their lifespan has passed and 1% are alive after two-thirds of their lifespan has passed?
_____

4. Give an example of a species that would have each type of survivorship curve.

X _____ Y _____ Z _____

SECTION 19-2 REVIEW

MEASURING POPULATIONS

VOCABULARY REVIEW Explain the relationship between the terms in each of the following groups of terms.

1. growth rate, birth rate, death rate _____

_____

_____

2. exponential growth, limiting factor _____

_____

_____

MULTIPLE CHOICE Write the correct letter in the blank.

_____ 1. If a country's per capita growth rate is 0.01 and its present population is 50,000,000, what will the population be one year from now?

    a. 500,000   **b.** 50,500,000   **c.** 60,000,000   **d.** 500,000,000

_____ 2. The exponential model of population growth applies

    a. when there are no limiting factors.
    b. if the birth rate increases as the population grows.
    c. when the population size exceeds the carrying capacity.
    d. to all real populations that exist in nature.

_____ 3. The logistic model of population growth

    a. reflects the fact that the carrying capacity fluctuates with environmental changes.
    b. does not accomodate the influence of limiting factors.
    c. reflects the fact that the birth rate decreases as the population grows.
    d. applies to all real populations that exist in nature.

_____ 4. One example of a density-dependent limiting factor is a

    a. forest fire.   **c.** period of very severe weather.
    b. flood.   **d.** shortage of nesting sites.

_____ 5. Which of the following is not a threat to the survival of small populations?

    a. breeding in captivity   **c.** habitat destruction
    b. inbreeding   **d.** disease outbreaks

Name _____ Class _____ Date _____

SHORT ANSWER Answer the questions in the space provided.

1. In 1996 in the United States, the number of live births was 4 million, the number of deaths was 2.4 million, and the population was 265 million. Calculate the per capita birth rate, death rate, and growth rate. Show your calculations. _____

_____

_____

2. What evidence did Charles Elton collect that suggested that fluctuations in hare and lynx populations were related? _____

_____

What other evidence indicates that these fluctuations may not have been related? _____

_____

3. Name three effects that inbreeding can have on a population. _____

_____

4. **Critical Thinking** If a population's per capita growth rate is 0.02 and its population is 100,000,000, how large will the population be in five years? Show your calculations. _____

_____

_____

STRUCTURES AND FUNCTIONS Use the figure to answer the following questions.

The graph below shows the growth of a population over time.

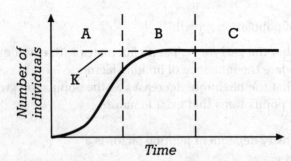

1. Describe the birth rate and death rate in region A. _____

2. Describe the birth rate and death rate in region C. _____

3. Identify the line labeled *K*. _____

4. What model best describes the growth of this population? _____

SECTION 19-3 REVIEW

HUMAN POPULATION GROWTH

VOCABULARY REVIEW Define the following terms.

1. hunter-gatherer lifestyle _____

_____

2. agricultural revolution _____

_____

3. developed country _____

_____

4. developing country _____

_____

MULTIPLE CHOICE Write the correct letter in the blank.

_____ 1. The hunter-gatherer lifestyle is associated with

    a. large populations.
    b. ancient human populations but is not found in human populations today.
    c. high mortality rates among infants and young children.
    d. high rates of population growth.

_____ 2. About 10,000 to 12,000 years ago, the human population began to grow more rapidly due to

    a. improvements in sanitation.   **c.** improved economic conditions.
    b. control of disease.   **d.** the agricultural revolution.

_____ 3. The global growth rate of the human population is

    a. no longer increasing.
    b. not important to people in developed countries.
    c. increasing but at a slower rate than in the mid-1960s.
    d. decreasing each year.

_____ 4. The current population growth rates of developed countries

    a. are lower than those of developing countries.
    b. are high because the death rate is low.
    c. are increasing because the fertility rate is increasing.
    d. are low because the death rate is high.

_____ 5. A country may have a negative growth rate if its

    a. population is mostly young people.   **c.** death rate is higher than its birth rate.
    b. birth rate is higher than its death rate.   **d.** population has access to health care.

SHORT ANSWER Answer the questions in the space provided.

1. Why did the development of agriculture have a major impact on the human population growth rate?

   _____

2. What factors caused human population growth to accelerate after 1650? _____

   _____

   _____

3. What features characterize most developing countries? _____

   _____

   _____

4. Why did population growth rates change after World War II? _____

   _____

5. **Critical Thinking** Under what conditions might the per capita birth and death rates not be

   enough to accurately predict future human population size? _____

   _____

STRUCTURES AND FUNCTIONS Use the figure to answer the following questions.

The graph below represents the hypothetical growth of a population over time. You may express
a time interval, for example, as "from A to B," or "from B to E."

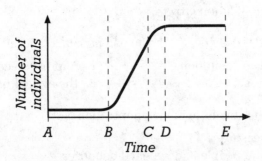

1. Which time interval best depicts human population growth over all of human history?

   _____

2. Which time interval best depicts human population growth until about 1650? _____

3. In which time interval is the birth rate approximately equal to the death rate? _____

4. In which time interval does the birth rate greatly exceed the death rate? _____

SECTION 20-1 REVIEW

SPECIES INTERACTIONS

VOCABULARY REVIEW Explain the relationship between the terms in each of the following pairs of terms.

1. predator, prey ——————————————————————————————————————

——

——

2. herbivore, secondary compound ——————————————————————————

——

3. parasite, host ——————————————————————————————————————

——

MULTIPLE CHOICE Write the correct letter in the blank.

—————— **1.** An example of mimicry that is important in anti-predator defenses is when

    a. a harmless species resembles a dangerous species.
    b. two harmless species look similar.
    c. a species resembles an inedible object.
    d. one individual uses bright colors to warn others of danger.

—————— **2.** One difference between predators and parasites is that parasites

    a. usually do not cause the immediate death of the organism they feed on.
    b. feed only on the inside of other organisms.
    c. are always microorganisms.
    d. are not anatomically or physiologically specialized.

—————— **3.** Magpies and crows are scavenger birds that feed on the same food sources and cannot live in the same community. This is an example of

    a. character displacement.   **c.** symbiosis.
    b. resource partitioning.   **d.** competitive exclusion.

—————— **4.** A change in anatomy that results when two species compete for the same resource is called

    a. mutualism.   **c.** competitive exclusion.
    b. character displacement.   **d.** resource partitioning.

—————— **5.** A symbiotic relationship in which one species benefits and the other is not affected is called

    a. commensalism.   **b.** mutualism.   **c.** parasitism.   **d.** competition.

SHORT ANSWER Answer the questions in the space provided.

1. How are secondary compounds useful to plants? _____

_____

2. What is the difference between the fundamental niche of a species and the realized niche of the

species? _____

_____

3. How do ectoparasites differ from endoparasites? _____

_____

_____

4. Explain how Darwin's finches illustrate the principle of character displacement. _____

_____

_____

5. **Critical Thinking** A biologist finds that when two species of paramecia are grown together in the laboratory, one species always outcompetes and eliminates the other. In ponds and other natural environments, however, the two species coexist. Suggest a hypothesis to explain this phenomenon.

_____

_____

_____

STRUCTURES AND FUNCTIONS Label each drawing below with the most appropriate term from the following list: pollinator, physical defense, secondary compound, endoparasite, ectoparasite, mimicry.

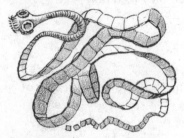

1. Tapeworm _____

2. Thorns _____

3. Kingsnake _____

4. Poison ivy _____

5. Deer tick _____

6. Butterfly _____

SECTION 20-2 REVIEW

PATTERNS IN COMMUNITIES

VOCABULARY REVIEW Define the following terms.

1. species richness _____

   _____

2. primary succession _____

   _____

3. species-area effect _____

   _____

MULTIPLE CHOICE Write the correct letter in the blank.

_____ 1. A community that has great species richness contains

   a. many different species.
   b. many individuals in each species.
   c. a few species whose members control most of the community's resources.
   d. species that are of great economic value.

_____ 2. The measure that relates the number of species in a community to the relative abundance of each species is called

   a. species richness.   **c.** community stability.
   b. species evenness.   **d.** community interaction.

_____ 3. Species that predominate early in the development of a community are called

   a. pioneer species.   **c.** dominant species.
   b. climax species.   **d.** succession species.

_____ 4. One explanation for the greater number of species in the Tropics than in temperate zones is that

   a. tropical habitats are younger than temperate habitats.
   b. there is more energy available to support more organisms in the Tropics.
   c. people have been cultivating species for much longer periods in the Tropics.
   d. the climate is more stable in temperate habitats.

_____ 5. The stable end point of succession is called

   a. staged community.   **c.** climatic change.
   b. climax community.   **d.** community development.

SHORT ANSWER Answer the questions in the space provided.

1. Why does primary succession often proceed very slowly? _____

_____

_____

2. How does species richness vary with latitude? _____

_____

3. Why are agricultural fields often less stable than natural communities in the same area? _____

_____

_____

_____

4. **Critical Thinking** A volcanic eruption removes all plant life from a valley below the volcano
   Explain why succession following the eruption is likely to occur more quickly on the valley floor

   than on the steep slopes that form the valley walls. _____

_____

_____

STRUCTURES AND FUNCTIONS The map below shows four hypothetical islands: A, B, C, and D. Rank the islands from 1 to 4 in terms of the species richness you would expect them to have, with the island that has the greatest richness as 1 and the island with the least richness as 4.

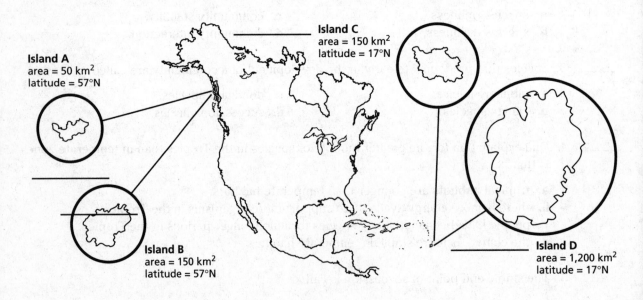

Island A
area = 50 km^2
latitude = 57°N

Island B
area = 150 km^2
latitude = 57°N

Island C
area = 150 km^2
latitude = 17°N

Island D
area = 1,200 km^2
latitude = 17°N

TERRESTRIAL BIOMES

VOCABULARY REVIEW Define the following terms.

1. biome _____

_____

2. tundra _____

_____

3. taiga _____

_____

4. savanna _____

_____

5. canopy _____

_____

MULTIPLE CHOICE Write the correct letter in the blank.

_____ 1. The biome that is characterized by the presence of permafrost is called

    a. savanna.   **b.** desert.   **c.** taiga.   **d.** tundra.

_____ 2. Plants living in the taiga are adapted for

    a. long, cold winters.   **c.** nutrient-rich soil.
    b. long summers.   **d.** very small amounts of precipitation.

_____ 3. Prairie, steppe, and veldt are different names for the biome known as

    a. tundra.   **c.** temperate deciduous forest.
    b. grassland.   **d.** taiga.

_____ 4. Which of the following is not an adaptation that limits water loss in desert plants?

    a. protective spines   **c.** broad, thin leaves
    b. a waxy coating   **d.** opening of stomata only at night

_____ 5. The amount of light that reaches the floor of a tropical rain forest is limited by the

    a. short growing season in the tropics.   **c.** dense growth of short vegetation that
    b. forest canopy.   covers most of the floor.
                                d. dense fog that exists within the forest.

Name _____ Class _____ Date _____

SHORT ANSWER Answer the questions in the space provided.

1. Name two factors that limit tree growth in the tundra. _____

_____

_____

2. What characteristic of grasses enables these plants to survive occasional fires and continuous

grazing by animals? _____

_____

3. How are the plants of savannas adapted to the rainfall patterns of this biome? _____

_____

4. Describe three adaptations of desert organisms that conserve water. _____

_____

_____

5. **Critical Thinking** Why aren't the forests of the taiga cut down and converted into farmland as

often as temperate deciduous forests? _____

_____

_____

6. **Critical Thinking** Why are vines so common in rain forests? _____

_____

_____

STRUCTURES AND FUNCTIONS The bar graphs below summarize the typical temperature range, annual precipitation, and soil-nutrient level of four biomes. Label each graph according to the biome it represents.

Temperature
Precipitation
Soil/nutrient content

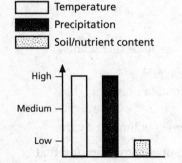

a _____

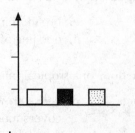

b _____

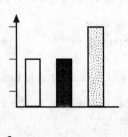

c _____

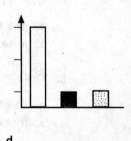

d _____

SECTION 21-2 REVIEW

AQUATIC ECOSYSTEMS

VOCABULARY REVIEW Distinguish between the terms in each of the following pairs of terms.

1. photic zone, aphotic zone _____

_____

2. neritic zone, oceanic zone _____

_____

_____

3. pelagic zone, benthic zone _____

_____

4. eutrophic lake, oligotrophic lake _____

_____

MULTIPLE CHOICE Write the correct letter in the blank.

_____ 1. Which of the following is not an environmental factor that organisms in the intertidal zone must cope with?

    a. periodic exposure to the air   **c.** constant darkness
    b. the force of crashing waves   **d.** the possibility of dehydration

_____ 2. Coral reefs form in the

    a. neritic zone.   **b.** intertidal zone.   **c.** pelagic zone.   **d.** aphotic zone.

_____ 3. There are fewer species in the oceanic zone than in the neritic zone because the oceanic zone

    a. receives very little sunlight.   **c.** is very cold.
    b. has low nutrient levels.   **d.** is under very high pressure.

_____ 4. A salt marsh is an example of a(n)

    a. pelagic zone.   **c.** estuary community.
    b. species-poor community.   **d.** oligotrophic zone.

_____ 5. Eutrophic lakes

    a. have very clear water.   **c.** contain little organic matter.
    b. generally do not contain fish.   **d.** are rich in vegetation.

SHORT ANSWER Answer the questions in the space provided.

1. What are some adaptations of intertidal organisms that enable them to survive in this zone?

_____

_____

2. Why is plankton important to aquatic ecosystems? _____

_____

3. Explain why the productivity of the oceanic zone is high, even though nutrient levels are low.

_____

_____

4. Explain how producers near deep-sea vents obtain energy. _____

_____

5. Critical Thinking Water that drains from agricultural fields during heavy rains or over-irrigation may contain high levels of nitrogen, phosphorus, and other nutrients. What effect might this water

have if it is allowed to enter an oligotrophic lake? _____

_____

_____

_____

STRUCTURES AND FUNCTIONS Identify the ocean zones labeled *a–g* in the diagram below.

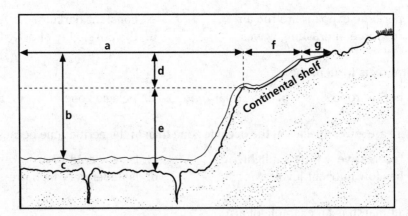

a _____   e _____

b _____   f _____

c _____   g _____

d _____

SECTION 22-1 REVIEW

AN INTERCONNECTED PLANET

VOCABULARY REVIEW Define the following terms.

1. biodiversity _____

_____

2. species evenness _____

_____

3. genetic diversity _____

_____

MULTIPLE CHOICE Write the correct letter in the blank.

_____ 1. Which of the following is NOT a measure of biodiversity?

    a. species evenness   **c.** genetic diversity
    b. genetic recombination   **d.** species richness

_____ 2. Of the following groups, which contains the greatest number of species?

    a. crustaceans   **b.** mammals   **c.** plants   **d.** insects

_____ 3. The mass extinction currently under way is different from previous mass extinctions because it

    a. is being caused largely by humans.
    b. involves the loss of fewer species.
    c. is occurring at a time when biodiversity is already low.
    d. is actually causing an increase in biodiversity.

_____ 4. The portion of Earth that includes all rivers, lakes, and the oceans is the

    a. geosphere.
    b. atmosphere.
    c. hydrosphere.
    d. biosphere.

_____ 5. The ozone layer in the upper atmosphere is important because it

    a. causes Earth to heat up.
    b. absorbs most of the sun's ultraviolet radiation.
    c. causes the greenhouse effect.
    d. causes Earth to cool.

SHORT ANSWER Answer the questions in the space provided.

1. Explain what makes up Earth's three major layers and the biosphere. _____

_____

_____

2. Why could a disease be more serious in a population with a low genetic diversity? _____

_____

3. What is the greenhouse effect? _____

_____

_____

4. **Critical Thinking** Why might botanists store the seeds of newly discovered plant species or

varieties in dry, refrigerated seed banks? _____

_____

_____

STRUCTURES AND FUNCTIONS Use the drawings below to answer the following
questions. The drawings show the number of individuals of four plant species found at
three sites. Each leaf represents one plant.

Site A   Site B   Site C

1. Which site has the greatest species richness? _____

2. Which site has the lowest species richness? _____

3. Which site has the greatest species evenness? _____

4. Which site has the lowest species evenness? _____

5. Which site has the greatest species diversity? _____

6. Which site has the lowest species diversity? _____

SECTION 22-2 REVIEW

ENVIRONMENTAL ISSUES

VOCABULARY REVIEW Define the following terms.

1. smog _____

_____

2. extinction _____

_____

3. keystone species _____

_____

4. chlorofluorocarbon _____

_____

MULTIPLE CHOICE Write the correct letter in the blank.

_____ 1. The increase in the concentration of pesticides in organisms at the top of the food chain is an example of

    a. extinction.   **c.** a keystone species.
    b. biological magnification.   **d.** pollution.

_____ 2. The ozone "hole" is a

    a. clearing in the smoggy air over a large city.
    b. zone of very low ozone concentration in the upper atmosphere over Antarctica.
    c. zone of very high ozone concentration in the lower atmosphere over Antarctica.
    d. circular patch of ozone in the upper atmosphere over the Arctic Ocean.

_____ 3. One of the likely effects of damage to the ozone layer is a(n)

    a. decrease in global temperatures.
    b. shift in wind patterns over North America.
    c. decrease in the amount of ultraviolet radiation that reaches Earth's surface.
    d. increase in the incidence of skin cancer in humans.

_____ 4. Since the 1960s the levels of atmospheric carbon dioxide have

    a. stayed the same.   **c.** decreased rapidly.
    b. increased rapidly.   **d.** increased slightly.

_____ 5. Doubling of the human population might

    a. hasten global warming.   **c.** All of the above
    b. decrease the amount of undeveloped land.   **d.** None of the above

SHORT ANSWER Answer the questions in the space provided.

1. What causes acid precipitation? _____

_____

_____

2. Identify three possible consequences of doubling Earth's human population. _____

_____

_____

3. What is sustainability? _____

_____

_____

4. **Critical Thinking** Increased CO_2 levels in the atmosphere are correlated with rising global tem-
peratures, leading many scientists to believe that the first phenomenon has caused the second.
What would it take to be certain that this correlation represents a cause-and-effect relationship?

_____

_____

_____

_____

STRUCTURES AND FUNCTIONS The flowcharts below represent some of the effects of
human activity on the environment. Each arrow indicates a known or suspected cause-
and-effect relationship. Complete the flowcharts by writing an appropriate response in
the space corresponding to each box.

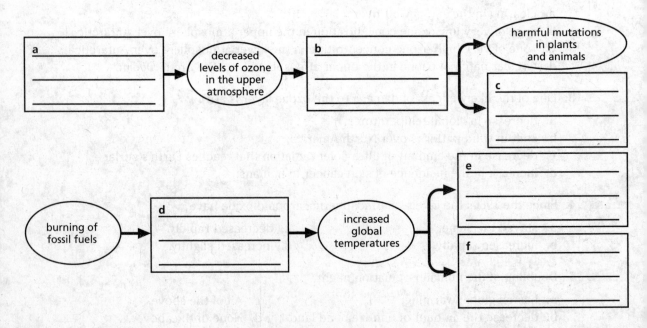

SECTION 22-3 REVIEW

ENVIRONMENTAL SOLUTIONS

VOCABULARY REVIEW Define the following terms.

1. conservation biology _____

_____

2. restoration biology _____

_____

MULTIPLE CHOICE Write the correct letter in the blank.

_____ 1. A species that is extremely sensitive to ecological changes is known as a(n)

    a. conservation species.
    b. bioindicator.
    c. keystone species.
    d. hotspot species.

_____ 2. In a debt-for-nature swap,

    a. developing countries destroy their natural ecosystems to build their economies.
    b. countries go into debt to pay for the conservation of their natural resources.
    c. richer countries pay off some of the debts of developing countries that take steps to preserve biodiversity.
    d. richer countries pay developing countries to convert their rain forests into farms.

_____ 3. Why are small aircraft used in captive breeding programs of whooping cranes?

    a. to teach young cranes their migration route
    b. to monitor whooping crane habitat
    c. to monitor the breeding habits of released cranes
    d. to scare off predators

_____ 4. Negative consequences of ecosystem alteration in southern Florida include

    a. the extinction of the melaleuca tree.   **c.** overgrowth of sea grass in Florida Bay.
    b. water shortages.   **d.** an increase in the populations of wading birds.

_____ 5. The plan for restoring the Everglades ecosystem involves

    a. building new drainage canals.
    b. planting more melaleuca trees.
    c. restoring the Kissimmee River to its original channel.
    d. adding fertilizer to the Everglades to increase its productivity.

SHORT ANSWER Answer the questions in the space provided.

1. What is a biodiversity hotspot? _____

_____

2. Why must efforts to protect migratory bird populations be international? _____

_____

3. What is ecotourism, and how can it be used to preserve biodiversity? _____

_____

_____

4. What human actions lead to the disappearance of much of the wetlands in the Everglades

ecosystem? _____

_____

_____

5. **Critical Thinking** What might be the value of the Everglade restoration plan? _____

_____

_____

STRUCTURES AND FUNCTIONS The flowcharts below represent some aspects of conservation and restoration biology. Complete the flowcharts by writing an appropriate response in each box.

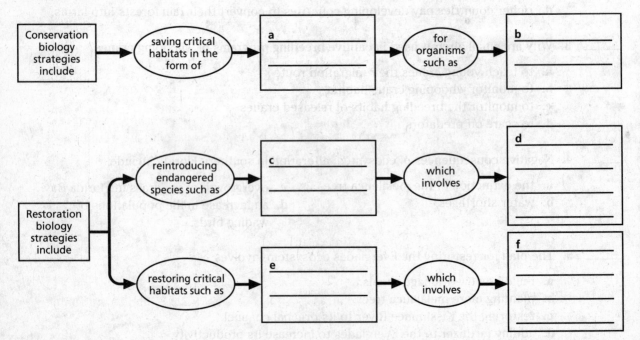

PROKARYOTES

VOCABULARY REVIEW Distinguish between the terms in each of the following groups of terms.

1. halophile, thermoacidophile _____

_____

2. bacillus, coccus, spirillum _____

_____

3. staphylococcus, streptococcus _____

_____

4. Gram-positive bacterium, Gram-negative bacterium _____

_____

MULTIPLE CHOICE Write the correct letter in the blank.

_____ 1. Fossil evidence indicates that the earliest prokaryotes on Earth lived about

    a. 1 billion years ago.   **c.** 2.5 billion years ago.
    b. 5 billion years ago.   **d.** None of the above

_____ 2. Which of the following types of bacteria would you be most likely to find in very salty water?

    a. chemoautotroph   **c.** cyanobacterium
    b. halophile   **d.** thermoacidophile

_____ 3. Archaea and Bacteria are placed in separate domains because

    a. Bacteria lack cell membranes.   **c.** proteins of Bacteria have no amino acids.
    b. Archaea have cells walls that   **d.** their rRNA sequences are different.
       contain peptidoglycan.

_____ 4. Actinomycetes are

    a. archaea that are spiral-shaped.
    b. proteobacteria that cause tooth decay.
    c. Gram-positive bacteria that form branching filaments.
    d. Gram-negative bacteria that are photosynthetic.

_____ 5. Which of the following types of bacteria would you be most likely to find in the human intestinal tract?

    a. spirochete   **b.** cyanobacterium   **c.** thermoacidophile   **d.** enteric bacterium

SHORT ANSWER Answer the questions in the space provided.

1. Why do some bacteria retain the Gram stain while others do not? _____

_____

2. Why are nitrogen-fixing bacteria important to plants? _____

_____

3. Identify two ecologically important characteristics of cyanobacteria. _____

_____

4. Identify one beneficial and one harmful role of Gram-negative enteric bacteria found in the human body.

_____

_____

5. Explain how the evolution of aerobic organisms depended on a metabolic product of cyano-

bacteria. _____

_____

_____

6. **Critical Thinking** How have explorations of saltwater lakes and hydrothermal vents on the ocean

floor led biologists to revise their ideas about the origin of eukaryotes? _____

_____

_____

_____

STRUCTURES AND FUNCTIONS Label each drawing below with the most appropriate term from the following list: coccus, streptococcus, spirochete, bacillus.

1. _____   2. _____   3. _____   4. _____

Name _____ Class _____ Date _____

BIOLOGY OF PROKARYOTES

VOCABULARY REVIEW Distinguish between the terms in each of the following pairs of terms.

1. capsule, endospore _____

_____

2. pilus, conjugation _____

_____

_____

3. obligate anaerobe, facultative anaerobe _____

_____

4. transformation, transduction _____

_____

MULTIPLE CHOICE Write the correct letter in the blank.

_____ 1. One structure you would not find in a bacterial cell is a

　　a. cell wall.　　　**b.** cell membrane.　　**c.** mitochondrion.　　**d.** chromosome.

_____ 2. Which of the following is not a method of movement used by bacteria?

　　a. gliding through a layer of slime
　　b. forceful expulsion of water from contractile vacuoles
　　c. producing a corkscrew-like motion
　　d. propulsion by flagella

_____ 3. Photoautotrophic bacteria obtain energy

　　a. from the sun.　　　　　　　　　**c.** by feeding on living organisms.
　　b. by oxidizing inorganic compounds.　　**d.** by feeding on dead and decaying material.

_____ 4. Which types of bacteria can live in the presence of oxygen?

　　a. only obligate anaerobes　　　　　**c.** only obligate aerobes and facultative
　　b. only obligate aerobes　　　　　　　　anaerobes
　　　　　　　　　　　　　　　　　　　　d. all bacteria

_____ 5. The process by which two living bacteria bind together and transfer genetic information is called

　　a. conjugation.　　**b.** transformation.　　**c.** transduction.　　**d.** encapsulation.

Name _____ Class _____ Date _____

SHORT ANSWER Answer the questions in the space provided.

1. Where does photosynthesis take place in a photoautotrophic bacterium? _____

_____

2. What is a glycocalyx, and what function does it serve? _____

_____

_____

3. Name three environmental factors that affect the growth of bacteria. _____

_____

4. What type of genetic recombination in bacteria involves DNA transfer by viruses? _____

_____

5. **Critical Thinking** Why are bacterial transformation, conjugation, and transduction not considered

   to be methods of reproduction? _____

_____

_____

STRUCTURES AND FUNCTIONS Briefly describe the function of each labeled structure in the drawing of a bacterial cell shown below.

1. Pilus _____

2. Capsule _____

3. Cell wall _____

4. Cell membrane _____

5. Chromosome _____

6. Plasmid _____

7. Flagellum _____

BACTERIA AND HUMANS

VOCABULARY REVIEW Define the following terms.

1. pathology _____

2. exotoxin _____

_____

3. endotoxin _____

_____

4. zoonosis _____

_____

5. bioremediation _____

_____

MULTIPLE CHOICE Write the correct letter in the blank.

_____ **1.** One bacterial disease that is transmitted by contaminated drinking water is

    a. Lyme disease.   **b.** gonorrhea.   **c.** tuberculosis.   **d.** cholera.

_____ **2.** A poison that is released from the outer membrane of dead Gram-negative bacteria is called

    a. a pathogen.   **c.** an endotoxin.
    b. an exotoxin.   **d.** a broad-spectrum toxin.

_____ **3.** Which of the following is not a way that bacteria cause disease in humans?

    a. destroying body tissues   **c.** damaging blood vessels
    b. conjugating with human cells   **d.** dissolving blood clots

_____ **4.** Bacteria can become resistant to antibiotics by

    a. secreting antibiotics.
    b. assisting the passage of antibiotics through the cell wall.
    c. acquiring an R-plasmid for resistance.
    d. growing only on Petri dishes.

_____ **5.** One of the positive ways bacteria affect our lives is by

    a. producing dental caries.
    b. consuming improperly preserved foods.
    c. preventing the decomposition of dead plants and animals.
    d. helping to clean up oil spills.

SHORT ANSWER Answer the questions in the space provided.

1. Identify three ways that bacteria can be transmitted from person to person. _____

_____

2. Name one bacterial disease that affects nerves, one that affects the intestine, and one that affects

the skin. _____

_____

3. Describe two ways that antibiotics work. _____

_____

_____

4. List four foods that are produced with the assistance of bacteria. _____

_____

5. **Critical Thinking** Why are broad-spectrum antibiotics often used to treat infections caused by

unidentified pathogens? What is the danger associated with overusing such antibiotics? _____

_____

_____

_____

STRUCTURES AND FUNCTIONS The diagram below shows a Petri dish containing a
bacterial culture and four paper disks (labeled *A–D*) treated with different antibiotics.
The concentrations of all four antibiotics are the same. Dark areas on the dish indicate
bacterial growth, and clear areas indicate inhibition of bacterial growth. State whether
the bacteria in this culture are very sensitive, moderately sensitive, or insensitive to each
antibiotic, and explain your reasoning.

A. _____

_____

B. _____

_____

C. _____

_____

D. _____

_____

SECTION 24-1 REVIEW

VIRAL STRUCTURE AND REPLICATION

VOCABULARY REVIEW Define the following terms.

1. virus ——

——

2. capsid ——

——

3. retrovirus ——

——

4. lytic cycle ——

——

5. lysogenic cycle ————————————————————————————————————

——

MULTIPLE CHOICE Write the correct letter in the blank.

———— **1.** Viruses are not alive because they

    a. do not grow.   **b.** lack cell parts.   **c.** do not metabolize. **d.** All of the above

———— **2.** Viruses can reproduce

    a. independently of host cells.
    b. independently of host cells if they first take up organelles from the host cells.
    c. only within host cells.
    d. only with the assistance of other viruses.

———— **3.** The enzyme reverse transcriptase uses

    a. DNA as a template to make more DNA.   **c.** RNA as a template to make more RNA.
    b. DNA as a template to make RNA.   **d.** RNA as a template to make DNA.

———— **4.** The grouping of viruses is based partly on the

    a. presence or absence of an envelope.   **c.** type of organism they infect.
    b. presence or absence of nucleic acid.   **d.** structure of their organelles.

———— **5.** Phage DNA that is integrated into a host cell's chromosome is a

    a. coronavirus.   **b.** retrovirus.   **c.** prophage.   **d.** capsid.

Name _____ Class _____ Date _____

SHORT ANSWER Answer the questions in the space provided.

1. What did Wendell Stanley's work suggest about the nature of viruses? _____

_____

_____

2. What kinds of factors can cause a prophage to become virulent? _____

_____

3. How does an RNA virus get viral DNA into a host cell's genome? _____

_____

_____

4. Why must a person receive a different flu vaccine each year to be protected against the flu?

_____

_____

5. **Critical Thinking** How does the structure and function of bacteriophages make these viruses

useful tools for genetic engineering? _____

_____

_____

STRUCTURES AND FUNCTIONS The diagrams below represent five steps in the lytic cycle of a bacteriophage. The order of the steps has been scrambled. Arrange the steps in their correct order by writing the letter of each step, and briefly describe what is happening in each step.

_____

_____

_____

  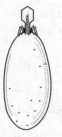  

a _____ b _____ c _____ d _____ e _____

SECTION 24-2 REVIEW

VIRAL DISEASES

VOCABULARY REVIEW Define the following terms.

1. inactivated virus _____

_____

2. attenuated virus _____

_____

3. oncogene _____

_____

4. proto-oncogene _____

_____

5. protease inhibitor _____

_____

MULTIPLE CHOICE Write the correct letter in the blank.

_____ 1. One viral disease that can occur in childhood and then reappear in adulthood in a more serious form is

    a. chickenpox.   **b.** smallpox.   **c.** rabies.   **d.** hepatitis.

_____ 2. The most successful approach to controlling viral diseases has been the use of

    a. antibiotics.   **b.** antiviral drugs.   **c.** viroids.   **d.** vaccines.

_____ 3. Which of the following viral diseases is now considered to be eradicated?

    a. chickenpox   **b.** smallpox   **c.** rabies   **d.** hepatitis

_____ 4. An emerging virus is one that arises

    a. from a host cell when the cell undergoes lysis.
    b. from a lysogenic cycle and enters a lytic cycle.
    c. when isolated habitats are developed by humans.
    d. on the skin after hiding inside nerve cells.

_____ 5. A disease-causing particle made of RNA without a capsid is called

    a. a viroid.   **c.** a prion.
    b. a retrovirus.   **d.** an envelope.

SHORT ANSWER Answer the questions in the space provided.

1. Name four viruses that can cause diseases that are often fatal. _____

_____

2. Explain the relationship between shingles and chickenpox. _____

_____

_____

3. Name two methods, other than vaccination, for controlling viral diseases. _____

_____

4. How are some viruses thought to cause cancer? _____

_____

5. Explain how an emerging virus might suddenly appear in a human population. _____

_____

_____

6. **Critical Thinking** Why would a drug that blocks DNA transcription not be a desirable method for

treating a viral disease? _____

_____

STRUCTURES AND FUNCTIONS Identify the structures labeled *a–e* in the diagram of the human immunodeficiency virus shown below.

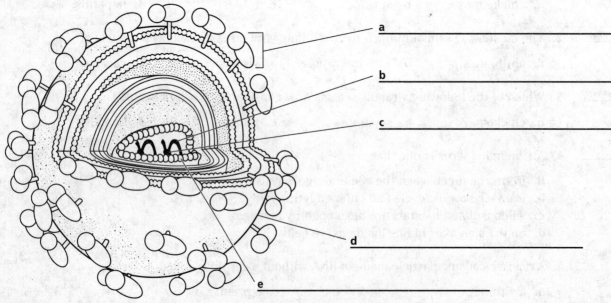

SECTION 25-1 REVIEW

CHARACTERISTICS OF PROTISTS

VOCABULARY REVIEW Define the following terms.

1. protist _____

_____

2. binary fission _____

_____

3. multiple fission _____

_____

4. conjugation _____

_____

MULTIPLE CHOICE Write the correct letter in the blank.

_____ **1.** Protozoans are members of the kingdom

    a. Animalia.   **b.** Plantae.   **c.** Fungi.   **d.** Protista.

_____ **2.** One characteristic that is not found in any protozoan is

    a. heterotrophy.   **b.** multicellularity.   **c.** motility.   **d.** parasitism.

_____ **3.** All protists are capable of

    a. asexual reproduction.   **c.** either asexual or sexual reproduction.
    b. sexual reproduction.   **d.** conjugation.

_____ **4.** All of the following are structures used for protist movement except

    a. cilia.
    b. flagella.
    c. zoospores.
    d. pseudopodia.

_____ **5.** Protists are thought to have evolved from

    a. early viruses.   **c.** ancient prokaryotes.
    b. early eukaryotes.   **d.** modern fungi.

SHORT ANSWER Answer the questions in the space provided.

1. Describe the two major ways by which protists obtain energy.

_____

_____

_____

2. How are protists classified?. _____

_____

3. What is endosymbiosis _____

_____

4. Critical Thinking Bacteria and protists both can undergo conjugation. Why is this process more

complex in protists than in bacteria? _____

_____

_____

STRUCTURES AND FUNCTIONS The diagram below represents asexual reproduction and sexual reproduction in *Chlamydomonas*. Label the two types of reproduction in the spaces provided.

a. _____   **b.** _____

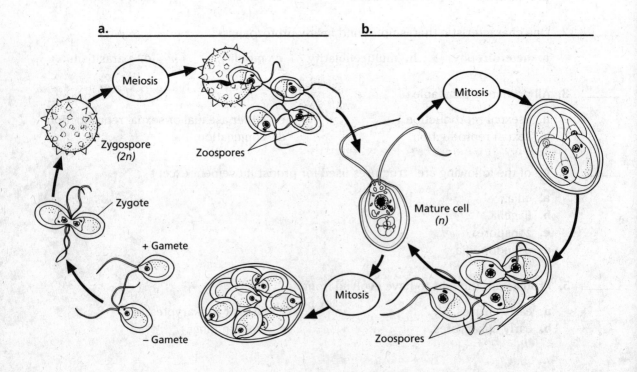

SECTION 25-2 REVIEW

ANIMAL-LIKE PROTISTS

VOCABULARY REVIEW Distinguish between the terms in each of the following pairs of terms.

1. cilia, flagella _____

_____

2. mouth pore, anal pore _____

_____

_____

3. macronucleus, micronucleus _____

_____

_____

MULTIPLE CHOICE Write the correct letter in the blank.

_____ 1. Amoebas move by means of a process known as

    a. vacuolar contracting.   **c.** flagellar whipping.

    b. cytoplasmic streaming.   **d.** ciliary beating.

_____ 2. Which of the following is formed from the tests of dead sarcodines?

    a. granite   **b.** limestone   **c.** sandstone   **d.** pearls

_____ 3. Sexual reproduction in ciliates involves

    a. binary fission and the formation of two identical offspring.

    b. the exchange of diploid macronuclei between two individuals.

    c. the exchange of haploid micronuclei between two individuals.

    d. the exchange of macronuclei and micronuclei between two individuals.

_____ 4. One disease caused by a mastigophoran is

    a. amebic dysentery.   **c.** sleeping sickness.

    b. malaria.   **d.** toxoplasmosis.

_____ 5. Most species in the phylum Apicomplexa are

    a. aquatic and move by using cilia.

    b. terrestrial and move by extending pseudopodia.

    c. parasitic and have complex life cycles.

    d. free-living and reproduce only asexually.

SHORT ANSWER Answer the questions in the space provided.

1. How have foraminifera and radiolarians contributed to the formation of sedimentary layers on

   the ocean floor? _____

   _____

2. Describe the processes of feeding and digestion in a paramecium. _____

   _____

   _____

3. Describe how protozoans use pseudopodia to move and to capture food. _____

   _____

   _____

4. **Critical Thinking** Although the protozoans that cause malaria are nonmotile, they parasitize two

   hosts during their life cycle. How do they accomplish this? _____

   _____

   _____

STRUCTURES AND FUNCTIONS Label each structure of the paramecium in the space indicated.

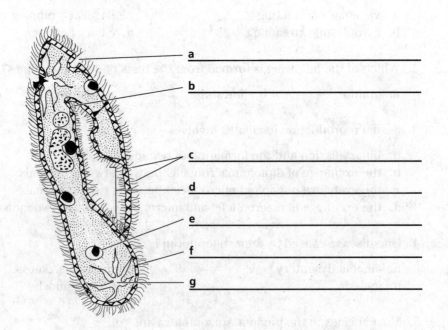

a _____

b _____

c _____

d _____

e _____

f _____

g _____

PLANTLIKE AND FUNGUSLIKE PROTISTS

VOCABULARY REVIEW Define the following terms.

1. fruiting body ——

——

2. gametangium ——

——

3. euglenoid ——

——

4. accessory pigment ——

——

MULTIPLE CHOICE Write the correct letter in the blank.

———— 1. Algae differ from protozoans in that algae are

    a. heterotrophic.   **c.** always multicellular.

    b. photosynthetic.   **d.** always unicellular.

———— 2. The body portion of a seaweed is called a

    a. pyrenoid.   **b.** holdfast.   **c.** sporophyte.   **d.** thallus.

———— 3. Algae are classified into phyla based on all of the following except their

    a. type of photosynthetic pigment.   **c.** presence or absence of flagella.

    b. form of food storage.   **d.** cell wall composition.

———— 4. A plasmodial slime mold will generally form a fruiting body when

    a. its host dies.

    b. the number of cells in the plasmodium becomes too large.

    c. the environment becomes too cold.

    d. food or water is scarce.

———— 5. Separate sperm-containing and egg-containing structures are produced by

    a. cellular slime molds.   **c.** water molds.

    b. plasmodial slime molds.   **d.** chytrids.

SHORT ANSWER Answer the questions in the space provided.

1. Describe two differences between green algae and plants. _____

_____

_____

2. Why is phytoplankton important to other organisms? _____

_____

_____

3. List the four body forms that algae can have. _____

_____

4. What structural features distinguish dinoflagellates from other algae? _____

_____

5. List two plantlike and two animal-like characteristics of euglenoids. _____

_____

_____

6. **Critical Thinking** Some biologists prefer to classify brown, red, and some green algae as plants rather than protists. What characteristics of these algae support such a classification?

_____

_____

_____

STRUCTURES AND FUNCTIONS Name the phylum of funguslike protists represented by each of the drawings below.

- Mass of cytoplasm with many nuclei
- Long filamentous bodies
- Flagellated gametes and zoospores
- Sluglike colony of many cells
- Fertilization tubes between reproductive structures

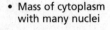

a _____   b _____   c _____   d _____

PROTISTS AND HUMANS

VOCABULARY REVIEW Distinguish between the terms in each of the following pairs of terms.

1. sporozoite, merozoite _____

_____

2. giardiasis, trichomoniasis _____

_____

3. alginate, agar _____

_____

MULTIPLE CHOICE Write the correct letter in the blank.

_____ **1.** Diatomaceous earth is valuable because it

   a. produces much of the Earth's oxygen.
   b. provides nutrients for many aquatic organisms.
   c. can be used to produce detergents, paint removers, and toothpaste.
   d. can be used as a source of petroleum.

_____ **2.** Which of the following is NOT an environmental role of protists?

   a. Protists produce large amounts of atmospheric oxygen.
   b. Photosynthetic protists are at the base of many food webs.
   c. Protists form important symbiotic relationships with other organisms.
   d. Protists form large amounts of cellulose.

_____ **3.** Algal blooms are caused by

   a. high nutrient concentrations.   **c.** low water temperature.
   b. low nutrient concentrations.   **d.** large numbers of fish.

_____ **4.** Malaria is characterized by

   a. severe chills, headache, fever, and fatigue.
   b. nerve damage.
   c. severe diarrhea, fever, and gastrointestinal hemorrhage.
   d. skin sores and swollen glands.

_____ **5.** Which of the following pathogens causes an intestinal tract disease?

   a. *Trypanosoma* sp.
   b. *Plasmodium* sp.
   c. *Entamoeba* sp.
   d. *Anopheles* sp.

Name _____ Class _____ Date _____

SHORT ANSWER Answer the questions in the space provided.

1. Describe two symbiotic relationships between a protist and another organism. _____
_____
_____

2. Why is carrageenan added to many commercial food products? _____
_____
_____

3. Why are scientists studying chemotaxis in cellular slime molds? _____
_____
_____

4. **Critical Thinking** Why are humans affected by red tides if they do not eat dinoflagellates?
_____
_____

STRUCTURES AND FUNCTIONS Identify the structures labeled *a–f* in the diagram of the life cycle of *Plasmodium* shown below.

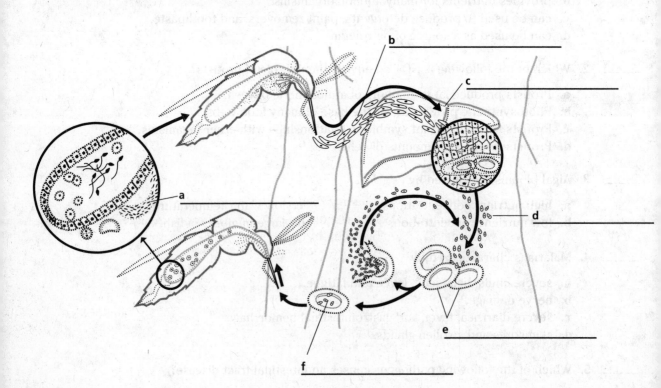

SECTION 26-1 REVIEW

OVERVIEW OF FUNGI

VOCABULARY REVIEW Define the following terms.

1. hypha _____

2. mycelium _____

_____

3. coenocyte _____

_____

4. sporangiophore _____

_____

5. conidium _____

_____

6. budding _____

_____

MULTIPLE CHOICE Write the correct letter in the blank.

_____ 1. All fungi are

    a. multicellular and prokaryotic.   **c.** eukaryotic and nonphotosynthetic.
    b. prokaryotic and photosynthetic.   **d.** unicellular and photosynthetic.

_____ 2. Unlike animals, fungi

    a. ingest their nutrients before digesting them.
    b. secrete enzymes and then absorb the digested nutrients through their cell wall.
    c. have cell walls made of cellulose without chitin.
    d. do not store energy in the form of glycogen.

_____ 3. Which of the following is NOT an asexual reproductive structure of a fungus?

    a. septum   **b.** sporangium   **c.** conidiophore   **d.** sporangiospore

_____ 4. Throughout most of their life cycle, most fungi are

    a. male.   **b.** female.   **c.** diploid.   **d.** haploid.

_____ 5. Biologists think that the first fungi on Earth arose from

    a. prokaryotes.   **b.** algae.   **c.** plants.   **d.** animals.

Name _____ Class _____ Date _____

SHORT ANSWER Answer the questions in the space provided.

1. How do the cell walls of fungi differ from those of plants? _____

_____

2. Describe an example of dimorphism in fungi. _____

_____

_____

3. Explain how a fungus reproduces through fragmentation. _____

_____

4. What do "plus" and "minus" mean when used in reference to fungi? _____

_____

_____

5. What characteristic do fungi share with animals? _____

_____

6. In what way are fungi resource recyclers? _____

_____

7. Critical Thinking In what ways are most fungi similar to unicellular protists? _____

_____

_____

STRUCTURES AND FUNCTIONS Identify the structures labeled *a–c*. In the spaces below the drawings, name the type of hyphae each drawing represents.

The drawings below depict two types of fungal hyphae.

a_____   b_____   c_____

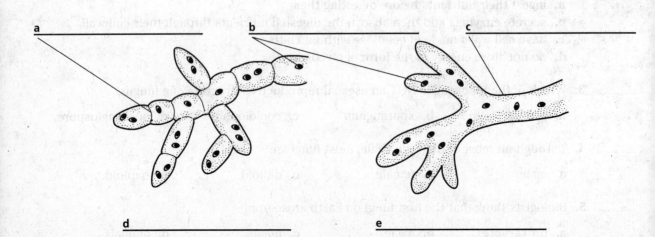

d_____   e_____

SECTION 26-2 REVIEW

CLASSIFICATION OF FUNGI

VOCABULARY REVIEW Distinguish between the terms in each of the following pairs of terms.

1. rhizoid, stolon _____

_____

2. basidium, basidiocarp _____

_____

3. ascogonium, antheridium _____

_____

4. ascocarp, ascus _____

_____

5. lichen, mycorrhiza _____

_____

MULTIPLE CHOICE Write the correct letter in the blank.

_____ 1. Fungi that have coenocytic hyphae and reproduce sexually through conjugation belong to the phylum

   a. Zygomycota. **b.** Basidiomycota. **c.** Ascomycota. **d.** Deuteromycota.

_____ 2. A mushroom is an example of a

   a. rhizoid. **b.** ascogonium. **c.** zygosporangium. **d.** basidiocarp.

_____ 3. Fungi that produce spores inside saclike compartments belong to the phylum

   a. Zygomycota. **b.** Basidiomycota. **c.** Ascomycota. **d.** Deuteromycota.

_____ 4. In the life cycle of an ascomycete, haploid nuclei fuse when

   a. conidia germinate.
   b. asci develop.
   c. a tube forms between the ascogonium and the antheridium.
   d. ascospores germinate.

_____ 5. One of the functions of the fungus in a mycorrhizal relationship is to

   a. perform photosynthesis   **c.** absorb phosphate and other ions.
   b. store sugars for the plant.   **d.** decompose rock to form soil.

SHORT ANSWER Answer the questions in the space provided.

1. How do the above-ground, sexual reproductive structures of basidiomycetes differ in appearance from those of ascomycetes? _____

   _____

2. How are fungi imperfecti different from other fungi? _____

3. Explain the difference between a mycorrhiza and a lichen. _____

   _____

   _____

4. What effect do lichens have on their physical environment? _____

   _____

5. Explain why mushrooms cannot be grouped with deuteromycetes. _____

   _____

6. What would be more beneficial to a growing plant, a mycorrhiza or lichen? Explain your answer.

   _____

   _____

   _____

7. **Critical Thinking** Why are fungi classified according to the sexual reproductive structures

   they form? _____

   _____

STRUCTURES AND FUNCTIONS Label each structure or process in the spaces provided.

The diagram below illustrates asexual and sexual reproduction in zygomycetes.

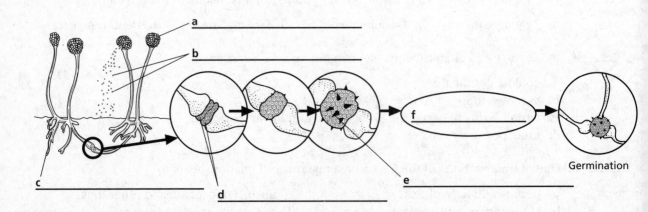

a _____

b _____

f _____

Germination

c _____

d _____

e _____

SECTION 26-3 REVIEW

FUNGI AND HUMANS

VOCABULARY REVIEW Answer the questions in the space provided.

1. What are aflatoxins? _____

2. What effect do aflatoxins have on humans? _____

3. Where are the organisms that produce aflatoxins found? _____

_____

4. What is a wheat rust? _____

_____

MULTIPLE CHOICE Write the correct letter in the blank.

_____ 1. Sniffling, sneezing, and respiratory distress may be symptoms of an allergic reaction to

    a. cortisone.
    b. the *Amanita* mushroom.
    c. the yeast *Candida albicans.*
    d. mold spores.

_____ 2. Which of the following is not a condition or disease that can be caused by fungi?

    a. athlete's foot   **b.** AIDS   **c.** ringworm   **d.** candidiasis

_____ 3. Fungal diseases that affect human internal organs are often caused by

    a. dimorphic fungi.   **b.** deuteromycetes.   **c.** truffles.   **d.** morels.

_____ 4. The yeast *Saccharomyces cerevisiae* is used to make all of the following except

    a. bread.   **b.** vaccines.   **c.** ethanol.   **d.** penicillin.

_____ 5. Fungi of the genus *Cephalosporium* are used to produce

    a. mushrooms.   **b.** cheese.   **c.** antibiotics.   **d.** soy products.

_____ 6. Which of the following is not a fungal product of importance to the food-processing industry?

    a. vitamin B_2 **b.** wheat rust   **c.** citric acid   **d.** gluconic acid

_____ 7. The automobile fuel gasohol is made in part with

    a. aflatoxins produced by *Amanita.*
    b. gluconic acid produced by *Saccharomyces cerevisiae.*
    c. ethanol produced by yeast.
    d. citric acid produced by yeast.

SHORT ANSWER Answer the questions in the space provided.

1. What conditions can cause *Candida albicans* to flourish? _____

   _____

2. Name four specific medical products that are produced by or with the use of fungi. _____

   _____

3. Name four types of foods that are produced by or with the use of fungi. _____

   _____

4. How is *Saccharomyces cerevisiae* induced to manufacture substances that it does not

   normally make? _____

   _____

   _____

5. **Critical Thinking** Some fungi produce substances with attractive odors or flavors. These
   substances are often concentrated in the reproductive structures of the fungi. Why might it be

   adaptive for a fungus to produce such substances? _____

   _____

   _____

STRUCTURES AND FUNCTIONS This flowchart illustrates the effects that fungi can have
on humans. Fill in the blanks to complete the chart.

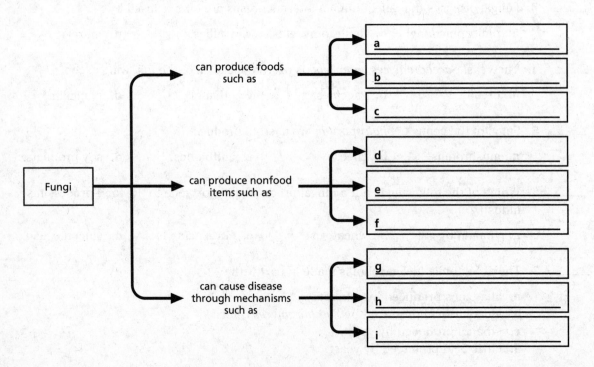

PLANTS AND PEOPLE

VOCABULARY REVIEW Distinguish between the terms in each of the following pairs of terms.

1. botany, agriculture _____

_____

2. cereal, root crop _____

_____

3. legume, nut _____

_____

4. fruit, vegetable _____

_____

MULTIPLE CHOICE Write the correct letter in the blank.

_____ 1. In cultivating wheat, early farmers selected wheat plants

    a. whose seeds were easily dispersed.
    b. whose stalks did not break easily in the wind.
    c. that produced the fewest grains.
    d. that had the largest seed pods.

_____ 2. Legumes are valuable crops because they have protein-rich seeds and because

    a. they improve the nitrogen content of soil.
    b. their leaves are used as herbs.
    c. their leaves are fed to livestock.
    d. their bark is a source of quinine.

_____ 3. Black pepper is the ground-up seed of a pepper plant, which makes pepper

    a. a fruit.   **b.** a flavoring.   **c.** an herb.   **d.** a spice.

_____ 4. All of the following plants are used for their medicinal value except the

    a. cinchona tree.   **b.** white willow.   **c.** coconut.   **d.** foxglove.

_____ 5. The artificial fabric rayon is made from

    a. rayon grass.   **c.** coal.
    b. processed wood fibers.   **d.** petroleum.

SHORT ANSWER Answer the questions in the space provided.

1. What is a cultivar? _____

_____

Give two examples of cultivars. _____

2. What nutrients are usually deficient in diets consisting of cereals and root crops?

_____

How can people supplement such diets to overcome this deficiency? _____

_____

3. Explain how grains can be used to produce fuel. _____

_____

4. **Critical Thinking** Why do you think root crops rather than cereals make up the major part of

the diet of people living in many parts of the world? _____

_____

STRUCTURES AND FUNCTIONS Label each of the food plants shown below according to one of the following food categories: cereal, root crop, legume, fruit, vegetable, nut, spice, herb.

_____   _____   _____   _____

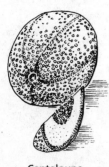

Cantaloupe

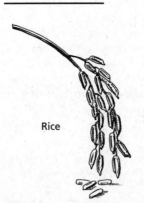

Rice

Celery

Nutmeg

_____   _____   _____   _____

Pecan

Potato

Lima bean

Oregano

SECTION 27-2 REVIEW

PLANTS AND THE ENVIRONMENT

VOCABULARY REVIEW Define the following terms.

1. plant ecology _____

_____

2. weed _____

_____

3. hay fever _____

_____

MULTIPLE CHOICE Write the correct letter in the blank.

_____ **1.** One of the inorganic nutrients recycled by plants is

    a. sugar.   **b.** starch.   **c.** phosphorus.   **d.** cellulose.

_____ **2.** Which of the following is *not* a reason why animals help pollinate plants?

    a. The animals want to help the plants reproduce successfully.
    b. The shape and color of the plants' flowers attract the animals.
    c. The animals obtain nectar as they pollinate the plants.
    d. The plants' flowers resemble females of the animals' species.

_____ **3.** Mycorrhizal fungi

    a. cause plant diseases that may result in major crop losses.
    b. infect plant roots without harming the roots.
    c. decrease a plant's ability to absorb water and inorganic nutrients.
    d. supply plants with energy in exchange for water.

_____ **4.** Plants that are harmful when eaten or touched include

    a. poison oak.   **c.** American mistletoe.
    b. holly.   **d.** All of the above

_____ **5.** Most of the problems associated with hay fever are caused by

    a. airborne pollen.   **c.** skin contact with weeds.
    b. ingested fruits and berries.   **d.** cotton clothing.

_____ **6.** Which of the following is *not* likely to cause hay fever?

    a. deciduous trees   **b.** wild grasses   **c.** cereal crops   **d.** large flowers

SHORT ANSWER Answer the questions in the space provided.

1. How do plants participate in the cycling of oxygen and carbon dioxide on Earth? _____
_____

_____

2. How do plants contribute to the formation and maintenance of soil? _____
_____

_____

3. What caused the near elimination of American chestnut trees in the early 1900s? _____
_____

4. What kinds of flowers usually produce allergy-inducing pollen? _____
_____

5. **Critical Thinking** Why have plants such as the water hyacinth and kudzu become so widespread

in some areas where they have been introduced by humans? _____

_____

_____

STRUCTURES AND FUNCTIONS The diagram below represents the cycling of inorganic
nutrients in the environment. Complete the diagram by filling in each space with one of
the following terms: inorganic nutrients, death, consumers, decomposers.

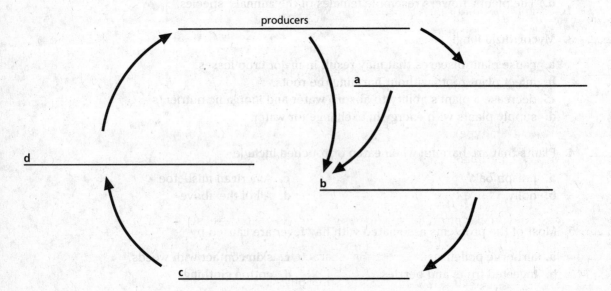

1. Which term describes the role of plants in the cycle? _____

2. Provide an example of a nutrient that could be recycled in this manner. _____

SECTION 28-1 REVIEW

OVERVIEW OF PLANTS

VOCABULARY REVIEW Distinguish between the terms in each of the following pairs of terms.

1. sporophyte, gametophyte _____

_____

2. spore, seed _____

_____

3. xylem, phloem _____

_____

4. vascular plant, nonvascular plant _____

_____

5. angiosperm, gymnosperm _____

_____

MULTIPLE CHOICE Write the correct letter in the blank.

_____ 1. Each of the following is a part of a seed except the

    a. embryo.   **b.** endosperm.   **c.** seed coat.   **d.** gametophyte.

_____ 2. The plant tissue that transports water from the roots to the leaves is the

    a. phloem.   **b.** xylem.   **c.** endosperm.   **d.** woody tissue.

_____ 3. Ferns are a type of

    a. vascular plant.   **b.** seed plant.   **c.** angiosperm.   **d.** gymnosperm.

_____ 4. Pine trees are a type of

    a. nonvascular plant.   **b.** angiosperm.   **c.** gymnosperm.   **d.** herbaceous plant.

_____ 5. The life cycle of a vascular plant is characterized by

    a. a large gametophyte and a small sporophyte.
    b. a large sporophyte and a small gametophyte.
    c. the absence of a sporophyte.
    d. the absence of a gametophyte.

Name _____ Class _____ Date _____

SHORT ANSWER Answer the questions in the space provided.

1. Name two adaptations plants have made to life on land, and briefly describe the advantage of each adaptation. _____

_____

_____

2. Describe three similarities between modern green algae and plants. _____

_____

_____

3. What structures or stages in the life cycle of a plant are haploid? _____

_____

4. **Critical Thinking** In what two ways are the spores of land plants different from the spores of algae, which you learned about in an earlier chapter? _____

_____

_____

STRUCTURES AND FUNCTIONS The diagram below is a phylogenetic diagram of plants and their algal ancestors. In the spaces provided, name the important adaptation(s) that evolved at each of the positions indicated on the phylogenetic diagram.

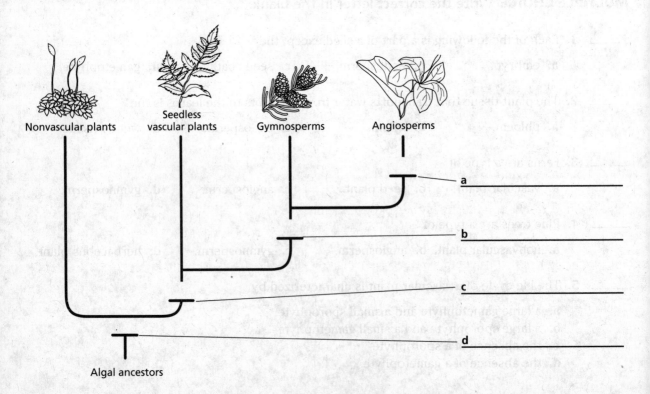

SECTION 28-2 REVIEW

NONVASCULAR PLANTS

VOCABULARY REVIEW Define the following terms.

1. bryophyte _____

_____

2. liverwort _____

_____

3. hornwort _____

_____

MULTIPLE CHOICE Write the correct letter in the blank.

_____ **1.** Bryophytes have

    a. true roots, stems, and leaves.   **c.** vascular tissue.
    b. an alternation-of-generations life cycle.   **d.** seeds.

_____ **2.** Bryophytes include all of the following plants except

    a. ferns.   **b.** hornworts.   **c.** liverworts.   **d.** mosses.

_____ **3.** Mosses are called pioneer plants because they

    a. are more closely related to algae than to plants.
    b. were the first plants to be cultivated by European settlers in North America.
    c. are often the first species to inhabit a barren area.
    d. gradually remove organic and inorganic matter from the surface of rocks.

_____ **4.** Peat bogs

    a. decompose rapidly.
    b. are composed mainly of algae and ferns.
    c. are found mostly in the southern hemisphere.
    d. are used as a source of fuel in many countries.

_____ **5.** The body forms of liverworts may include all of the following except

    a. thin leaflike structures arranged along a stemlike axis.
    b. clusters of leaves and flowers at the end of a woody stem.
    c. a flat body with distinguishable upper and lower surfaces.
    d. an umbrella-shaped structure that holds reproductive cells.

SHORT ANSWER Answer the questions in the space provided.

1. What phase of the bryophyte life cycle is dominant? _____

2. Why do bryophytes require a moist environment for sexual reproduction? _____

   _____

3. Describe three ways that humans use peat moss. _____

   _____

   _____

4. How are hornworts similar to algae and different from other plants? _____

   _____

   _____

5. Explain how mosses benefit an environmentally disturbed area. _____

   _____

   _____

6. **Critical Thinking** In what type of environment would you expect to find liverworts with a thalloid

   body form? Explain your answer. _____

   _____

   _____

STRUCTURES AND FUNCTIONS The drawing below illustrates the main parts of a moss. Identify the phases of the moss life cycle represented by *a* and *b*, and name the structure labeled *c*.

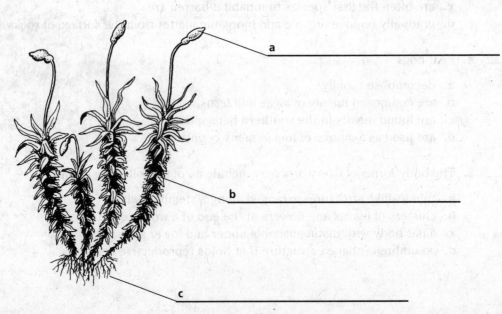

a _____

b _____

c _____

SECTION 28-3 REVIEW

VASCULAR PLANTS

VOCABULARY REVIEW Distinguish between the terms in each of the following pairs of terms.

1. fiddlehead, frond _____

_____

2. monocot, dicot _____

_____

3. parallel venation, net venation _____

_____

MULTIPLE CHOICE Write the correct letter in the blank.

_____ **1.** The mobile sexual reproductive parts of all seedless plants are

    a. rhizomes.   **b.** cones.   **c.** spores.   **d.** epiphytes.

_____ **2.** One of the adaptive advantages of seeds is that seeds

    a. do not remain inactive for long periods of time.
    b. can germinate without water.
    c. lack a tough outer coat.
    d. contain a nutrient supply.

_____ **3.** Naked seeds are produced by plants in the phylum

    a. Coniferophyta.   **b.** Lycophyta.   **c.** Anthophyta.   **d.** Pteridophyta.

_____ **4.** One of the differences between angiosperms and gymnosperms is that

    a. most gymnosperms can reach maturity in a single growing season.
    b. angiosperms have a more efficient vascular system.
    c. gymnosperms are more likely to be associated with mycorrhizae.
    d. angiosperms are less diverse than gymnosperms.

_____ **5.** Most monocots

    a. bear their seeds in cones.
    b. have vascular bundles that are arranged in a circle.
    c. do not produce flowers.
    d. have parallel venation.

SHORT ANSWER Answer the questions in the space provided.

1. Identify two ways that vascular plants differ from nonvascular plants. _____

   _____

   _____

2. Briefly describe the distinguishing characteristics of gymnosperms in the phyla Cycadophyta,

   Ginkgophyta, and Coniferophyta. _____

   _____

   _____

3. How do the reproductive structures of angiosperms differ from those of gymnosperms?

   _____

   _____

4. **Critical Thinking** There are many more species of ferns (phylum Pteridoophyta) than there are
   species in the other three phyla of seedless vascular plants. Propose a hypothesis to explain this fact.

   _____

   _____

STRUCTURES AND FUNCTIONS Write the phylum name of the type of vascular plant represented by each of the drawings. Choose the name from the list of phylum names below.

Lycophyta	Pteridoophyta	Coniferophyta
Psilophyta	Cycadophyta	Gnetophyta
Sphenophyta	Ginkgophyta	Anthophyta

Ginkgo

Whisk fern

Cycad

Pine

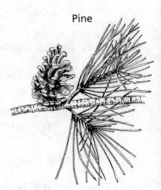

a _____   b _____   c _____   d _____

SECTION 29-1 REVIEW

PLANT CELLS AND TISSUES

VOCABULARY REVIEW Distinguish between the terms in each of the following groups of terms.

1. parenchyma cells, collenchyma cells, sclerenchyma cells _____

_____

_____

2. dermal tissue system, ground tissue system, vascular tissue system _____

_____

_____

3. apical meristems, intercalary meristems, lateral meristems _____

_____

_____

MULTIPLE CHOICE Write the correct letter in the blank.

_____ 1. Which of the following plant cells is dead at maturity?

    a. epidermal cell   **b.** companion cell   **c.** vessel element   **d.** collenchyma cell

_____ 2. The conducting parenchyma cell of angiosperm phloem is called a

    a. sieve tube member.   **c.** stoma.
    b. tracheid.   **d.** cuticle.

_____ 3. Intercalary meristems are found in some

    a. conifers.   **b.** gymnosperms.   **c.** dicots.   **d.** monocots.

_____ 4. In woody stems and roots, the epidermis is replaced by

    a. the vascular cambium.   **c.** apical meristems.
    b. cork cells.   **d.** sieve plates.

_____ 5. Primary growth refers to

    a. the germination of a seedling.
    b. an increase in the length of a plant.
    c. an increase in the diameter of a stem.
    d. growth produced by the lateral meristems.

SHORT ANSWER Answer the questions in the space provided.

1. What type of parenchyma cell is found in the nonwoody parts of plants, and what are the functions

   of this cell type? _____

   _____

2. Describe the appearance, primary function, and location of collenchyma cells. _____

   _____

   _____

3. In what parts of a plant would you expect to find sclerenchyma cells? _____

   _____

4. What kinds of meristems are found in monocots, and where are they located? _____

   _____

   What kinds of meristems are found in dicots, and where are they located? _____

   _____

5. **Critical Thinking** Why is it advantageous for plants to have water-transporting cells that are dead?

   _____

   _____

STRUCTURES AND FUNCTIONS The drawings below depict the major components of xylem and phloem. Identify the structures labeled *a–d*. In the spaces below the drawings labeled *e–g*, name the type of component each drawing represents.

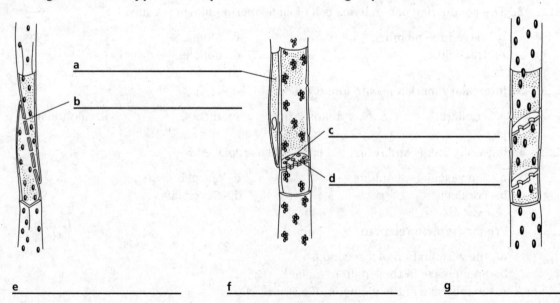

e _____   f _____   g _____

ROOTS

VOCABULARY REVIEW Define the following terms.

1. adventitious root _____

_____

2. cortex _____

_____

3. pericycle _____

_____

4. macronutrient _____

_____

5. micronutrient _____

_____

MULTIPLE CHOICE Write the correct letter in the blank.

_____ 1. One example of a plant with a fibrous root system is a

  a. carrot.   **b.** cottonwood.   **c.** radish.   **d.** grass.

_____ 2. All of the following adaptations increase the ability of roots to absorb water except

  a. root caps.   **c.** fibrous root systems.
  b. root hairs.   **d.** mycorrhizal associations.

_____ 3. The cortex of a primary root is made of

  a. epidermal cells.   **b.** parenchyma cells.   **c.** vascular tissues.   **d.** pith.

_____ 4. Roots perform all of the following functions except

  a. absorbing water and minerals from the soil.
  b. anchoring the plant in the soil.
  c. carrying out the light reactions of photosynthesis.
  d. storing water and organic compounds.

_____ 5. One of the micronutrients plants absorb is

  a. manganese.   **b.** nitrogen.   **c.** potassium.   **d.** carbon.

SHORT ANSWER Answer the questions in the space provided.

1. What kind of tissue forms the innermost cylinder of a root? _____

   _____

2. What cells divide to form lateral roots? _____

   _____

3. Where does a vascular cambium form during secondary growth in roots? _____

   _____

4. What structures does this vascular cambium produce, and where are they produced? _____

   _____

   _____

5. Name four macronutrients in plants. _____

   _____

6. **Critical Thinking** Would you expect water absorption to be greater in parts of roots that have

   undergone secondary growth or in parts that have not? Explain your reasoning. _____

   _____

   _____

STRUCTURES AND FUNCTIONS The drawings below show cross sections of a monocot root and a dicot root. Identify the structures labeled *a–f*. In the spaces below the drawings, name the type of root each drawing represents.

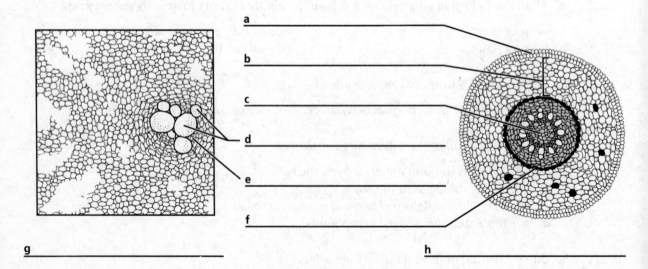

a _____

b _____

c _____

d _____

e _____

f _____

g _____

h _____

SECTION 29-3 REVIEW

STEMS

VOCABULARY REVIEW Distinguish between the terms in each of the following pairs of terms.

1. heartwood, sapwood _____

   _____

2. springwood, summerwood _____

   _____

3. source, sink _____

   _____

4. translocation, transpiration _____

   _____

5. pith, wood _____

   _____

MULTIPLE CHOICE Write the correct letter in the blank.

_____ 1. Which of the following are found in both roots and stems?

   a. buds **b.** vascular tissues **c.** nodes **d.** internodes

_____ 2. Lateral stems arise from meristems located

   a. randomly along the main stem. **c.** between the bark and the wood.
   b. deep inside the main stem. **d.** at nodes on the surface of the main stem.

_____ 3. One difference between monocot stems and dicot stems is that monocot stems usually

   a. have vascular bundles arranged in a ring.
   b. replace primary tissues with secondary tissues.
   c. retain the primary growth pattern their entire lives.
   d. have secondary growth.

_____ 4. In a stem cross section, an annual ring represents an abrupt change between

   a. summerwood and springwood. **c.** bark and cork.
   b. heartwood and sapwood. **d.** xylem and phloem.

_____ 5. The driving force for transpiration is provided by

   a. water pressure in the roots. **c.** the evaporation of water from the leaves.
   b. water tension in the stems. **d.** the hydrolysis of ATP.

SHORT ANSWER Answer the questions in the space provided.

1. What structures on a stem are analogous to the root cap on a root? _____

   _____

   How do these structures differ from a root cap? _____

   _____

2. Explain how evaporation, tension, cohesion, and adhesion are involved in the movement of water

   through a plant. _____

   _____

   _____

3. **Critical Thinking** Besides serving as a conduit for water, what other function does wood have
   in trees and other woody plants? How is this function important in stimulating photosynthesis?

   _____

   _____

STRUCTURES AND FUNCTIONS The diagram below represents the movement of carbohydrates in a plant as described by the pressure-flow model. Identify the structures
labeled *a–d* and the substances that are transported along the arrows labeled *e–i.*

a _____

b _____

c _____

d _____

e _____

f _____

g _____

h _____

i _____

SECTION 29-4 REVIEW

LEAVES

VOCABULARY REVIEW Define the following terms.

1. petiole _____

_____

2. mesophyll _____

_____

3. guard cell _____

_____

MULTIPLE CHOICE Write the correct letter in the blank.

_____ 1. A leaf that is divided into leaflets is called a

    a. simple leaf.   **b.** compound leaf.   **c.** veined leaf.   **d.** parallel leaf.

_____ 2. Leaves consist of

    a. dermal tissue only.
    b. dermal tissue and ground tissue only.
    c. ground tissue and vascular tissue only.
    d. dermal tissue, ground tissue, and vascular tissue.

_____ 3. One adaptation that reduces water loss from leaves without reducing the rate of photo-synthesis is the

    a. closure of stomata during the night.
    b. closure of stomata during a water shortage.
    c. presence of large numbers of stomata.
    d. presence of epidermal hairs.

_____ 4. Most photosynthesis occurs in a portion of the leaf called the

    a. vascular bundle.   **c.** palisade mesophyll.
    b. spongy mesophyll.   **d.** upper epidermis.

_____ 5. Leaves that develop in full sun

    a. are thicker.
    b. have a larger area per leaf.
    c. have fewer chloroplasts per unit area.
    d. have minimal shading of one chloroplast by another.

SHORT ANSWER Answer the questions in the space provided.

1. Describe three adaptations of leaves for functions besides photosynthesis. _____

_____

_____

2. What is the usual function of the epidermal hairs on a leaf? _____

_____

_____

3. What are the products of photosynthesis in a leaf used for, and where are they used within the plant?

_____

_____

4. Explain how potassium ions are involved in the opening of stomata. _____

_____

_____

5. **Critical Thinking** Why would an agricultural practice that eliminated transpirational water loss

be disadvantageous for plants? _____

_____

_____

_____

STRUCTURES AND FUNCTIONS Identify the structures labeled *a–f* in the drawing of the internal structure of a leaf shown below.

a _____

b _____

c _____

d _____

e _____

f _____

SECTION 30-1 REVIEW

PLANT LIFE CYCLES

VOCABULARY REVIEW Distinguish between the terms in each of the following pairs of terms.

1. antheridium, archegonium _____

_____

2. homospory, heterospory _____

_____

3. integument, micropyle _____

_____

MULTIPLE CHOICE Write the correct letter in the blank.

_____ 1. Which of the following is the correct order of formation of structures in the life cycle of a moss?

   a. archegonium and antheridium, spores, sporophyte, egg and sperm, zygote
   b. zygote, spores, sporophyte, archegonium and antheridium, egg and sperm
   c. sporophyte, spores, archegonium and antheridium, egg and sperm, zygote
   d. egg and sperm, archegonium and antheridium, zygote, spores, sporophyte

_____ 2. The production of a single type of spore is a characteristic of the life cycles of

   a. mosses and most ferns.
   b. mosses and most gymnosperms.
   c. most ferns and gymnosperms.
   d. mosses, most ferns, and most gymnosperms.

_____ 3. One structure that is found in ferns but not in mosses or conifers is

   a. an ovule.   **b.** a pollen grain.   **c.** a sporophyte.   **d.** a sorus.

_____ 4. The dominant stage in the life cycle of a conifer is the

   a. gametophyte.   **b.** sporophyte.   **c.** megasporangium. **d.** microsporangium.

_____ 5. Sexual reproduction in conifers and other seed plants is independent of seasonal rains because

   a. these plants grow only near streams and rivers.
   b. pollinators carry the sperm to the eggs.
   c. fertilization occurs inside structures within the sporophyte.
   d. fertilization always involves eggs and sperm of the same plant.

SHORT ANSWER Answer the questions in the space provided.

1. Which of the following structures in a moss life cycle are haploid and which are diploid: sporophyte, spore, archegonium, antheridium, gametophyte, zygote? _____

_____

Which structure represents the dominant phase of the life cycle? _____

2. How do the sperm of conifers differ from those of mosses and ferns? _____

_____

How do the spores of conifers differ from those of mosses and most ferns? _____

_____

3. What kind of cell division results in the production of spores? _____

What kind of cell division results in the production of gametes? _____

4. **Critical Thinking** Why must mosses and ferns live in environments that are wet during at least

part of the year? _____

_____

STRUCTURES AND FUNCTIONS Identify the structures labeled *a–h* in the diagram of the life cycle of a fern shown below.

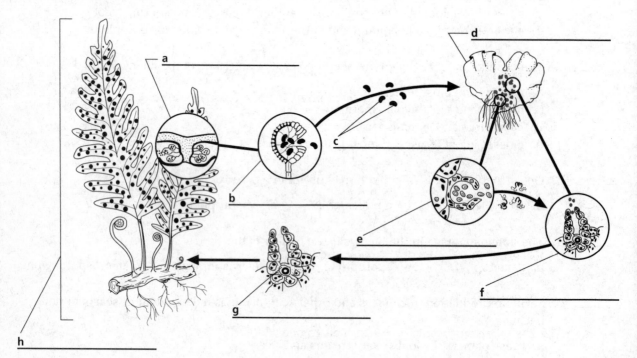

SECTION 30-2 REVIEW

SEXUAL REPRODUCTION IN FLOWERING PLANTS

VOCABULARY REVIEW Explain the relationship between the terms in each of the following pairs of terms.

1. anther, filament _____

_____

2. stigma, style _____

_____

3. polar nuclei, double fertilization _____

_____

MULTIPLE CHOICE Write the correct letter in the blank.

_____ **1.** During ovule formation in a flowering plant, the resulting structure contains

    a. four megaspores.
    b. one megaspore mother cell with four nuclei.
    c. one egg cell and two polar nuclei.
    d. four megaspores and four egg cells.

_____ **2.** In a flowering plant, the female gametophyte is referred to as

    a. an embryo sac.   **c.** an ovule.
    b. a megaspore mother cell.   **d.** a carpel.

_____ **3.** During pollen formation in a flowering plant, the resulting structure contains

    a. two sperm cells.   **c.** one microspore mother cell.
    b. a generative cell and a tube cell.   **d.** four microspores.

_____ **4.** Successful wind pollination usually requires

    a. large, colorful flowers.
    b. the release of small amounts of pollen.
    c. wet weather.
    d. the relative proximity of individuals to one another.

_____ **5.** In a flowering plant, one sperm fertilizes the polar nuclei to form the

    a. micropyle.   **b.** endosperm.   **c.** pollen tube.   **d.** zygote.

SHORT ANSWER Answer the questions in the space provided.

1. What happens to the four megaspores produced during ovule formation? _____
_____

What happens to the four microspores produced during pollen grain formation? _____
_____

2. Which of the following structures and events occur in both gymnosperms and angiosperms, and which occur only in angiosperms: wind pollination, animal pollination, pollen grain, pollen tube, fertilization quickly following pollination, double fertilization, embryo sac, endosperm?
_____
_____
_____
_____

3. What adaptive advantage does a plant gain by producing nectar? _____
_____

4. What is the function of endosperm? _____
_____

5. **Critical Thinking** Are plants that are pollinated by moths and bats more likely to have colorful flowers or fragrant flowers? Explain your reasoning. _____
_____

STRUCTURES AND FUNCTIONS Identify the structures labeled *a–i* in the diagram of a flower shown below.

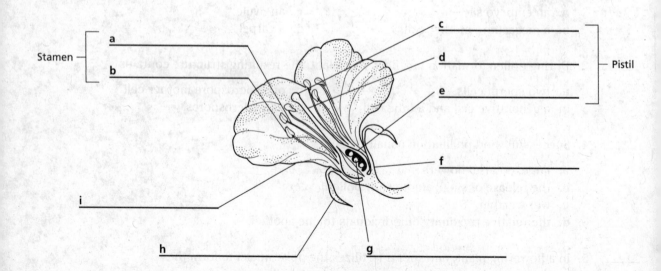

SECTION 30-3 REVIEW

DISPERSAL AND PROPAGATION

VOCABULARY REVIEW Define the following terms.

1. radicle _____

2. hypocotyl _____

_____

3. epicotyl _____

_____

4. plumule _____

_____

5. hilum _____

_____

MULTIPLE CHOICE Write the correct letter in the blank.

_____ 1. One structure that is not an adaptation for fruit or seed dispersal is the

    a. "parachute" on a milkweed seed.   **c.** air chamber in a coconut.
    b. pair of wings on a pine seed.   **d.** cotyledon of a corn grain.

_____ 2. Fruits are classified partly on the basis of how

    a. they are dispersed.   **c.** many pistils or flowers form the fruit.
    b. many seeds they contain.   **d.** large they are.

_____ 3. Which of the following plants has mature seeds that contain endosperm?

    a. corn   **b.** lima bean   **c.** pea   **d.** pine

_____ 4. The first visible sign of seed germination is the

    a. growth of the shoot.
    b. emergence of the radicle.
    c. appearance of the cotyledons above the soil.
    d. unfolding of the plumule's embryonic leaves.

_____ 5. Vegetative propagation refers to the

    a. sexual reproduction of plants that are consumed as vegetables.
    b. growth of the leaves and stems of a plant.
    c. use of vegetative structures to produce new plants.
    d. crossing of two strains of plants to produce hybrid vegetables.

SHORT ANSWER Answer the questions in the space provided.

1. Name the category of fruit to which each of the following belongs: raspberry, pineapple, pea pod.

_____

_____

2. Identify four environmental factors or conditions that are required for the germination of at least

some seeds. _____

_____

3. What is the main advantage of asexual reproduction? _____

_____

What is the main disadvantage of asexual reproduction? _____

_____

4. Name four plant structures that are adapted for vegetative reproduction. _____

_____

5. Name three common methods of seed dispersal, and give an example of each method.

_____

_____

6. **Critical Thinking** Because plants make their own food through photosynthesis, why is it

necessary for plant seeds to contain food reserves? _____

_____

STRUCTURES AND FUNCTIONS Identify the structures labeled *a–f* in the diagram of a corn grain shown below.

a _____

b _____

c _____

d _____

e _____

f _____

SECTION 31-1 REVIEW

PLANT HORMONES

VOCABULARY REVIEW Define the following terms.

1. plant hormone _____

_____

2. apical dominance _____

_____

3. ethephon _____

_____

4. abscission _____

_____

5. cytokinin _____

_____

MULTIPLE CHOICE Write the correct letter in the blank.

_____ 1. The major effect of indoleacetic acid is to

    a. inhibit the enlargement of fruit.   **c.** stimulate dormancy.
    b. stimulate cell growth.   **d.** inhibit germination.

_____ 2. After a shoot has had its tip removed, apical dominance can be maintained artificially by the application of

    a. GA.   **b.** 2,4-D.   **c.** ABA.   **d.** NAA.

_____ 3. One of the effects of gibberellins is to stimulate

    a. germination.   **b.** ripening.   **c.** dormancy.   **d.** abscission.

_____ 4. Ethylene differs from other plant hormones in that it

    a. has only inhibitory effects on plants.   **c.** is a gas at room temperature.
    b. is produced only in seeds.   **d.** affects only the plant that produces it.

_____ 5. By varying the ratio of auxins to cytokinins in a tissue-culture medium, botanists can selectively stimulate the formation of

    a. roots or shoots.   **c.** flowers or fruits.
    b. stems or leaves.   **d.** seeds or lateral buds.

Name _____ Class _____ Date _____

SHORT ANSWER Answer the questions in the space provided.

1. Why does the removal of seeds from a strawberry fruit prevent the fruit from enlarging? _____
_____

2. Identify three agricultural uses of gibberellins. _____
_____

3. Identify three agricultural uses of ethylene or ethephon. _____
_____

4. How is it adaptive for a water-stressed plant to produce ABA? _____
_____
_____

5. Critical Thinking Abscisic acid was originally named "dormin." Why was that an appropriate

name for this hormone? _____
_____
_____

STRUCTURES AND FUNCTIONS The drawings below show two plants of the same
species and the same age. The plant on the right was treated with a hormone. The plant
on the left was not. Which of the five major groups of plant hormones was used to treat
the plant on the right? Explain your answer.

_____

_____

_____

_____

_____

_____

_____

PLANT MOVEMENTS

VOCABULARY REVIEW Define the following terms, and provide one example of a type of plant or a plant part to which each term applies.

1. thigmotropism _____

_____

2. thigmonastic movement _____

_____

3. nyctinastic movement _____

_____

MULTIPLE CHOICE Write the correct letter in the blank.

_____ 1. The positive phototropism shown by shoots is caused by the movement of

    a. auxin to the shaded side of the shoot.   **c.** ethylene to the shaded side of the shoot.
    b. auxin to the lighted side of the shoot.   **d.** ethylene to the lighted side of the shoot.

_____ 2. The coiling of a morning glory stem around a fence post is an example of

    a. phototropism.   **c.** thigmotropism.
    b. chemotropism.   **d.** a thigmonastic movement.

_____ 3. The opposite responses of stems and roots to gravity are thought to be due to the

    a. inhibition of cell elongation in the lower side of the stems and the stimulation of cell elongation in the lower side of the roots.
    b. stimulation of cell elongation in the lower side of the stems and the inhibition of cell elongation in the lower side of the roots.
    c. inhibition of cell elongation in the lower side of both the stems and the roots.
    d. stimulation of cell elongation in the lower side of both the stems and the roots.

_____ 4. Unlike tropisms, nastic movements are

    a. always positive.   **c.** restricted to flowers.
    b. always negative.   **d.** independent of the direction of stimuli.

_____ 5. The daily change in the orientation of the prayer plant's leaves is an example of

    a. solar tracking.   **c.** a thigmonastic movement.
    b. a nyctinastic movement.   **d.** gravitropism.

SHORT ANSWER Answer the questions in the space provided.

1. What is the adaptive advantage of positive phototropism? _____

   _____

   What is the adaptive advantage of positive gravitropism? _____

   _____

2. What type of plant hormone is thought to be involved in all plant tropisms that involve

   cell elongation? _____

3. What cellular events make nastic movements possible? _____

   _____

4. What are three adaptive advantages of thigmonastic movements? _____

   _____

5. **Critical Thinking** The Venus' flytrap obtains nitrogen and minerals by closing its leaves around
   insects and then digesting the insects. Why would a thigmonastic movement be more useful than

   thigmotropism for this type of plant response? _____

   _____

STRUCTURES AND FUNCTIONS Use the diagram of a seedling below to answer the
following questions.

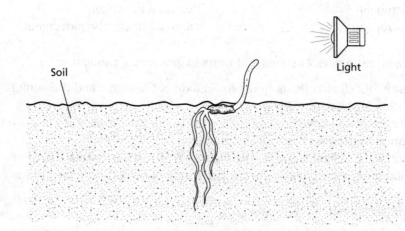

1. What tropisms are being exhibited by the various parts of this seedling? _____

   _____

2. What hormones are involved in these responses? _____

   _____

SEASONAL RESPONSES

VOCABULARY REVIEW Define the following terms.

1. photoperiodism ——————————————————————————————

——

2. vernalization ————————————————————————————————

——

3. bolting ———————————————————————————————————

——

4. critical night length ————————————————————————————

——

MULTIPLE CHOICE Write the correct letter in the blank.

————— 1. Long-day plants flower

    a. in the fall.
    b. when the day length is longer than 12 hours.
    c. when the night length is shorter than a critical number of hours.
    d. when the night length is longer than a critical number of hours.

————— 2. Flower growers can induce winter flowering in a long-day plant by

    a. spraying the plant with gibberellin.
    b. exposing the plant to low temperatures.
    c. covering the plant in the late afternoon with an opaque cloth.
    d. exposing the plant to a low level of light in the middle of the night.

————— 3. Plants monitor changes in day length with the pigment

    a. anthocyanin.   **b.** phytochrome.   **c.** chlorophyll.   **d.** carotenoid.

————— 4. Crop plants whose flowering is stimulated by vernalization are usually sown in the

    a. fall.   **b.** winter.   **c.** spring.   **d.** summer.

————— 5. The fall colors displayed by many tree leaves are caused partly by the

    a. stimulation of carotenoid synthesis that occurs only in the fall.
    b. disappearance of chlorophyll, which allows the carotenoids to become visible.
    c. migration of chlorophyll from the stems into the leaves.
    d. replacement of carotenoids by anthocyanins.

Name _____ Class _____ Date _____

SHORT ANSWER Answer the questions in the space provided.

1. Identify three processes that are affected by photoperiodism in at least some plant species.

_____

_____

2. Name one short-day plant and identify the time of year when it flowers. _____

_____

Name one long-day plant and identify the time of year when it flowers. _____

_____

3. Identify three plant processes in which phytochrome is involved. _____

_____

4. How can plants whose flowering is stimulated by vernalization be prevented from flowering?

_____

_____

5. Critical Thinking Spinach is a long-day plant with a critical night length of 10 hours. Why is

spinach not usually grown in the northern United States during the summer? _____

_____

_____

STRUCTURES AND FUNCTIONS Use the diagram below to fill in lines *a–f.*

The diagrams below represent three different conditions of day and night length. A short-day
plant, with a critical night length of 14 hours, and a long-day plant, with a critical night length of
8 hours, are grown under each condition. On the lines, indicate whether each plant will flower
under each condition.

	Does short-day plant flower?	Does long-day plant flower?
17 hr light | 7 hr dark	a _____	b _____
9 hr light | 15 hr dark	c _____	d _____
9 hr light | 7 hr dark | 7 hr dark	e _____	f _____
1 hr light		

THE NATURE OF ANIMALS

VOCABULARY REVIEW Define the following terms.

1. vertebrate _____

_____

2. ingestion _____

_____

3. dorsal nerve cord _____

_____

4. cephalization _____

_____

MULTIPLE CHOICE Write the correct letter in the blank.

_____ 1. Which of the following statements accurately describes animals?

    a. All animals are multicellular, all are heterotrophic, and all lack cell walls.
    b. All animals are multicellular, some are heterotrophic, and some lack cell walls.
    c. Some animals are multicellular, all are heterotrophic, and all lack cell walls.
    d. Some animals are multicellular, some are heterotrophic, and some lack cell walls.

_____ 2. An animal's ability to move results from the interrelationship between

    a. dermal tissue and vascular tissue.   **c.** nervous tissue and muscle tissue.
    b. vascular tissue and nervous tissue.   **d.** muscle tissue and ground tissue.

_____ 3. Scientists infer that the first invertebrates evolved from

    a. simple vertebrates.   **c.** loosely connected fungi.
    b. large groups of bacteria.   **d.** colonial protists.

_____ 4. Cephalization is associated with

    a. bilaterally symmetrical animals.   **c.** sponges.
    b. radially symmetrical animals.   **d.** hydras.

_____ 5. A body cavity aids in an animal's movement by

    a. anchoring the animal firmly to objects in its environment.
    b. providing a firm structure against which muscles can contract.
    c. giving rise to muscle tissue during embryonic development.
    d. secreting a fluid that allows the animal to glide over surfaces.

SHORT ANSWER Answer the questions in the space provided.

1. Explain the relationship between differentiation and specialization. _____

_____

_____

_____

2. On what basis do taxonomists group animals into phyla? _____

_____

_____

3. Why is cephalization important to animals? _____

_____

_____

4. Name three functions of a coelom. _____

_____

_____

5. **Critical Thinking** Why is it important for a taxonomist to look at patterns of development when

trying to classify animals? _____

_____

_____

STRUCTURES AND FUNCTIONS In the drawing of a prairie dog shown below, label the animal's anterior and posterior ends and its dorsal and ventral sides in spaces *a–d*.

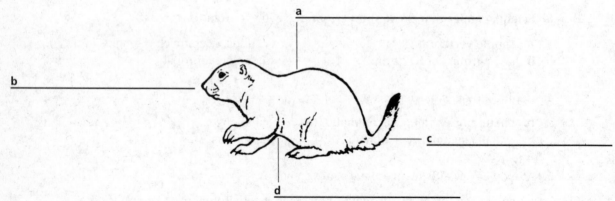

What type of symmetry does this animal have? _____

Name _____ Class _____ Date _____

INVERTEBRATES AND VERTEBRATES

VOCABULARY REVIEW Explain the relationship between the terms in each of the following pairs of terms.

1. segmentation, vertebrae _____

_____

2. integument, exoskeleton _____

_____

MULTIPLE CHOICE Write the correct letter in the blank.

_____ **1.** In a closed circulatory system,

    a. cells exchange nutrients directly with the environment.
    b. the bloodlike circulatory fluid never leaves the coelom.
    c. blood circulates through the body in tubular vessels.
    d. the blood carries gases but not nutrients or wastes.

_____ **2.** A gut is a

    a. structure specialized for gas exchange in water.
    b. simple excretory organ of invertebrates.
    c. digestive chamber with one opening.
    d. digestive tract that runs through the body.

_____ **3.** A hermaphrodite is an organism that

    a. produces only male gametes.   **c.** produces both male and female gametes.
    b. produces only female gametes.   **d.** does not produce any gametes.

_____ **4.** The moist skin of an amphibian functions as

    a. a respiratory organ.   **c.** an insulating material.
    b. a structure for conserving water.   **d.** a rigid exoskeleton.

_____ **5.** Development of zygotes outside the body of the female parent is a characteristic of

    a. all fishes and amphibians.
    b. many fishes, amphibians, reptiles, and birds.
    c. all reptiles and birds.
    d. reptiles, birds, and some amphibians.

SHORT ANSWER Answer the questions in the space provided.

1. Name two animal phyla whose members show segmentation. _____

_____

2. What waste excretion problem is shared by invertebrates and vertebrates? _____

_____

_____

How do some invertebrates and vertebrates deal with this problem? _____

_____

_____

3. Explain how the legs of a deer and the integument of a reptile are adaptations for life on land.

_____

_____

_____

4. What is one advantage of the multichambered heart that is found in some vertebrates?

_____

_____

5. **Critical Thinking** Name one advantage and one disadvantage of being a hermaphrodite.

_____

_____

_____

STRUCTURES AND FUNCTIONS The table below summarizes the functions of some vertebrate structures. Complete the table by filling in the missing structures and functions.

Structure	Function
a _____	filters wastes from the blood
Lung or gill	b _____
c _____	provides a barrier against the environment
Brain	d _____
e _____	provides structural support for the body

SECTION 32-3 REVIEW

FERTILIZATION AND DEVELOPMENT

VOCABULARY REVIEW Distinguish between the terms in each of the following pairs of terms.

1. archenteron, blastopore _____

_____

2. pseudocoelom, coelom _____

_____

_____

3. protostome, deuterostome _____

_____

4. schizocoely, enterocoely _____

_____

_____

MULTIPLE CHOICE Write the correct letter in the blank.

_____ **1.** The eggs of different animal species vary greatly in size, depending on

    a. whether the egg and sperm are haploid or diploid.
    b. how long the food supply in the yolk must last.
    c. the number of chromosomes in the egg.
    d. the number of chromosomes in the sperm.

_____ **2.** The central cavity of a blastula is called a

    a. blastocoel.   **b.** coelom.   **c.** blastopore.   **d.** gastrula.

_____ **3.** Body parts formed by the mesoderm include the

    a. lungs.   **b.** liver.   **c.** muscles.   **d.** pancreas.

_____ **4.** Animals in which the anus develops from the blastopore include

    a. mollusks.   **b.** arthropods.   **c.** annelids.   **d.** chordates.

_____ **5.** Animals that develop from three germ layers without a body cavity are called

    a. coelomates.   **c.** acoelomates.
    b. pseudocoelomates.   **d.** schizocoelomates.

SHORT ANSWER Answer the questions in the space provided.

1. Contrast the structure of a blastula with that of a gastrula. _____
_____
_____

2. Name the three germ layers in order, from outside to inside. _____
_____

3. What features of development indicate that echinoderms and chordates are more closely related
to each other than they are to other animals? _____
_____

4. **Critical Thinking** Why is it important to have a mechanism that prevents more than one sperm
from entering an egg? _____
_____
_____

STRUCTURES AND FUNCTIONS The diagrams below show coelom formation during the
two distinct patterns of development that most animals can undergo. In spaces a and b,
name each pattern of development. In spaces c and d, name each type of coelom formation. In spaces e and f, name the structure that the opening at the bottom becomes.

a _____   b _____

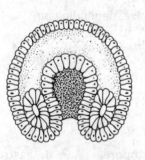 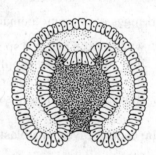

c _____   d _____

e _____   f _____

SECTION 33-1 REVIEW

PORIFERA

VOCABULARY REVIEW Define the following terms.

1. choanocyte _____

_____

2. osculum _____

_____

3. spicule _____

_____

4. amoebocyte _____

_____

MULTIPLE CHOICE Write the correct letter in the blank.

_____ 1. Invertebrates are animals that lack

    a. true tissues.   **b.** true organs.   **c.** a skeleton.   **d.** a backbone.

_____ 2. Adult sponges are sessile, which means that they

    a. have no gastrula stage.   **c.** use a jellylike substance for body support.
    b. attach to a surface and do not move.   **d.** produce both eggs and sperm.

_____ 3. Choanocytes perform all of the following functions except

    a. pumping water into the interior of the sponge.
    b. engulfing and digesting food that is filtered from the water.
    c. passing nutrients to amebocytes.
    d. distributing nutrients throughout the rest of the body.

_____ 4. Sponges eliminate carbon dioxide and cellular wastes by

    a. allowing them to diffuse into the water that passes through the sponge.
    b. excreting them into the surrounding water through pores in the body wall.
    c. transporting them to an excretory organ that empties into the osculum.
    d. converting them into usable carbohydrates.

_____ 5. After a sponge egg is fertilized, it develops into a(n)

    a. external bud.   **b.** gemmule.   **c.** larva.   **d.** gastrula.

SHORT ANSWER Answer the questions in the space provided.

1. On what basis are animals placed into the invertebrate category? _____

   _____

   _____

2. What are the two substances that a sponge's skeleton may be made of? _____

   _____

   How do these substances differ? _____

   _____

   _____

3. How do choanocytes participate in the sexual reproduction of sponges? _____

   _____

   _____

4. Why is hermaphroditism beneficial in sponges even though they rarely self-fertilize?

   _____

   _____

5. **Critical Thinking** Would gemmules or larvae be better at distributing a population of sponges

   through an area? Explain your reasoning. _____

   _____

   _____

   _____

STRUCTURES AND FUNCTIONS Identify the structures labeled *a–e* in the diagram of a sponge shown below.

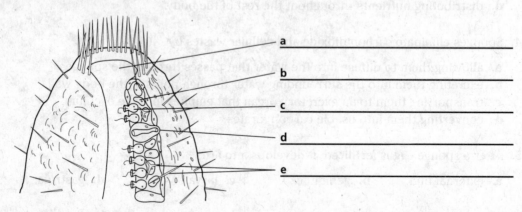

a _____

b _____

c _____

d _____

e _____

SECTION 33-2 REVIEW

CNIDARIA AND CTENOPHORA

VOCABULARY REVIEW Distinguish between the terms in each of the following pairs of terms.

1. polyp, medusa _____

_____

2. epidermis, gastrodermis _____

_____

3. mesoglea, planula _____

_____

4. cnidocyte, nematocyst _____

_____

5. colloblast, apical organ _____

_____

MULTIPLE CHOICE Write the correct letter in the blank.

_____ 1. Cnidarians and ctenophores are more complex than sponges because, unlike sponges, they have

    a. tissues and organs.
    b. both asexual and sexual reproduction.
    c. a skeleton.
    d. a backbone.

_____ 2. The structure that coordinates the complex activities of a cnidarian's body is the

    a. gastrovascular cavity.
    b. colloblast.
    c. nerve net.
    d. tentacle.

_____ 3. An example of a cnidarian in the class Hydrozoa is a

    a. coral.
    b. sea anemone.
    c. jellyfish.
    d. Portuguese man-of-war.

_____ 4. Corals exist in a symbiotic relationship with

    a. fungi.   **b.** algae.   **c.** hydras.   **d.** mosses.

_____ 5. Ctenophores move through the water by

    a. somersaulting.
    b. contracting their bell-shaped bodies.
    c. beating their cilia.
    d. rotating like a propeller.

SHORT ANSWER Answer the questions in the space provided.

1. How are nematocysts adapted for capturing prey? _____

_____

_____

2. List three differences between hydras and most other hydrozoans. _____

_____

_____

3. What is the dominant body form in the life cycle of a scyphozoan? _____

What is the dominant body form in the life cycle of an anthozoan? _____

4. Describe two examples of symbiosis found among cnidarians. _____

_____

_____

5. How do coral polyps produce a coral reef? _____

_____

_____

6. **Critical Thinking** Would you expect to find green hydras in a cave pond that receives little or

no light? Explain your reasoning. _____

_____

_____

STRUCTURES AND FUNCTIONS Identify the structures labeled *a–f* in the diagram of a cnidarian body shown below.

a _____

b _____

c _____

d _____

e _____

f _____

Which body form is represented by this diagram? _____

SECTION 34-1 REVIEW

PLATYHELMINTHES

VOCABULARY REVIEW Distinguish between the terms in each of the following pairs of terms.

1. proglottid, tegument _____

_____

2. cerebral ganglia, eyespots _____

_____

3. primary host, intermediate host _____

_____

MULTIPLE CHOICE Write the correct letter in the blank.

_____ 1. Flatworms are the simplest animals with

    a. a backbone.   **c.** bilateral symmetry.
    b. a coelom.   **d.** radial symmetry.

_____ 2. The gastrovascular cavity of a flatworm

    a. has no opening to the outside.
    b. has a single opening.
    c. has two openings.
    d. is connected to the outside by numerous pores.

_____ 3. One difference between free-living flatworms and parasitic flatworms is that

    a. free-living flatworms have proglottids.
    b. free-living flatworms do not have a gastrovascular cavity.
    c. parasitic flatworms have simpler life cycles.
    d. parasitic flatworms have a tegument.

_____ 4. The eggs of the blood fluke *Schistosoma*

    a. leave the primary host in feces or urine.
    b. are produced by hermaphroditic adults.
    c. must be deposited on dry land to develop.
    d. are ingested by the intermediate host.

_____ 5. The primary hosts of beef tapeworms are

    a. cows.   **b.** snails.   **c.** pigs.   **d.** humans.

SHORT ANSWER Answer the questions in the space provided.

1. How do planarians eliminate excess water from their bodies? _____

_____

_____

2. How do planarians and tapeworms differ in their ability to detect light? _____

_____

_____

3. What are the primary host and the intermediate host of a blood fluke? _____

_____

    How does a blood fluke enter its primary host? _____

_____

4. What stage of the beef tapeworm life cycle is spent inside a cyst? _____

5. **Critical Thinking** Some people mistakenly believe that all organisms are perfectly adapted to their environments. What aspect of blood fluke reproduction suggests that these flatworms are

    not perfectly adapted to the environment inside their human hosts? _____

_____

_____

STRUCTURES AND FUNCTIONS Identify the structures labeled *a–g* in the diagram of a tapeworm shown below.

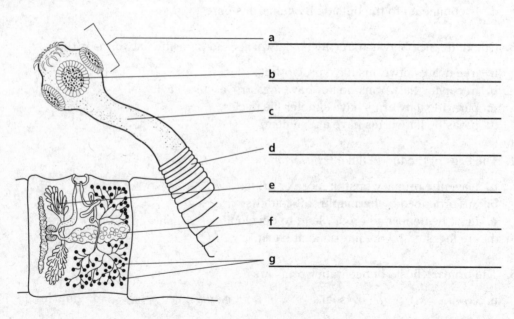

a _____

b _____

c _____

d _____

e _____

f _____

g _____

SECTION 34-2 REVIEW

NEMATODA AND ROTIFERA

VOCABULARY REVIEW Define the following terms.

1. trichinosis ——

——

2. filarial worm ——

——

3. mastax ——

——

MULTIPLE CHOICE Write the correct letter in the blank.

———— 1. Pseudocoelomates have a hollow, fluid-filled cavity that is

    a. lined by ectoderm on the outside and mesoderm on the inside.
    b. lined by mesoderm on the outside and endoderm on the inside.
    c. completely surrounded by mesoderm.
    d. completely surrounded by endoderm.

———— 2. The roundworm digestive tract

    a. has no opening.   **c.** has two openings.
    b. has a single opening.   **d.** is absent in parasitic roundworms.

———— 3. *Ascaris* eggs enter the body of a human host when the

    a. host ingests contaminated food or water.
    b. eggs attach to the bare sole of a human foot.
    c. eggs are inhaled as spores.
    d. cysts rupture inside uncooked meat.

———— 4. Hookworms normally reach the human intestine after they

    a. are ingested as cysts in contaminated meat.
    b. bore directly from the skin of the abdomen to the intestine.
    c. enter the host's anus and migrate to the intestine.
    d. travel through the blood to the lungs and throat and are then swallowed.

———— 5. A rotifer's excretory system includes

    a. flame cells and excretory tubules.   **c.** a single, small kidney.
    b. contractile vacuoles.   **d.** many excretory pores on the body surface.

Name _____ Class _____ Date _____

SHORT ANSWER Answer the questions in the space provided.

1. What advantage does a digestive tract have over a gastrovascular cavity? _____
_____

2. Compare the sites where eggs hatch in the life cycles of *Ascaris,* hookworms, and pinworms.
_____
_____

3. What insect carries the roundworm that causes elephantiasis? _____

4. What structure on a rotifer looks like a pair of rotating wheels? _____

   What is the function of this structure? _____
   _____

5. **Critical Thinking** Most roundworms that parasitize the digestive tract live in the small intestine, which is close to the stomach. What is the adaptive advantage of living in the small intestine for a

   worm that does not feed directly on its host's tissues? _____
   _____

STRUCTURES AND FUNCTIONS Identify the structures labeled *a–g* in the diagram of a rotifer shown below.

a _____

e _____

b _____

c _____

f _____

d _____

g _____

SECTION 35-1 REVIEW

MOLLUSCA

VOCABULARY REVIEW Explain the relationship between the terms in each of the following pairs of terms.

1. visceral mass, mantle _____

_____

_____

2. hemolymph, hemocoel _____

_____

_____

3. incurrent siphon, excurrent siphon _____

_____

_____

MULTIPLE CHOICE Write the correct letter in the blank.

_____ **1.** One advantage of a coelom over a pseudocoelom is that a coelom

    a. contains fluid while a pseudocoelom does not.
    b. is completely surrounded by endoderm.
    c. eliminates the need for a circulatory system.
    d. allows body wall muscles to contract without hindering digestion.

_____ **2.** One feature that is shared by many mollusks and annelids is the

    a. radula.   **b.** mantle cavity.   **c.** trochophore.   **d.** pseudopodium.

_____ **3.** Mollusks in the class Gastropoda

    a. lack a distinct head.   **c.** do not have a hemocoel.
    b. have an open circulatory system.   **d.** are usually sessile.

_____ **4.** Bivalves have all of the following structures except

    a. a radula.   **b.** adductor muscles.   **c.** siphons.   **d.** gills.

_____ **5.** An octopus generally moves by

    a. pumping a jet of water through its incurrent siphon.
    b. crawling along the bottom with its tentacles.
    c. gliding on a layer of mucus with the help of cilia.
    d. repeatedly opening its valves and snapping them shut.

SHORT ANSWER Answer the questions in the space provided.

1. Identify the two main regions of a typical mollusk's body. _____

   _____

   Which region contains most of the internal organs? _____

   Which region is directly involved with locomotion? _____

2. What is the usual function of the mantle in a snail or clam? _____

   _____

3. Contrast the feeding methods of gastropods and bivalves. _____

   _____

   _____

   _____

4. Contrast sexual reproduction of marine clams and most freshwater clams. _____

   _____

   _____

5. **Critical Thinking** A cephalopod called the paper nautilus makes a type of shell with its foot. This shell, which consists largely of protein, is formed only by the female and is used to protect

   the eggs. List four reasons why this shell is not a typical molluskan shell. _____

   _____

   _____

   _____

STRUCTURES AND FUNCTIONS Identify the structures labeled *a–h* in the diagram of the basic body plan of a mollusk shown below.

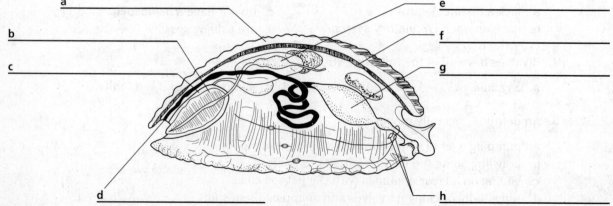

SECTION 35-2 REVIEW

ANNELIDA

VOCABULARY REVIEW Define the following terms.

1. seta _____

_____

2. parapodium _____

_____

3. typhlosole _____

_____

4. nephridium _____

_____

MULTIPLE CHOICE Write the correct letter in the blank.

_____ 1. Segmentation is an advantage for annelid worms because it

    a. requires the whole body to move as a single unit.
    b. reduces the number of setae on the parapodia.
    c. divides the pseudocoelom into multiple compartments.
    d. is accompanied by the duplication of some internal organs.

_____ 2. Contraction of an earthworm's longitudinal muscles

    a. pushes the anterior end forward.   **c.** pulls the posterior end forward.
    b. pulls the anterior end backward.   **d.** pushes the posterior end backward.

_____ 3. An earthworm uses its setae to

    a. grip the soil surface.   **c.** contract in a longitudinal direction.
    b. contract in a circular direction.   **d.** form a protective case for its eggs.

_____ 4. One difference between leeches and polychaetes is that leeches

    a. do not have segments.   **c.** have parapodia.
    b. do not have setae.   **d.** are never carnivorous.

_____ 5. All annelids in the classes Oligochaeta and Hirudinea have

    a. gills.   **c.** a segmented coelom.
    b. parapodia.   **d.** an open circulatory system.

Name _____ Class _____ Date _____

SHORT ANSWER Answer the questions in the space provided.

1. How does the function of an earthworm's crop differ from that of its gizzard? _____
_____
_____

2. List three benefits of earthworm activity. _____
_____
_____

3. What is the function of an earthworm's aortic arches? _____
_____

4. Describe the locomotion of a leech on land. _____
_____
_____

5. **Critical Thinking** Some parasitic leeches are attracted by warmth. What type of host would you expect such leeches to have, and what would be the adaptive advantage of this attraction?
_____
_____
_____

STRUCTURES AND FUNCTIONS Identify the structures labeled *a–h* in the diagram of an earthworm shown below.

a _____   c _____

b _____   d _____

                              e _____

f _____

g _____

h _____

SECTION 36-1 REVIEW

PHYLUM ARTHROPODA

VOCABULARY REVIEW Define the following terms.

1. arthropod _____

_____

2. compound eye _____

` _____

3. tagma _____

_____

4. chelicera _____

_____

MULTIPLE CHOICE Write the correct letter in the blank.

_____ 1. An arthropod's exoskeleton performs all of the following functions except

    a. producing gametes.   **c.** supporting the animal's weight.

    b. protecting internal organs.   **d.** helping prevent desiccation.

_____ 2. One feature that arthropods share with annelids is

    a. a closed circulatory system.   **c.** a ventral nerve cord.

    b. jointed appendages.   **d.** a lack of cephalization.

_____ 3. An arthropod sheds its old exoskeleton when

    a. the old exoskeleton wears out.

    b. the new exoskeleton exerts pressure on the epidermis.

    c. the animal is 1–2 years old.

    d. a hormone is produced that induces molting.

_____ 4. Ancestral arthropods probably had

    a. no coelom.

    b. one pair of appendages on every segment.

    c. bodies consisting of a few, highly specialized tagmata.

    d. endoskeletons.

_____ 5. The subphylum Crustacea includes

    a. insects.   **b.** spiders.   **c.** ticks.   **d.** shrimps.

SHORT ANSWER Answer the questions in the space provided.

1. What substance makes an arthropod's exoskeleton repel water, and where is this substance located?

   _____

2. What substance makes some arthropods' exoskeletons hard, and where is this substance located?

   _____

3. List two examples of arthropod appendages. _____

4. Identify three ways that arthropods show cephalization. _____

   _____

   _____

5. **Critical Thinking** The extinct animal *Marella* is thought to have been a distant ancestor of some living arthropods. *Marella* had branched legs and unbranched antennae. Why is it difficult

   to place *Marella* in any of the subphyla of living arthropods? _____

   _____

   _____

STRUCTURES AND FUNCTIONS The figure below shows a phylogenetic diagram of living arthropods. In the blank spaces at the top of the diagram, write the names of the animals that belong on each branch of the tree. Some branches will have more than one name. Choose the names from the following list:

spider	mite	horseshoe crab	sea spider
shrimp	insect	millipede	scorpion
centipede			

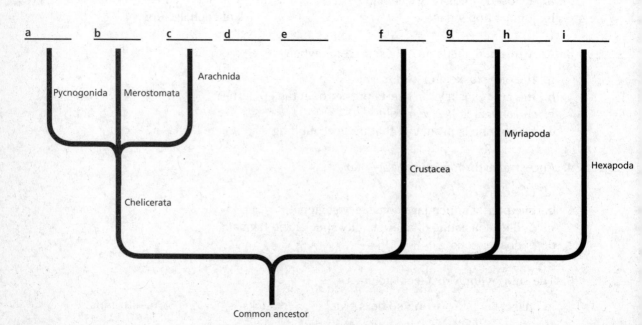

SECTION 36-2 REVIEW

SUBPHYLUM CRUSTACEA

VOCABULARY REVIEW Distinguish between the terms in each of the following pairs of terms.

1. cirrus, cheliped _____

_____

2. cephalothorax, thorax _____

_____

3. antenna, antennule _____

_____

4. telson, swimmeret _____

_____

MULTIPLE CHOICE Write the correct letter in the blank.

_____ 1. Crustaceans are the only arthropods that have

    a. three pairs of legs.
    b. two pairs of feeling appendages on their head.
    c. chitin in their exoskeleton.
    d. chelicerae.

_____ 2. Freshwater crustaceans include

    a. copepods and barnacles.   **c.** water fleas and crayfish.
    b. barnacles and water fleas.   **d.** crayfish and sow bugs.

_____ 3. A crayfish uses its swimmerets to

    a. defend itself.   **c.** manipulate food.
    b. propel itself during tailflips.   **d.** create water currents.

_____ 4. A crayfish has teeth in its

    a. stomach.   **b.** esophagus.   **c.** uropods.   **d.** green glands.

_____ 5. The hairs that project from the exoskeleton of a crayfish are used to

    a. create water currents over the surface of the crayfish.
    b. sense vibrations and chemicals in the water.
    c. retain body heat within the crayfish.
    d. protect the crayfish from predators.

SHORT ANSWER Answer the questions in the space provided.

1. Describe the structural features of a nauplius. _____

_____

2. Explain how a barnacle feeds. _____

_____

_____

3. List the functions of the mandibles, maxillae, and maxillipeds in a crayfish. _____

_____

_____

4. Describe the path of hemolymph flow through a crayfish, beginning with the heart. _____

_____

_____

5. **Critical Thinking** In a stagnant pool of water, a crayfish may spend much of its time lying with one side of its carapace near the surface of the water. In this position, it will move the walking legs on that side in a rhythmic back-and-forth motion. Explain the likely function of this behavior.

_____

_____

STRUCTURES AND FUNCTIONS Identify the structures labeled *a–g* in the diagram of the internal structure of a crayfish shown below.

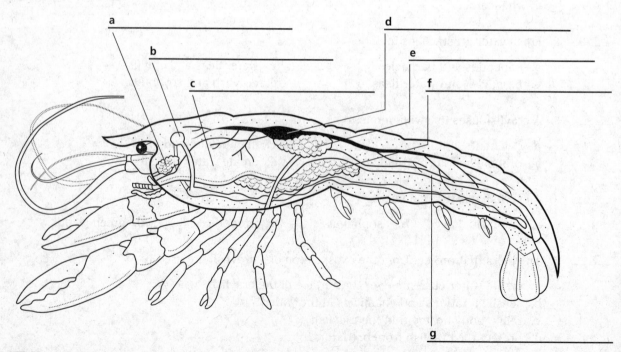

SECTION 36-3 REVIEW

SUBPHYLA CHELICERATA AND MYRIAPODA

VOCABULARY REVIEW Define the following terms.

1. arachnid _____

2. pedipalp _____

_____

3. spiracle _____

_____

4. Malpighian tubule _____

_____

5. spinneret _____

_____

6. book lung _____

_____

MULTIPLE CHOICE Write the correct letter in the blank.

_____ **1.** How many pairs of appendages are on the cephalothorax of most arachnids?

    a. two   **b.** four   **c.** six   **d.** eight

_____ **2.** A spider's respiratory system may include

    a. tracheae.   **b.** spinnerets.   **c.** pedipalps.   **d.** chelicerae.

_____ **3.** One difference between scorpions and spiders is that scorpions

    a. are herbivores.   **c.** are not venomous.
    b. have large pincerlike pedipalps.   **d.** do not have an abdomen.

_____ **4.** A chigger is the larva of a

    a. centipede.   **b.** spider.   **c.** tick.   **d.** mite.

_____ **5.** Millipedes have

    a. two pairs of legs on most body segments.
    b. long antennae.
    c. a flattened body.
    d. a waxy exoskeleton.

SHORT ANSWER Answer the questions in the space provided.

1. Name three ways that spiders use silk. _____

_____

2. Describe the structure and function of book lungs. _____

_____

3. Identify the two spiders in the United States whose bites are poisonous to humans, and describe

the appearance of these spiders. _____

_____

_____

4. How are centipedes adapted to a predatory way of life? _____

_____

_____

5. **Critical Thinking** Some biologists believe that smaller animals can occupy a greater variety of habitats and are more abundant than larger animals. Which group of arthropods is an example of this idea? Explain your reasoning, and list the habitats occupied by that group.

_____

_____

_____

STRUCTURES AND FUNCTIONS Identify the structures labeled *a–h* in the diagram of the internal structure of a spider shown below.

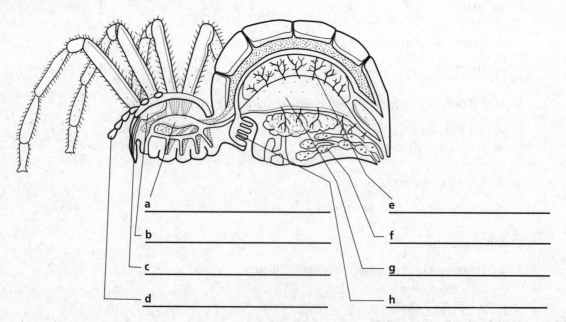

a _____   e _____

b _____   f _____

c _____   g _____

d _____   h _____

THE INSECT WORLD

VOCABULARY REVIEW Distinguish between the terms in each of the following pairs of terms.

1. labrum, labium _____

_____

2. tympanum, ovipositor _____

_____

_____

3. incomplete metamorphosis, complete metamorphosis _____

_____

_____

4. nymph, pupa _____

_____

_____

MULTIPLE CHOICE Write the correct letter in the blank.

_____ 1. One of the most important factors responsible for the success of insects is their

    a. large size.   **c.** long life span.
    b. heavy exoskeleton.   **d.** ability to fly.

_____ 2. The protozoan that causes malaria is transmitted by

    a. fleas.   **b.** mosquitoes.   **c.** flies.   **d.** cockroaches.

_____ 3. Which of the following is a structure that insects do not share with spiders?

    a. chelicera.   **b.** trachea.   **c.** Malpighian tubule. **d.** abdomen.

_____ 4. The life cycle of an insect that undergoes complete metamorphosis may include all of the following stages except a(n)

    a. adult.   **b.** pupa.   **c.** nymph.   **d.** larva.

_____ 5. The bombardier beetle defends itself by

    a. dropping seeds on its enemies.   **c.** resembling the plants on which it feeds.
    b. spraying a noxious chemical.   **d.** resembling a bumblebee.

SHORT ANSWER Answer the questions in the space provided.

1. List three characteristics that insects share with other members of the subphylum Myriapoda.

   _____

   _____

   List two differences between insects and other members of the subphylum Myriapoda. _____

   _____

2. What beneficial function do termites serve in wild habitats? _____

   _____

3. Describe the roles of the salivary glands and the gastric ceca in digestion in a grasshopper.

   _____

   _____

4. How does a chrysalis differ from a cocoon? _____

   _____

5. **Critical Thinking** Female mosquitoes feed on blood, while male mosquitoes feed on plant sap or nectar. How is this difference in feeding behavior important for the reproductive success

   of mosquitoes? _____

   _____

   _____

STRUCTURES AND FUNCTIONS Identify the structures labeled *a–c* in the drawing of a grasshopper shown below.

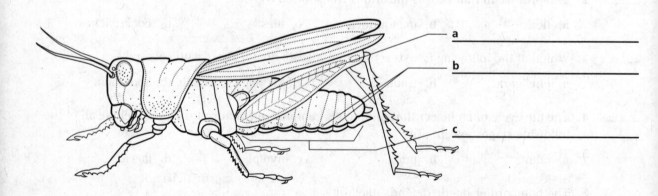

SECTION 37-2 REVIEW

INSECT BEHAVIOR

VOCABULARY REVIEW Define the following terms.

1. pheromone ————————————————————————————————————

——

2. innate behavior ————————————————————————————————

——

3. royal jelly ————————————————————————————————————

——

4. queen factor ————————————————————————————————————

——

5. kin selection ————————————————————————————————————

——

MULTIPLE CHOICE Write the correct letter in the blank.

————— 1. Insects that communicate at a distance by producing sounds include

    a. ants.   **b.** mosquitoes.   **c.** silkworm moths.   **d.** fireflies.

————— 2. Honeybees that develop from unfertilized eggs are called

    a. workers.   **b.** queens.   **c.** nurse bees.   **d.** drones.

————— 3. A queen honeybee stops producing the queen factor when the

    a. first worker hatches from its egg.   **c.** hive becomes overcrowded.
    b. first drone hatches from its egg.   **d.** hive population drops below about 20 bees.

————— 4. Which body part does a scout bee move from side to side when the bee performs a waggle dance?

    a. abdomen   **b.** labrum   **c.** thorax   **d.** antenna

————— 5. The stinging behavior of worker honeybees is

    a. learned from the queen.   **c.** not an altruistic behavior.
    b. learned from the drones.   **d.** an innate behavior.

Name _____ Class _____ Date _____

SHORT ANSWER Answer the questions in the space provided.

1. In which of the following kinds of insects does the male use its antennae to find distant females:

   cricket, mosquito, moth, firefly? _____

   Name the communication signal detected by the antennae in each case. _____

   _____

2. What mechanism ensures that female crickets are attracted to males of the same species? _____

   _____

3. Which of the three types of bees in a honeybee colony is (are) female? _____

   Which of the three types is (are) sterile? _____

4. Under what conditions will worker honeybees kill drones? _____

   _____

5. **Critical Thinking** For an altruistic behavior to be maintained in a population over time, it must

   be directed at close relatives. Why is that so? _____

   _____

   _____

   _____

STRUCTURES AND FUNCTIONS The diagrams below show two types of dances performed by honeybees. In the space below each diagram, identify the dance and briefly describe the information it conveys.

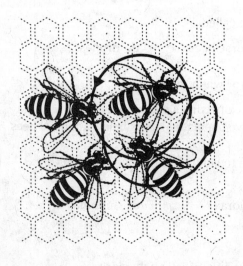

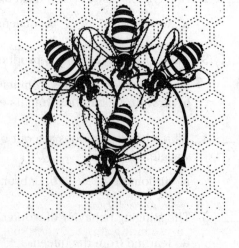

a _____   b _____

_____   _____

ECHINODERMS

VOCABULARY REVIEW Explain the relationship between the terms in each of the following pairs of terms.

1. ossicle, test _____

_____

2. tube foot, ampulla _____

_____

3. cardiac stomach, pyloric stomach _____

_____

4. water-vascular system, radial canal _____

_____

MULTIPLE CHOICE Write the correct letter in the blank.

_____ **1.** Both echinoderms and chordates

    a. lack a coelom.   **c.** have bilateral symmetry as adults.

    b. have radially symmetrical larvae.   **d.** are deuterostomes.

_____ **2.** One characteristic that is found only in echinoderms is

    a. a nerve net.

    b. the presence of only two tissue layers during development.

    c. a water-vascular system.

    d. an endoskeleton.

_____ **3.** Members of the class Echinoidea include

    a. sea urchins.   **b.** sea cucumbers.   **c.** sea stars.   **d.** sea lilies.

_____ **4.** The surface that is opposite the mouth in a sea star is called the

    a. oral surface.   **b.** aboral surface.   **c.** posterior surface.   **d.** dorsal surface.

_____ **5.** Sexual reproduction among sea stars usually involves

    a. separate sexes and internal fertilization.

    b. separate sexes and external fertilization.

    c. hermaphrodites and internal fertilization.

    d. hermaphrodites and external fertilization.

Name _____ Class _____ Date _____

SHORT ANSWER Answer the questions in the space provided.

1. What do the larvae of echinoderms indicate about the evolution of echinoderms? _____

_____

_____

2. Name the class of each of the following echinoderms: basket star, sea star, feather star, brittle star.

_____

_____

3. Describe the organization of a sea star's nervous system. _____

_____

_____

4. How do sea stars reproduce sexually? _____

_____

5. How do sea stars use their ability to regenerate as a defensive mechanism? _____

_____

6. **Critical Thinking** Why is the lack of cephalization not a disadvantage for a sea star? _____

_____

_____

STRUCTURES AND FUNCTIONS Identify the structures labeled a–f in the drawing of part of a sea star shown below.

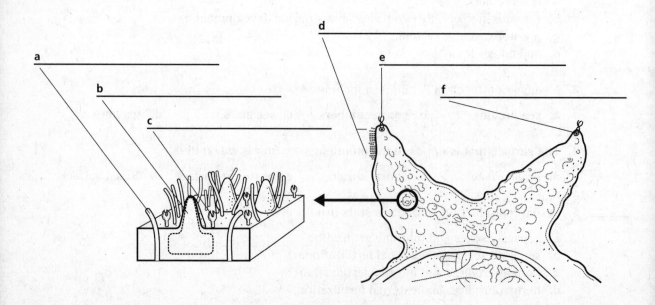

SECTION 38-2 REVIEW

INVERTEBRATE CHORDATES

VOCABULARY REVIEW Define the following terms.

1. notochord _____

_____

2. lancelet _____

_____

3. tunicate _____

_____

4. atriopore _____

_____

MULTIPLE CHOICE Write the correct letter in the blank.

_____ **1.** In most chordates, the function of the notochord is taken over by the

    a. vertebral column. **b.** brain.   **c.** spinal cord.   **d.** pharynx.

_____ **2.** The gill chambers of aquatic chordates evolved from the

    a. dorsal nerve cord.   **c.** pharyngeal pouches.
    b. backbone.   **d.** postanal tail.

_____ **3.** Animals in the subphyla Cephalochordata and Urochordata live

    a. only in fresh water.   **c.** only on land.
    b. only in the ocean.   **d.** in fresh water, in the ocean, and on land.

_____ **4.** A lancelet feeds by

    a. pursuing and capturing small animals with its tentacles.
    b. sucking blood from the skin of a larger animal.
    c. digesting nutrients contained in the bottom sediments it swallows.
    d. filtering food particles from the water that passes through its pharynx.

_____ **5.** Unlike adult lancelets, adult tunicates

    a. have segmented muscles in their tail.   **c.** are usually sessile.
    b. are radially symmetrical.   **d.** have separate sexes.

Name _____ Class _____ Date _____

SHORT ANSWER Answer the questions in the space provided.

1. List the chordate characteristics that lancelets have as adults. _____

_____

2. How do lancelets use their tail? _____

_____

3. How did tunicates receive their name? _____

_____

4. What behavior do tunicates exhibit when touched? _____

_____

5. How does the structure of a larval tunicate differ from that of an adult tunicate? _____

_____

6. **Critical Thinking** How are most adult tunicates similar to sponges, and how are they different

from sponges? _____

_____

_____

_____

STRUCTURES AND FUNCTIONS Identify the structures labeled *a–f* in the diagram of a lancelet shown below.

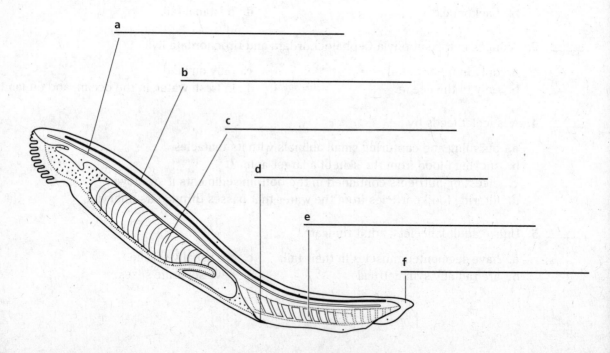

a _____

b _____

c _____

d _____

e _____

f _____

SECTION 39-1 REVIEW

INTRODUCTION TO VERTEBRATES

VOCABULARY REVIEW Define the following terms.

1. vertebra _____

_____

2. cranium _____

_____

3. gill arch _____

_____

MULTIPLE CHOICE Write the correct letter in the blank.

_____ 1. All of the following are vertebrate characteristics except

    a. a post-anal tail.   **c.** a ventral hollow nerve cord.
    b. pharyngeal pouches.   **d.** an endoskeleton.

_____ 2. Skates belong to the class

    a. Myxini.   **b.** Chondrichthyes.   **c.** Reptilia.   **d.** Amphibia.

_____ 3. Which of the following fishes is jawless?

    a. hagfish   **b.** ray   **c.** guppy   **d.** catfish

_____ 4. The earliest vertebrates were

    a. bony fishes.   **c.** amphibians with thin, moist skin.
    b. spiny fishes with skeletons of cartilage.   **d.** jawless fishes.

_____ 5. The evolution of paired fins was important to early fishes because paired fins

    a. led directly to the evolution of gill arches.
    b. led directly to the evolution of paired legs in mammals.
    c. increased the stability and maneuverability of the fishes.
    d. allowed the fishes to seize and manipulate prey.

_____ 6. Jaws are thought to have evolved from the

    a. second and third vertebrae.   **c.** first pair of fins.
    b. first pair of gill arches.   **d.** anterior half of the pharynx.

SHORT ANSWER Answer the questions in the space provided.

1. Compare modern jawless fishes with those that lived 500 million years ago. _____

_____

2. Compare and contrast the skin of amphibians with the skin of reptiles. _____

_____

3. Name the class to which horses belong, and describe two major characteristics of the animals in

   that class. _____

_____

4. What two important evolutionary events occurred in fishes about 450 million years ago?

_____

5. **Critical Thinking** Explain why the class Chondrichthyes contains many more species than

   the class Cephalaspidomorphi. _____

_____

_____

_____

STRUCTURES AND FUNCTIONS The figure below shows a phylogenetic diagram of vertebrates. In the blank space at the end of each branch of the diagram, write the name of the vertebrate class represented by that branch.

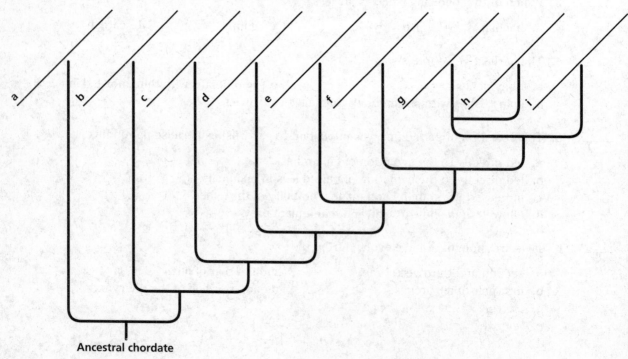

Ancestral chordate

SECTION 39-2 REVIEW

JAWLESS AND CARTILAGINOUS FISHES

VOCABULARY REVIEW Define the following terms.

1. lateral line _____

_____

2. cartilage _____

_____

3. placoid scale _____

_____

4. chemoreception _____

_____

MULTIPLE CHOICE Write the correct letter in the blank.

_____ **1.** Fishes obtain the oxygen they need by absorbing it through their

    a. kidneys.   **b.** gills.   **c.** skin.   **d.** rectal gland.

_____ **2.** The body of a freshwater fish usually

    a. tends to gain chloride ions through diffusion.
    b. tends to gain sodium ions through diffusion.
    c. tends to lose water through osmosis.
    d. has a higher concentration of solutes than the surrounding water does.

_____ **3.** One characteristic of many lampreys but not of hagfishes is

    a. a parasitic lifestyle.   **c.** the presence of unpaired fins.
    b. a cartilaginous skeleton.   **d.** the presence of jaws.

_____ **4.** Fishes in the class Chondrichthyes

    a. have skeletons composed of bone.   **c.** have movable jaws.
    b. are usually herbivores.   **d.** usually live in fresh water.

_____ **5.** Some cartilaginous fishes store lipids in their liver as an adaptation that

    a. increases buoyancy.
    b. increases the overall density of their body.
    c. removes toxic ammonia from their body.
    d. allows the fishes to swim continuously.

Name _____ Class _____ Date _____

SHORT ANSWER Answer the questions in the space provided.

1. Describe the feeding behavior of a hagfish. _____

_____

_____

2. Describe how some sharks' teeth are adapted to capturing large fish or mammals. _____

_____

_____

3. Describe two methods by which cartilaginous fishes can cause water to flow across their gills.

_____

_____

4. Contrast fertilization in lampreys with that in cartilaginous fishes. _____

_____

5. **Critical Thinking** Which type of fishes would you expect to produce more gametes each time

   they reproduce—jawless fishes or cartilaginous fishes? Explain your reasoning. _____

_____

_____

STRUCTURES AND FUNCTIONS Identify the structures labeled a–i in the drawing of a shark shown below.

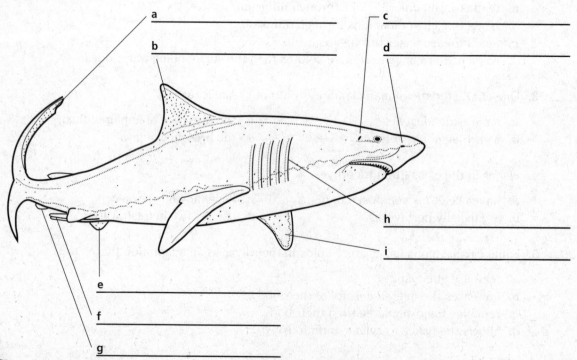

a _____

b _____

c _____

d _____

e _____

f _____

g _____

h _____

i _____

BONY FISHES

VOCABULARY REVIEW Define the following terms.

1. swim bladder ————————————————————————————————————
   ——

2. lobe-finned fish ———————————————————————————————————
   ——

3. ray-finned fish ————————————————————————————————————
   ——

4. countercurrent flow ———————————————————————————————
   ——

MULTIPLE CHOICE Write the correct letter in the blank.

——————— 1. One of the functions of the scales on a bony fish is to

    a. help reduce water resistance.   **c.** absorb salt from the surrounding water.
    b. conserve body heat.   **d.** sense vibrations in the water.

——————— 2. The coelacanth is an example of a

    a. primitive, fishlike amphibian.   **c.** lobe-finned fish.
    b. jawless fish.   **d.** ray-finned fish.

——————— 3. The part of a fish's digestive tract that secretes bile is the

    a. intestine.   **b.** liver.   **c.** stomach.   **d.** pancreas.

——————— 4. In a fish, the blood that leaves the heart goes first to the

    a. kidneys.   **b.** brain.   **c.** muscles.   **d.** gills.

——————— 5. Fish gills are efficient organs for gas exchange because they

    a. have a small surface area.
    b. have no other functions besides gas exchange.
    c. can transport oxygen out of the body at the same time they transport carbon dioxide into the body.
    d. operate on the principle of countercurrent flow.

SHORT ANSWER Answer the questions in the space provided.

1. Explain how the scales of a bony fish can respond to changes in the food supply. _____

_____

_____

2. What two organs are involved in maintaining water and ion balance in a bony fish? _____

_____

_____

3. How does a bony fish adjust its buoyancy? _____

_____

_____

4. Where does fertilization occur in bony fishes? _____

_____

_____

5. **Critical Thinking** Why would a fish with faulty valves in its conus arteriosus probably suffer

from a lack of energy? _____

_____

_____

STRUCTURES AND FUNCTIONS Identify the structures labeled *a–d* in the diagram of a fish's heart shown below. Draw three arrows on the diagram to show where blood enters and leaves the heart.

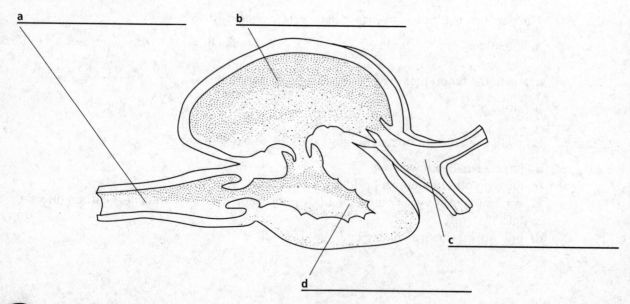

a _____   b _____

c _____

d _____

ORIGIN AND EVOLUTION OF AMPHIBIANS

VOCABULARY REVIEW Define the following terms.

1. preadaptation _____

_____

2. tadpole _____

MULTIPLE CHOICE Write the correct letter in the blank.

_____ 1. One factor that may have favored the evolution of land-dwelling amphibians from aquatic vertebrates was the

    a. decreasing temperature of the world's oceans.

    b. decreasing competition for food in lakes, rivers, and ponds.

    c. increasing abundance of food sources on land.

    d. increasing presence of predators on land.

_____ 2. The teeth of *Ichthyostega* indicate that it ate

    a. fish.

    b. insects.

    c. plants.

    d. plankton.

_____ 3. Most amphibian eggs

    a. are fertilized internally.

    b. have a shell around them.

    c. are surrounded by membranes.

    d. are laid in water or in moist places.

_____ 4. The feet of most amphibians

    a. are webbed.

    b. have claws.

    c. have eight toes.

    d. are homologous to the fins of fishes.

_____ 5. Caecilians detect prey by

    a. using their keen eyesight.

    b. sensing electric fields generated by prey.

    c. using their forelimbs to feel for prey in the mud.

    d. using chemosensory tentacles on their head.

Name _____ Class _____ Date _____

SHORT ANSWER Answer the questions in the space provided.

1. Explain why scientists think that amphibians evolved from lobe-finned fishes. _____
_____
_____

2. What evidence suggests that *Ichthyostega* spent most of its time in the water? _____
_____
_____

3. Name three ways that amphibians carry out gas exchange. _____
_____
_____

4. Compare the skin and body shape of a frog with those of a salamander. _____
_____
_____

5. Critical Thinking Many frogs are both poisonous and very colorful. What function does their

coloration likely serve? _____
_____

STRUCTURES AND FUNCTIONS The diagram below summarizes the division of the class Amphibia into its three orders. In spaces *a–c*, write the scientific name of each order. In spaces *d–g*, fill in the common names of the animals in each order.

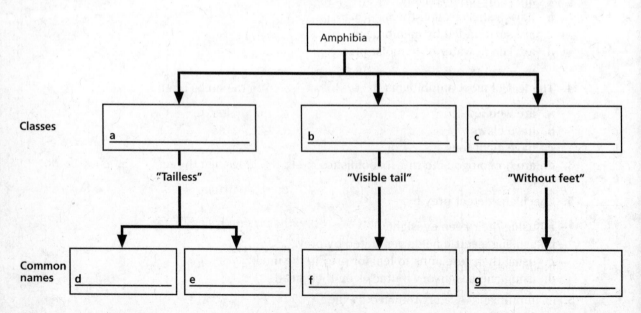

SECTION 40-2 REVIEW

CHARACTERISTICS OF AMPHIBIANS

VOCABULARY REVIEW Distinguish between the terms in each of the following pairs of terms.

1. pulmonary circulation, systemic circulation _____

   _____

2. pulmonary respiration, cutaneous respiration _____

   _____

3. duodenum, ileum _____

   _____

4. mesentery, columella _____

   _____

5. nictitating membrane, tympanic membrane _____

   _____

MULTIPLE CHOICE Write the correct letter in the blank.

_____ 1. An amphibian's mucous glands

    a. filter nitrogenous wastes from the blood.
    b. produce enzymes that help break down food.
    c. secrete poisonous substances that repel predators.
    d. supply a lubricant that keeps the skin moist in air.

_____ 2. The weight of an amphibian's body is transferred to the limbs by the

    a. cervical vertebra.   **c.** radio-ulna.
    b. pectoral and pelvic girdles.   **d.** tibiofibula.

_____ 3. The part of a frog's heart that pumps blood to the lungs and the rest of the body is the

    a. ventricle.   **b.** left atrium.   **c.** right atrium.   **d.** sinus venosus.

_____ 4. The direction that air flows when a frog breathes is controlled by the

    a. conus arteriosus.   **c.** nostrils.
    b. floor of the mouth.   **d.** lungs.

_____ 5. In amphibians, bile is produced by the

    a. cloaca.   **b.** liver.   **c.** pancreas.   **d.** duodenum.

Name _____ Class _____ Date _____

SHORT ANSWER Answer the questions in the space provided.

1. Explain how the vertebrae of a frog's spine help the frog to live on land. _____

_____

2. Why does oxygenated blood reach muscles and organs more rapidly in an amphibian than it

does in a fish? _____

_____

3. Identify the function of each of the following parts of the amphibian nervous system: cerebrum,

cerebellum, optic lobes, medulla oblongata. _____

_____

_____

4. **Critical Thinking** The ventral muscles of the belly are more developed in amphibians than they

are in fishes. Explain why. _____

_____

STRUCTURES AND FUNCTIONS Identify the structures labeled *a–f* in the diagram of a frog's skeleton shown below.

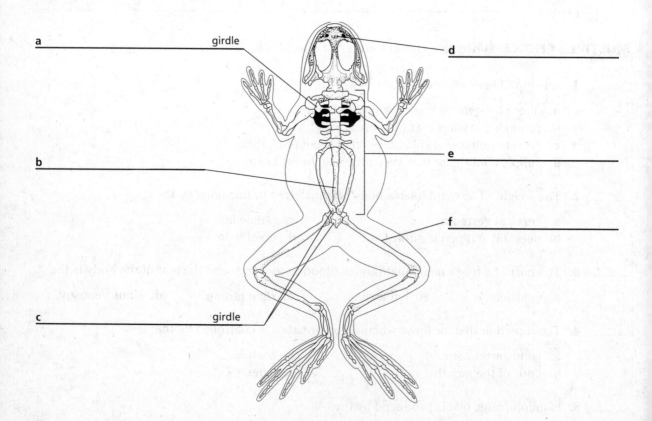

a _____ girdle

d _____

b _____

e _____

f _____

c _____ girdle

SECTION 40-3 REVIEW

REPRODUCTION IN AMPHIBIANS

VOCABULARY REVIEW Define the following terms.

1. amplexus _____

   _____

2. thyroxine _____

   _____

MULTIPLE CHOICE Write the correct letter in the blank.

_____ 1. In a female frog, immature eggs are contained in a pair of lobed
   a. ovaries.
   b. oviducts.
   c. testes.
   d. kidneys.

_____ 2. A frog croaks by

   a. rapidly rubbing its hind legs together.
   b. brushing its forelegs against its vocal sacs.
   c. moving air back and forth between its mouth and lungs.
   d. forcing air out of its nostrils under positive pressure.

_____ 3. One factor that increases the chances of successful fertilization in frogs is that

   a. eggs can be fertilized by sperm of any frog species.
   b. the female produces a single egg.
   c. fertilization occurs internally.
   d. fertilization occurs while the male grasps firmly onto the female.

_____ 4. A newly hatched tadpole lives off

   a. nutrients in the ovaries of its mother.
   b. yolk stored in its body.
   c. plants that grow underwater.
   d. flying insects that land on the water's surface.

_____ 5. Metamorphosis in amphibians

   a. involves a slow change from adult to larva.
   b. is triggered by the disappearance of the lungs.
   c. is stimulated by a hormone.
   d. occurs in all species that produce eggs.

SHORT ANSWER Answer the questions in the space provided.

1. List two reasons why male frogs call during the breeding season. _____

   _____

2. List three changes that occur in the body of a tadpole during metamorphosis. _____

   _____

3. Describe two varieties of amphibian development that do not involve metamorphosis. _____

   _____

   _____

4. Why do some species of frogs sit on their eggs? _____

   _____

5. **Critical Thinking** The jellylike material that surrounds the eggs of many frogs and toads is often very sticky. Suggest an adaptive advantage that this stickiness may provide.

   _____

   _____

   _____

STRUCTURES AND FUNCTIONS The drawings below represent the stages in the life cycle of a frog. Place the stages in the correct order by writing the numbers 1–6 in the spaces beneath the drawings, beginning with the stage that shows fertilization.

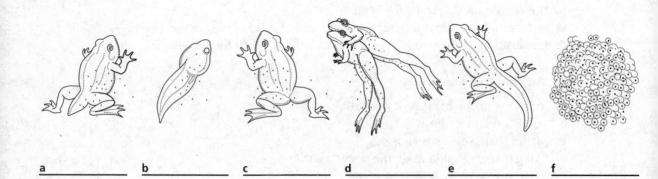

a _____   b _____   c _____   d _____   e _____   f _____

SECTION 41-1 REVIEW

ORIGIN AND EVOLUTION OF REPTILES

VOCABULARY REVIEW Define the following terms.

1. amnion _____

   _____

2. allantois _____

   _____

3. chorion _____

   _____

4. albumen _____

   _____

5. keratin _____

   _____

MULTIPLE CHOICE Write the correct letter in the blank.

_____ 1. One group of extinct reptiles that could fly were the

      a. dinosaurs.   **b.** pterosaurs.   **c.** plesiosaurs.   **d.** ichthyosaurs.

_____ 2. The asteroid-impact hypothesis proposes that

      a. all dinosaur fossils more than 65 million years old were destroyed by an asteroid.
      b. all reptiles were destroyed by an asteroid 65 million years ago.
      c. the ancestors of dinosaurs were brought to Earth on an asteroid.
      d. the sudden extinction of dinosaurs was caused by an asteroid that hit Earth.

_____ 3. Birds are thought to be most closely related to

      a. dinosaurs.   **b.** lizards.   **c.** crocodiles.   **d.** turtles.

_____ 4. The amniotic egg is found only in

      a. reptiles.   **c.** reptiles, mammals, and birds.
      b. reptiles and birds.   **d.** amphibians, reptiles, mammals, and birds.

_____ 5. Gas exchange in reptiles takes place in the

      a. gills.   **b.** lungs.   **c.** skin.   **d.** lungs and skin.

Name ——————————————————————— Class ——————————— Date ————————

SHORT ANSWER Answer the questions in the space provided.

1. List two pieces of evidence that support the asteroid-impact hypothesis. ——————

——

——

——

2. What functions are performed by the shell of a reptilian egg? ——————————

——

3. Why is the skin of a reptile better adapted to a terrestrial environment than is the skin of an

amphibian? ——

——

4. **Critical Thinking** At one time, all of Earth's land masses were joined in a supercontinent called
Pangaea. About 180 million years ago, Pangaea began to break up into separate continents, which
slowly drifted apart. Fossil evidence indicates that dinosaurs became much more diverse after this
time. Explain how the breakup of Pangaea may have contributed to the increase in dinosaur diversity.

——

——

——

STRUCTURES AND FUNCTIONS The phylogenetic diagram below provides a hypothesis
for how modern reptiles are related to each other and to dinosaurs and birds. In the
blank spaces, write the names of the animals that belong on each branch of the diagram.
Choose the names from the following list:

birds   crocodiles   dinosaurs   lizards   snakes   tuataras   turtles

Early reptiles

SECTION 41-2 REVIEW

CHARACTERISTICS OF REPTILES

VOCABULARY REVIEW Define the following terms.

1. alveoli _____

2. Jacobson's organ _____

_____

3. ectotherm _____

_____

4. viviparity _____

_____

5. placenta _____

_____

MULTIPLE CHOICE Write the correct letter in the blank.

_____ 1. Unlike the heart of a lizard, the heart of a crocodile has

    a. no atria.   **c.** a single ventricle that is partially divided.
    b. no conus arteriosus.   **d.** two separate ventricles.

_____ 2. A snake uses its columella to

    a. inject venom.   **b.** detect odors.   **c.** hear.   **d.** detect heat.

_____ 3. Ectotherms require less energy than endotherms because

    a. their muscles are very efficient.   **c.** they have very large fat reserves.
    b. their metabolism is very slow.   **d.** their cellular activities do not require ATP.

_____ 4. The body temperature of a lizard is

    a. usually maintained within a narrow range.
    b. usually equal to the environmental temperature.
    c. always lower than the environmental temperature.
    d. always higher than the environmental temperature.

_____ 5. A female snake that retains her fertilized eggs within her body exhibits a pattern of reproduction called

    a. oviparity.   **b.** ovoviviparity.   **c.** viviparity.   **d.** vovoparity.

Name _____ Class _____ Date _____

SHORT ANSWER Answer the questions in the space provided.

1. List three conditions under which a reptile might redirect blood away from its lungs. _____

_____

_____

2. Explain how a snake detects ground vibrations. _____

_____

3. Explain how a pit viper detects warm objects. _____

_____

4. List three things a lizard might do to regulate its body temperature. _____

_____

5. List three ways a female crocodile provides parental care. _____

_____

_____

6. **Critical Thinking** Why is internal fertilization necessary in reptiles? _____

_____

_____

STRUCTURES AND FUNCTIONS Identify the structures labeled *a–d* in the diagram of a turtle's heart shown below. In the rectangles labeled *e–g*, draw an arrow to indicate the direction in which blood normally flows through that part of the heart.

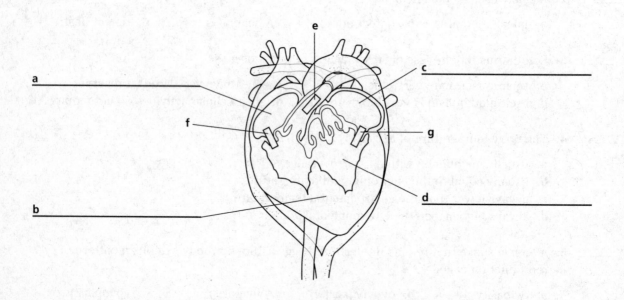

SECTION 41-3 REVIEW

MODERN REPTILES

VOCABULARY REVIEW Define the following terms.

1. carapace _____

_____

2. autotomy _____

_____

3. constrictor _____

_____

4. elapid _____

_____

MULTIPLE CHOICE Write the correct letter in the blank.

_____ 1. One difference between turtles and other reptiles is that turtles

    a. have their pelvic and pectoral girdles within their ribs.
    b. fertilize their eggs externally.
    c. do not produce amniotic eggs.
    d. respire with gills rather than lungs.

_____ 2. The living reptiles most closely related to dinosaurs are

    a. turtles.   **b.** lizards.   **c.** crocodiles.   **d.** tuataras.

_____ 3. Crocodilians usually capture prey by

    a. chasing after prey on land.
    b. digging prey out of the mud at the bottom of a lake.
    c. lying in wait until the prey approaches.
    d. using bait to lure prey into a pit.

_____ 4. Lizards live on every continent except

    a. Africa.   **b.** Asia.   **c.** Australia.   **d.** Antarctica.

_____ 5. An example of a constrictor is a

    a. cobra.   **b.** king snake.   **c.** rattlesnake.   **d.** coral snake.

SHORT ANSWER Answer the questions in the space provided.

1. Explain how the shell and limbs of water-dwelling turtles are adapted to an aquatic environment.

   _____

   _____

2. How can a snake swallow an object that is larger in diameter than the snake's head? _____

   _____

   _____

3. How does a viper immoblize its prey? _____

   _____

4. Why is *tuatara* an appropriate name for reptiles in the order Rhynchocephalia? _____

   _____

5. **Critical Thinking** Explain why snakes have a difficult time moving forward if they are placed on

   a very smooth surface. _____

   _____

   _____

STRUCTURES AND FUNCTIONS The table below lists several structures found in reptiles. Complete the table by identifying a reptilian order in which each structure is found and briefly describing the function of each structure.

Structure	Order	Function
Fangs in back of mouth	a _____	b _____
Valve at back of throat	c _____	d _____
Forked tongue	e _____	f _____
Domed carapace	g _____	h _____
Pads on fingers and toes	i _____	j _____
Elastic ligaments in jaw and skull	k _____	l _____

SECTION 42-1 REVIEW

ORIGIN AND EVOLUTION OF BIRDS

VOCABULARY REVIEW Define the following terms.

1. furcula _____

_____

2. beak _____

_____

MULTIPLE CHOICE Write the correct letter in the blank.

_____ 1. Feathers are composed mainly of

    a. albumen.   **b.** chitin.   **c.** keratin.   **d.** cellulose.

_____ 2. Which of the following statements about a bird's skeleton is untrue?

    a. The skeleton is very flexible because none of the bones are fused.
    b. Many of the bones are thin-walled and hollow.
    c. Air sacs from the respiratory system penetrate some of the bones.
    d. The bones are lighter than those of nonflying animals.

_____ 3. Bird reproduction is characterized by

    a. ovoviviparity.
    b. oviparity.
    c. viviparity.
    d. both oviparity and viviparity.

_____ 4. Birds are thought to have evolved from

    a. small, tree-dwelling mammals.
    b. small, fast-running dinosaurs.
    c. ancient, flying reptiles.
    d. modern, two-legged reptiles.

_____ 5. One characteristic that *Archaeopteryx* shared with modern birds is the presence of

    a. teeth.   **c.** a long, bony tail.
    b. claws on its forelimbs.   **d.** a fused collarbone.

_____ 6. One characteristic that *Sinornis* shared with modern birds is the presence of

    a. wings that could be folded against the body.
    b. ectothermic metabolism.
    c. a long, bony tail.
    d. solid, thick-walled bones.

SHORT ANSWER Answer the questions in the space provided.

1. List two functions for which feathers are important. _____

_____

_____

2. What makes a bird's respiratory system more efficient than the respiratory systems of other

terrestrial vertebrates? _____

_____

_____

3. List three similarities between birds and some dinosaurs. _____

_____

_____

4. Describe two hypotheses for the evolution of flight in birds. _____

_____

_____

_____

5. **Critical Thinking** Compared with other vertebrates, birds are poorly represented in the fossil

record. Propose a possible explanation for this observation. _____

_____

STRUCTURES AND FUNCTIONS The phylogenetic diagram at right shows how birds could be related to some other groups of vertebrates. In the blank spaces, write the name of the animals that belong on each branch. Choose the name from the following list:

Birds
Dinosaurs
Mammals
Reptiles

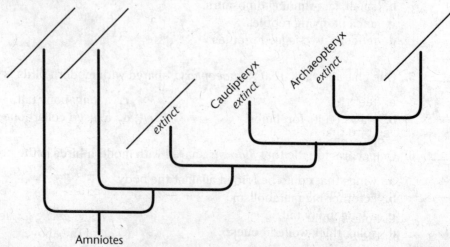

extinct

Caudipteryx
extinct

Archaeopteryx
extinct

Amniotes

SECTION 42-2 REVIEW

CHARACTERISTICS OF BIRDS

VOCABULARY REVIEW Distinguish between the terms in each of the following pairs of terms.

1. shaft, vane _____

_____

2. barb, barbule _____

_____

3. sternum, pygostyle _____

_____

4. proventriculus, gizzard _____

_____

5. precocial, altricial _____

_____

MULTIPLE CHOICE Write the correct letter in the blank.

_____ 1. Birds use their beaks to rub their feathers with oil secreted by the

    a. follicles.   **b.** preen gland.   **c.** crop.   **d.** vasa deferentia.

_____ 2. The humerus, radius, and ulna are part of a bird's

    a. furcula.   **b.** leg.   **c.** wing.   **d.** pelvic girdle.

_____ 3. In a bird, the breakdown of food begins in the

    a. proventriculus.   **b.** esophagus.   **c.** small intestine.   **d.** cloaca.

_____ 4. When a bird breathes, air moves from the posterior air sacs to the

    a. anterior air sacs.   **b.** lungs.   **c.** trachea.   **d.** outside of the bird.

_____ 5. One bird that bears precocial young is the

    a. hawk.   **b.** parrot.   **c.** pigeon.   **d.** duck.

_____ 6. Modifications for flight in the skeleton of a bird include

    a. hollow bones.   **c.** a fused pelvic girdle.
    b. the pygostyle.   **d.** All of the above

SHORT ANSWER Answer the questions in the space provided.

1. What functions does a bird's tail perform during flight? _____

_____

_____

2. How do birds eliminate nitrogenous waste? _____

_____

_____

3. Explain the advantage of having eyes located near the front of the head. _____

_____

_____

4. Name three navigation cues that may be used by migrating birds. _____

_____

_____

5. **Critical Thinking** What might happen to a bird with a defective preen gland? _____

_____

_____

_____

STRUCTURES AND FUNCTIONS Identify the structures labeled *a–g* in the diagram of a bird shown below.

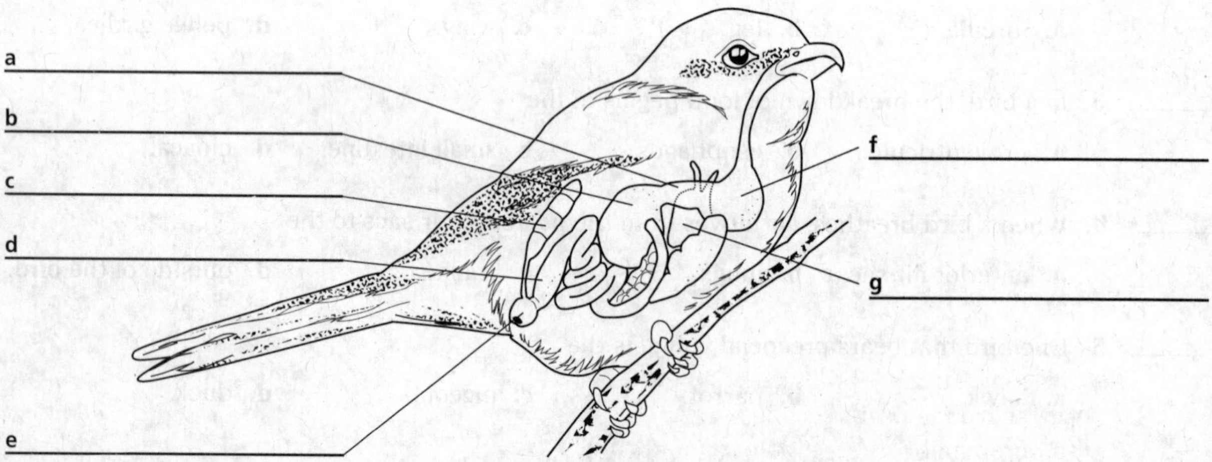

a _____

b _____

c _____

d _____

f _____

g _____

e _____

SECTION 42-3 REVIEW

CLASSIFICATION

VOCABULARY REVIEW Define the following terms.

1. syrinx _____

_____

2. crop milk _____

_____

MULTIPLE CHOICE Write the correct letter in the blank.

_____ 1. The cardinal has a beak that is specialized for

  a. tearing flesh.
  b. feeding on nectar.
  c. sifting through mud.
  d. cracking seeds.

_____ 2. Hummingbirds are found only in

  a. the Western Hemisphere.   c. Asia.
  b. South America.   d. Africa.

_____ 3. Toucans and woodpeckers belong to the order

  a. Anseriformes.   c. Piciformes.
  b. Strigiformes.   d. Apodiformes.

_____ 4. Due to habitat destruction and excessive collecting for the pet trade, extinction is threatening many species in the order
  a. Struthioniformes.   c. Falconiformes.
  b. Psittaciformes.   d. Columbiformes.

_____ 5. The bird order that contains the greatest number of species is
  a. Ciconiiformes.   c. Sphenisciformes.
  b. Galliformes.   d. Passeriformes.

_____ 6. Which of the following characteristics can be observed in the order Struthioniformes?

  a. a large wingspread for flying.
  b. long, strong legs for running.
  c. sharp talons for seizing prey.
  d. crop milk for feeding their young.

Name _____ Class _____ Date _____

SHORT ANSWER Answer the questions in the space provided.

1. Contrast the feet of a kestrel with those of a goose. _____

_____

2. What are raptors, and where are they found? _____

_____

3. Describe the unusual construction of a passerine's feet, and explain the usefulness of this feature.

_____

_____

4. **Critical Thinking** When a homing pigeon is released some distance from its loft with a small magnet tied to its back, it has no difficulty finding its way back to the loft on a sunny day but becomes disoriented and lost on an overcast day. What do these observations suggest about

   how homing pigeons navigate? _____

_____

_____

STRUCTURES AND FUNCTIONS In the spaces below, write the name that corresponds to the order of the bird shown. Choose the names from the following list:

Anseriformes   Passeriformes
Apodiformes   Piciformes
Ciconiiformes   Psittaciformes
Columbiformes   Strigiformes
Galliformes   Struthioniformes

_____ _____

Great blue heron   Great horned owl

_____

Red-tailed hawk   Blue jay   Mallard

SECTION 43-1 REVIEW

ORIGIN AND EVOLUTION OF MAMMALS

VOCABULARY REVIEW Define the following terms.

1. mammary gland _____

_____

2. monotreme _____

_____

3. marsupial _____

_____

MULTIPLE CHOICE Write the correct letter in the blank.

_____ 1. The heart of a mammal

    a. contains two chambers, like the heart of a bird.
    b. contains four chambers, like the heart of an amphibian.
    c. has two completely separate ventricles.
    d. allows deoxygenated blood to mix with oxygenated blood.

_____ 2. The lower jaw of a mammal

    a. is composed of a single bone.
    b. contains teeth that are uniform in size.
    c. contains teeth that are uniform in shape.
    d. does not usually leave a trace in the fossil record.

_____ 3. Some therapsids are believed to have had all of the following features except

    a. limbs positioned under the body.   **c.** endothermy.
    b. moist, wet skin.   **d.** hair.

_____ 4. Two groups of vertebrates that appeared at about the same time during the Triassic period were

    a. synapsids and fishes.   **c.** mammals and reptiles.
    b. therapsids and amphibians.   **d.** mammals and dinosaurs.

_____ 5. Early mammals are thought to have avoided competition with dinosaurs by feeding on

    a. insects at night.   **c.** plants during the day.
    b. plants at night.   **d.** small vertebrates during the day.

SHORT ANSWER Answer the questions in the space provided.

1. Describe a function of hair. _____

_____

2. List three characteristics of *Dimetrodon*. _____

_____

_____

3. Why are modern terrestrial mammals considered more like *Lycaenops* than *Dimetrodon*?

_____

4. What kind of animal constituted most of the large terrestrial carnivores and herbivores during

the Cretaceous period, and what kind of animal fills these roles today? _____

What biological event is responsible for this change over time? _____

_____

5. **Critical Thinking** Although hair is not preserved in fossils, scientists are fairly certain that the

first mammals had hair. How can scientists be so certain about this? _____

_____

_____

_____

STRUCTURES AND FUNCTIONS The drawings below show the fossilized skulls of two
extinct vertebrates. One of the skulls is from an animal in the group that gave rise to
modern reptiles. The other skull is from an animal in the group that gave rise to
mammals. Identify the group that each skull belongs to, and give two reasons that
support your identification.

_____

_____

_____

_____

Eye socket   Eye socket

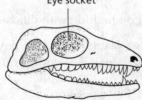 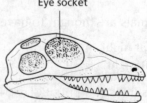

SECTION 43-2 REVIEW

CHARACTERISTICS OF MAMMALS

VOCABULARY REVIEW Define the following terms.

1. diaphragm _____

_____

2. baleen _____

_____

3. echolocation _____

_____

4. rumen _____

_____

MULTIPLE CHOICE Write the correct letter in the blank.

_____ 1. One place where you would expect to find mammals but not reptiles is

    a. a desert.   **b.** the Arctic.   **c.** a rain forest.   **d.** the ocean.

_____ 2. One mammalian feature that is an adaptation for endothermy is

    a. a four-chambered heart.   **c.** a single lower jawbone.
    b. the presence of specialized teeth.   **d.** oviparity.

_____ 3. Which of the following is NOT true about the cecum?

    a. It branches from the small intestine.
    b. It acts as a fermentation chamber.
    c. It is found in mammals that chew cud.
    d. It contains microorganisms that complete digestion.

_____ 4. The lungs of a mammal

    a. expel air when the diaphragm contracts.
    b. contain a few large but very efficient alveoli.
    c. supply blood to placental mammals even before they are born.
    d. have a much larger surface area than the lungs of a reptile.

_____ 5. At hatching, a monotreme is

    a. very small and only partially developed.
    b. small but fully developed.
    c. nearly adult-sized but only partially developed.
    d. nearly adult-sized and fully developed.

SHORT ANSWER Answer the questions in the space provided.

1. Explain how the respiratory system of a mammal helps sustain a rapid metabolism. _____

_____

2. How are microorganisms beneficial to herbivorous mammals? _____

_____

3. Name the largest part of a mammalian brain, and list three of its functions. _____

_____

_____

4. How does a placenta form? _____

_____

5. **Critical Thinking** The ears, feet, and tail of North American mammals are often smaller in northern species than they are in southern species. Explain the adaptive advantage of these size differences.

_____

_____

_____

STRUCTURES AND FUNCTIONS Identify the structures labeled *a–e* in the diagram of a mammalian heart shown below. In the rectangles labeled *f–l,* draw an arrow to indicate whether blood is flowing toward the heart or away from the heart.

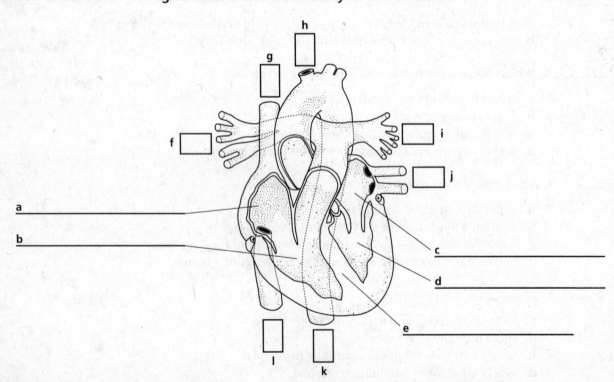

DIVERSITY OF MAMMALS

VOCABULARY REVIEW Define the following terms.

1. pinniped ——

——

2. ungulate ——

——

MULTIPLE CHOICE Write the correct letter in the blank.

———— 1. The only egg-laying mammals are found in the order

    a. Monotremata.   **b.** Marsupialia.   **c.** Sirenia.   **d.** Rodentia.

———— 2. The fossil record indicates that marsupials once dominated South America but were gradually displaced by

    a. monotremes.   **c.** dinosaurs.

    b. placental mammals.   **d.** opossums.

———— 3. The teeth of insectivores are adapted for

    a. chiseling through roots and twigs.
    b. grinding plant material.
    c. consuming a variety of foods.
    d. grasping and piercing prey.

———— 4. Mammals in the order Chiroptera are commonly called

    a. sloths.   **b.** manatees.   **c.** bats.   **d.** whales.

———— 5. Mammals with streamlined bodies adapted for efficient swimming are found in the orders

    a. Edentata, Lagomorpha, and Sirenia.
    b. Carnivora, Cetacea, and Sirenia.
    c. Cetacea, Proboscidea, and Artiodactyla.
    d. Artiodactyla, Perissodactyla, and Rodentia.

———— 6. Which of the following mammals is a tapir most closely related to?

    a. horse   **b.** pig   **c.** walrus   **d.** porcupine

SHORT ANSWER Answer the questions in the space provided.

1. A large mammal is standing in a meadow chewing its cud. Identify the order to which this

   mammal belongs. _____

   Is this mammal more likely to have three toes or four? _____

2. Name the mammalian order to which humans belong.

   _____

3. **Critical Thinking** Shrews are the smallest mammals, some weighing as little as 2 g (0.07 oz). They also eat constantly and must hunt for food both day and night. Explain why shrews have

   such a voracious appetite. _____

   _____

   _____

STRUCTURES AND FUNCTIONS In the space above each drawing below, write the name that corresponds to the order of the mammal shown in that drawing. Choose the names from the following list:

Artiodactyla	Chiroptera	Marsupialia	Primates	Sirenia
Carnivora	Insectivora	Monotremata	Proboscidea	Xenarthra
Cetacea	Lagomorpha	Perissodactyla	Rodentia	

_____   _____   _____

_____   _____   _____

Name _____ Class _____ Date _____

PRIMATES AND HUMAN ORIGINS

VOCABULARY REVIEW Define the following terms.

1. prehensile appendage _____

_____

2. opposable thumb _____

_____

3. bipedalism _____

_____

4. hominid _____

_____

MULTIPLE CHOICE Write the correct letter in the blank.

_____ 1. Which of the following is NOT a primate characteristic?

    a. large brain relative to body size   **c.** teeth specialized for a carnivorous diet
    b. binocular vision   **d.** opposable thumbs

_____ 2. Primates that exhibit bipedalism include

    a. humans.   **c.** the great apes.
    b. New World monkeys.   **d.** All of the above

_____ 3. The oldest known australopithecine is

    a. Lucy.   **c.** *Australopithecus africanus.*
    b. *Australopithecus anamensis.*   **d.** *Australopithecus robustus.*

_____ 4. Similarities between *Homo habilis* and modern humans include

    a. height.   **c.** facial structure.
    b. brain capacity.   **d.** ability to use tools.

_____ 5. According to the multiregional hypothesis

    a. local populations of *H. erectus* gave rise to local populations of *H. sapiens.*
    b. *H. sapiens* evolved from *H. erectus* in Africa.
    c. *H. sapiens* evolved from *H. erectus* in Asia.
    d. *H. sapiens* evolved from at least two species of hominids.

SHORT ANSWER Answer the questions in the space provided.

1. List three characteristics of primates. _____

_____

2. Describe two anthropoid adaptations. _____

_____

3. How is the human skeleton adapted to bipedalism? _____

_____

_____

4. Contrast the multiregional hypothesis with the recent-African-origin hypothesis.

_____

_____

5. **Critical Thinking** Why is it considered inaccurate to refer to a "missing link" with respect to human evolution?

_____

_____

_____

STRUCTURES AND FUNCTIONS The table below compares several physical traits between humans and chimpanzees. Complete the table by filling in the missing information.

Physical Traits	Human	Chimpanzee
Cranial capacity	**a**	500 cm^3
Spine	S-shaped	**b**
Pelvis	**c**	flat
Toes	aligned	**d**
Jaw	**e**	larger

SECTION 44-1 REVIEW

DEVELOPMENT OF BEHAVIOR

VOCABULARY REVIEW Define the following terms.

1. innate behavior _____

_____

2. fixed action pattern _____

_____

3. habituation _____

_____

4. operant conditioning _____

_____

5. imprinting _____

_____

MULTIPLE CHOICE Write the correct letter in the blank.

_____ **1.** A biologist who studies behavior is
    a. called a psychologist.
    b. called an ethnographer.
    c. called an ethologist.
    d. concerned only with the genetics of behavior.

_____ **2.** Removal of infected young from a bee hive is an example of behavior that is

    a. unresponsive to environmental conditions, or fixed.
    b. triggered only by environmental stimuli.
    c. mostly learned.
    d. both genetic and triggered by environmental conditions.

_____ **3.** A fixed action pattern

    a. continues from start to finish without modification.
    b. is adaptive.
    c. may be triggered by an environmental stimulus.
    d. All of the above

_____ **4.** Learning to associate a reward with a predictive stimulus, such as a hamburger with the sight of a neon sign, is an example of

    a. classical conditioning.
    b. operant conditioning.
    c. imprinting.
    d. reasoning.

_____ **5.** Which of the following is an example of imprinting?

    a. a salmon's ability to recognize chemical cues in the water when returning to the stream where it was born to spawn

    b. a chimpanzee stacking boxes to reach a banana

    c. an octopus using its arms to unscrew a jar lid and eat the fish inside the jar

    d. a dog salivating in response to a bell

SHORT ANSWER Answer the questions in the space provided.

1. List four questions that ethologists ask about an animal's behavior. _____

_____

_____

2. Describe an example of how natural selection shapes behavior. _____

_____

3. Give two examples of innate behaviors. _____

_____

4. How is habituation adaptive? _____

_____

5. Critical Thinking What kinds of behaviors might be involved in using a computer?

_____

_____

STRUCTURES AND FUNCTIONS The table below compares several kinds of behavior. Complete the table by filling in the missing information.

Behavior	Learned or Innate	Example
Fixed action pattern	a	b
c	d	Not hearing planes overhead
Operant conditioning	e	f
Classical conditioning	g	h
i	j	An octopus opening a jar for fish
k	l	Goslings following their mother

SECTION 44-2 REVIEW

TYPES OF ANIMAL BEHAVIOR

VOCABULARY REVIEW Define the following terms.

1. dominance hierarchy _____

_____

2. aposematic coloration _____

_____

3. pheromone _____

_____

4. circadian rhythm _____

_____

MULTIPLE CHOICE Write the correct letter in the blank.

_____ 1. The optimality hypothesis helps to explain

    a. courtship behavior.   **c.** parental behavior.

    b. dominance hierarchies.   **d.** feeding behavior.

_____ 2. An animal may establish and defend a territory by using

    a. chemical signals.   **b.** vocal signals.   **c.** visual signals.   **d.** All of the above

_____ 3. A mating system in which a male mates with multiple females is called

    a. male polygamy.   **b.** female polygamy.   **c.** monogamy.   **d.** sexual selection.

_____ 4. Social behavior is defined as an interaction that involves

    a. several species.

    b. sacrificing one's own security to help another.

    c. two or more animals of the same species.

    d. None of the above

_____ 5. Hibernation is associated with

    a. circadian rhythms.

    b. annual biological cycles.

    c. migration.

    d. days becoming longer in the springtime.

SHORT ANSWER Answer the questions in the space provided.

1. What is the usual outcome of aggressive behavior? ——————————————

———

2. Describe a situation in which monogamy would be favored. ——————————

———

3. Contrast the costs and benefits of parental care. ————————————————

———

———

4. List the criteria that must be met for communication to be considered language. ————

———

5. **Critical Thinking** Crossbills are birds that use their beaks to eat the seeds of pine cones. One day, a flock of crossbills feeds in a single pine tree for several hours. On another day, the same flock moves from tree to tree as it feeds. Explain these behaviors.

———

———

STRUCTURES AND FUNCTIONS The table below lists several examples of behaviors. Complete the table by filling in the missing behavior.

Behavior	Example
a	A ground squirrel giving an alarm call
b	Owls hunting at night and resting during the day
c	Monarch butterflies traveling to Mexico for the winter
d	Male and female mourning doves bowing and cooing to each other
e	Head-butting in bighorn sheep
f	A cat urinating on bushes in its neighborhood
g	Pecking orders in chickens

SECTION 45-1 REVIEW

THE HUMAN BODY PLAN

VOCABULARY REVIEW Describe the functions of the tissues listed below.

1. nervous tissue _____

_____

2. muscular tissue _____

_____

3. skeletal muscle _____

_____

4. epithelial tissue _____

_____

5. connective tissue _____

_____

MULTIPLE CHOICE Write the correct letter in the blank.

_____ **1.** Nervous tissue contains specialized cells called

    a. transmitters.   **b.** messenger cells.   **c.** neurons.   **d.** cardiac cells.

_____ **2.** Tissue that binds, supports, and protects structures is called

    a. connective tissue.   **c.** skeletal tissue.
    b. muscle tissue.   **d.** epithelial tissue.

_____ **3.** Organ systems consist of

    a. tissues.   **b.** cells.   **c.** organs.   **d.** All of the above

_____ **4.** The body cavity that contains the heart, esophagus, and organs of the respiratory system is the

    a. cranial cavity.   **c.** abdominal cavity.
    b. spinal cavity.   **d.** thoracic cavity.

_____ **5.** Which organ system includes the kidneys, ureters, bladder, urethra, lungs, and skin?

    a. integumentary system   **c.** excretory system
    b. digestive system   **d.** endocrine system

SHORT ANSWER Answer the questions in the space provided.

1. List three types of muscle tissue. _____

    _____

2. Describe how body tissues, organs, and organ systems are related. _____

    _____

    _____

3. Describe the composition of connective tissue. _____

    _____

4. Describe two functions of nervous tissue. _____

    _____

    _____

5. **Critical Thinking** Can an organ be part of more than one organ system? Explain your answer.

    _____

    _____

    _____

STRUCTURES AND FUNCTIONS Use the figure below to answer the following questions.

1. Label each part of the figure in the spaces provided.

2. Which of the labeled body cavities contain the central nervous system? _____

    _____

3. What is the function of the body cavities? _____

    _____

    _____

a _____

b _____

c _____

d _____

e _____

SECTION 45-2 REVIEW

SKELETAL SYSTEM

VOCABULARY REVIEW Explain the relationship between the terms in each of the following pairs of terms.

1. axial skeleton, appendicular skeleton _____

_____

2. periosteum, compact bone _____

_____

3. bone marrow, spongy bone _____

_____

4. ossification, epiphyseal plate _____

_____

5. joint, ligament _____

_____

MULTIPLE CHOICE Write the correct letter in the blank.

_____ 1. The process in which bone cells gradually replace cartilage is called

    a. ossification.   **c.** restoration.
    b. osteoarthritis.   **d.** None of the above

_____ 2. The axial skeleton includes bones of the

    a. arms.   **b.** legs.   **c.** ribs.   **d.** All of the above

_____ 3. Semimovable joints are found

    a. in the knees.   **c.** in the thumbs.
    b. between vertebrae.   **d.** in the elbows.

_____ 4. Tough bands of connective tissue that hold bones in place are called

    a. ligaments.   **b.** tendons.   **c.** gliding joints.   **d.** muscles.

_____ 5. Osteoarthritis is characterized by

    a. stretching of ligaments.   **c.** fracturing of bones.
    b. autoimmunity.   **d.** thinning of cartilage.

Name _____ Class _____ Date _____

SHORT ANSWER Answer the questions in the space provided.

1. Describe three functions of bones. _____

_____

_____

2. List three types of joints, and give an example of each type. _____

_____

_____

3. Describe the importance of bone marrow. _____

_____

4. **Critical Thinking** Why is dietary calcium important to bone growth and maintenance?

_____

_____

STRUCTURES AND FUNCTIONS Use the figure
of the human skeleton at right to answer the
following questions.

1. Label each part of the figure in the spaces
   provided.

2. What are the primary functions of the

   skeleton? 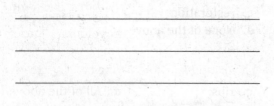 _____

   _____

   _____

   _____

   _____

3. How do bones elongate? _____

   _____

   _____

   _____

   _____

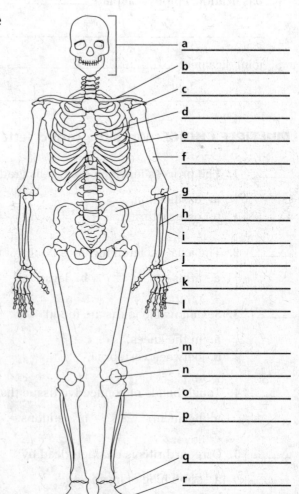

a _____
b _____
c _____
d _____
e _____
f _____
g _____
h _____
i _____
j _____
k _____
l _____
m _____
n _____
o _____
p _____
q _____
r _____
s _____

SECTION 45-3 REVIEW

MUSCULAR SYSTEM

VOCABULARY REVIEW Distinguish between the terms in each of the following pairs of terms.

1. voluntary muscle, involuntary muscle _____

_____

2. origin, insertion _____

_____

3. flexor, extensor _____

_____

4. actin, myosin _____

_____

5. muscle fatigue, oxygen debt _____

_____

MULTIPLE CHOICE Write the correct letter in the blank.

_____ 1. Which of the following types of muscle tissues is found in the walls of the stomach, intestines, and blood vessels?

    a. cardiac muscle   **b.** smooth muscle   **c.** skeletal muscle   **d.** voluntary muscle

_____ 2. Which of the following types of muscle tissues is responsible for moving most parts of the body?

    a. cardiac muscle   **b.** smooth muscle   **c.** skeletal muscle   **d.** involuntary muscle

_____ 3. A sarcomere

    a. is the functional unit of muscle contraction.   **c.** uses ATP.
    b. consists of myofibrils.   **d.** All of the above

_____ 4. Muscles that cause a joint to bend are called

    a. flexors.   **b.** origins.   **c.** extensors.   **d.** insertions.

_____ 5. Which of the following happens when a skeletal muscle contracts?

    a. Sarcomeres shorten.   **c.** Myosin heads attach to actin filaments.
    b. Myosin heads bend outward.   **d.** All of the above

Name _____ Class _____ Date _____

SHORT ANSWER Answer the questions in the space provided.

1. How does a runner acquire an oxygen debt? _____

_____

2. How does a muscle contract? _____

_____

_____

3. Distinguish between the three types of muscle tissue. _____

_____

_____

_____

4. **Critical Thinking** Why are flexors and extensors considered antagonistic muscles?

_____

_____

STRUCTURES AND FUNCTIONS Use the figure of the human arm below to answer the following questions.

1. Label each part of the figure in the spaces provided.

a _____

b _____

c _____

d _____

e _____

f _____

g _____

h _____

2. Which muscle is a flexor and which muscle is an extensor? _____

_____

3. Where is the insertion of *a* located? Where is the origin of *a* located? _____

_____

_____

INTEGUMENTARY SYSTEM

VOCABULARY REVIEW Define the following terms.

1. exocrine gland ——————————————————————————————————

——

2. melanin ——————————————————————————————————————

——

3. sebum ——————————————————————————————————————

——

4. keratin ——————————————————————————————————————

——

5. sweat gland ————————————————————————————————————

——

MULTIPLE CHOICE Write the correct letter in the blank.

———— 1. The dermis

    a. covers the epidermis.
    b. produces melanin.
    c. contains nervous tissue and blood vessels.
    d. consists mostly of dead cells.

———— 2. Which of the following is secreted by oil glands in the skin?

    a. melanin   **b.** sebum   **c.** keratin   **d.** sweat

———— 3. Which of the following is *not* a function of the layer of fat cells beneath the dermis?

    a. produces oil
    b. provides an energy reserve
    c. absorbs shock
    d. insulates the body

———— 4. Hair and nails are composed primarily of

    a. sebum.   **b.** keratin.   **c.** glands.   **d.** All of the above

———— 5. Sweat glands

    a. secrete sebum into the bloodstream.
    b. stimulate hair follicles.
    c. help maintain a steady body temperature.
    d. insulate the body.

Name _____ Class _____ Date _____

SHORT ANSWER Answer the questions in the space provided.

1. Describe the functions of the skin. _____

_____

2. How does exposure to ultraviolet light influence melanin production in the skin? _____

_____

_____

3. Describe the functions of the epidermis. _____

_____

4. How are hair and nails similar in structure? _____

_____

5. Critical Thinking What causes freckles and pigmented moles? _____

_____

_____

STRUCTURES AND FUNCTIONS Use the figure below to answer the following questions.

1. Label each part of the figure in the spaces provided.

2. Which structures contain keratin? _____

_____

3. Explain how the dermis enables the body to interact with the external environment.

_____

_____

SECTION 46-1 REVIEW

THE CIRCULATORY SYSTEM

VOCABULARY REVIEW Distinguish between the terms in each of the following pairs of terms.

1. ventricle, atrium _____

_____

2. sinoatrial node, atrioventricular node _____

_____

3. artery, vein _____

_____

4. pulmonary circulation, systemic circulation _____

_____

MULTIPLE CHOICE Write the correct letter in the blank.

_____ 1. Which of the following is most important to the heartbeat?

    a. aortic valve   **b.** sinoatrial node   **c.** lymph node   **d.** tricuspid valve

_____ 2. During its circulation from the left atrium to the left ventricle, what percentage of the blood enters the pulmonary circulation?

    a. 25%   **b.** 50%   **c.** 100%   **d.** None of the above

_____ 3. Exchange of nutrients and waste between blood and body tissues occurs across

    a. arterioles.   **b.** capillaries.   **c.** arteries.   **d.** veins.

_____ 4. Which one of the following characteristics is unique to the pulmonary circulation?

    a. capillaries that exchange gases with the surrounding tissue
    b. arteries that carry blood away from the heart
    c. an artery that originates at the right ventricle
    d. an artery that originates at the right atrium

_____ 5. The lymphatic system is important for the normal function of the body because it

    a. carries newly formed blood to the cardiovascular system.
    b. returns excess intercellular fluid to the cardiovascular system.
    c. provides an alternate route for blood during strenuous exercise.
    d. carries oxygen to the lymph nodes.

SHORT ANSWER Answer the questions in the space provided.

1. Trace the flow of blood through the heart. _____

_____

_____

_____

2. Describe the function of the lymphatic system. _____

_____

_____

3. **Critical Thinking** If the aortic valve could not close completely, would the diastolic pressure or

systolic pressure be affected the most? Explain your answer. _____

_____

_____

STRUCTURES AND FUNCTIONS Use the figure of the human heart below to answer the following questions.

1. Label each part of the figure in the spaces provided.

a _____

b _____

c _____

d _____

e _____

f _____

g _____

h _____

i _____

j _____

k _____

2. How would a defect of the mitral valve affect circulation? _____

_____

SECTION 46-2 REVIEW

BLOOD

VOCABULARY REVIEW Explain the relationship between the terms in each of the
following pairs of terms.

1. leukocyte, phagocyte _____

_____

2. antigen, antibody _____

_____

3. erythrocyte, hemoglobin _____

_____

4. platelet, fibrin _____

_____

MULTIPLE CHOICE Write the correct letter in the blank.

_____ **1.** When oxygen is carried by the blood, it is bonded to

    a. platelets.   **b.** antibodies.   **c.** plasma.   **d.** hemoglobin.

_____ **2.** Phagocytes

    a. carry hemoglobin.   **c.** engulf microorganisms.
    b. synthesize erythrocytes.   **d.** produce antibodies.

_____ **3.** Platelets

    a. are formed in lymph nodes.   **c.** produce hemoglobin.
    b. are involved with blood clotting.   **d.** are whole cells.

_____ **4.** Mature red blood cells

    a. live for several years.   **c.** promote clotting.
    b. are the largest cells in the blood.   **d.** do not have a nucleus.

_____ **5.** If someone is receiving a blood transfusion, which of the following is most important
to know?

    a. the number of erythrocytes in the donated blood
    b. if the father of the blood donor is Rh$^+$
    c. the donor's blood type
    d. if the blood recipient has eaten within the last six hours

Name _____ Class _____ Date _____

SHORT ANSWER Answer the questions in the space provided.

1. How is oxygen transported in the blood? _____

_____

2. List two structural differences and two functional differences between erythrocytes and leukocytes.

_____

_____

3. Explain why a person with type AB blood can donate blood only to a person with the same

   blood type. _____

_____

4. Describe the role of platelets in blood clotting. _____

_____

5. **Critical Thinking** How might lack of dietary iron affect the oxygen-carrying capacity of the blood?

_____

_____

_____

STRUCTURES AND FUNCTIONS Use the table below to answer the following questions.

Blood types	Antigen on red blood cells	Can give blood to
A	A	A, AB
B	B	B, AB
AB	A and B	AB
O	none	A, B, AB, O

1. Explain why type O blood can be donated in a blood transfusion regardless of the recipient's

   blood type. _____

_____

2. Describe the antibody-antigen interactions that would occur if an Rh^- person with type B blood

   received blood from an Rh^+ person with type AB blood. _____

_____

_____

THE RESPIRATORY SYSTEM

VOCABULARY REVIEW Explain the relationship between the terms in each of the following pairs of terms.

1. epiglottis, trachea _____

_____

2. expiration, larynx _____

_____

3. bronchi, bronchioles _____

_____

4. alveoli, inspiration _____

_____

MULTIPLE CHOICE Write the correct letter in the blank.

_____ 1. Cilia that line the walls of air passageways

    a. move the inspired air to the alveoli.   **c.** moisten the expired air.
    b. move the expired air to the nasal cavity.   **d.** clean the inspired air.

_____ 2. The exchange of gases that occurs at an alveolus depends on

    a. elevated blood pressure.   **c.** concentration gradients.
    b. mucus carrying dissolved oxygen.   **d.** bronchioles closing during expiration.

_____ 3. Carbon dioxide is transported in the blood

    a. bound to hemoglobin.   **c.** as bicarbonate ions.
    b. plasma.   **d.** All of the above

_____ 4. Inspiration occurs when

    a. the diaphragm pushes upward.   **c.** blood pressure increases.
    b. thoracic volume increases.   **d.** thoracic pressure increases.

_____ 5. The rate of breathing is controlled by cells within

    a. a specialized node located in the bronchus.
    b. the diaphragm.
    c. the brain.
    d. stretch receptors located between the ribs.

SHORT ANSWER Answer the questions in the space provided.

1. Is the nasal cavity a part of the respiratory system? Explain your answer. _____
_____
_____

2. How is most carbon dioxide transported in the blood? _____
_____
_____

3. Describe how the skeleton is involved with expiration. _____
_____
_____

4. **Critical Thinking** Oxygen deficiency is called hypoxia. Suggest two possible causes of

   inadequate delivery of oxygen to body tissues. _____
_____
_____

STRUCTURES AND FUNCTIONS Use the figure below to answer the following questions.

1. What drives the diffusion of oxygen into the blood
   and carbon dioxide from a blood cell to an alveolus?

   _____

   _____

   _____

2. In the lungs, is carbon dioxide more concentrated in
   the alveoli or in the blood? Explain your answer.

   _____

   _____

   _____

3. Does the exchange of carbon dioxide depend on the concentration of oxygen in the alveoli and

   the blood? Explain your answer. _____
_____
_____

SECTION 47-1 REVIEW

NONSPECIFIC DEFENSES

VOCABULARY REVIEW Define the following terms.

1. Koch's postulates _____

_____

2. interferon _____

_____

3. histamine _____

_____

4. natural killer cell _____

_____

MULTIPLE CHOICE Write the correct letter in the blank.

_____ 1. Mucus serves as a nonspecific defense to pathogens by

    a. being secreted by the skin.   **c.** digesting pathogens.
    b. capturing pathogens.   **d.** secreting cytokines.

_____ 2. Which of the following statements is *false?*

    a. Fever stimulates the body's defense mechanisms.
    b. Fever suppresses the growth of certain bacteria.
    c. Fever activates cellular enzymes.
    d. Fever promotes the action of white blood cells.

_____ 3. Macrophages

    a. are white blood cells.   **c.** engulf and destroy large pathogens.
    b. cross blood-vessel walls.   **d.** All of the above

_____ 4. Natural killer cells are

    a. specialized red blood cells.   **c.** phagocytes.
    b. infected cells.   **d.** None of the above

_____ 5. An inflammatory response is initiated by

    a. release of histamines.   **c.** fever.
    b. pathogens.   **d.** drying of mucous membranes.

Name _____ Class _____ Date _____

SHORT ANSWER Answer the questions in the space provided.

1. How are neutrophils involved in the body's defense against pathogens? _____

_____

_____

2. How does interferon inhibit viruses? _____

_____

_____

3. How does the first line of defense protect the body against pathogens? _____

_____

_____

4. **Critical Thinking** Why might taking aspirin to reduce fever slow rather than hasten your

recovery from a bacterial infection? _____

_____

_____

STRUCTURES AND FUNCTIONS Use the table below to answer the following questions.

1. The table lists the steps that occur in the inflammatory response. Put the steps in the correct order by writing in the numbers 1–5 in the table under the column labeled "Order."

Order	Events of inflammatory response
	Damaged cells secrete histamine.
	White blood cells attack and destroy the pathogens.
	Pathogens enter the body by penetrating the skin.
	White blood cells move to the infected area.
	Flow of blood to the infected area increases.

2. Why is an increase in the permeability of capillaries essential to the inflammatory response?

_____

_____

3. How would applying ice to a wounded area to reduce blood flow to the area affect the inflammatory

response? _____

_____

SPECIFIC DEFENSES: THE IMMUNE SYSTEM

VOCABULARY REVIEW Define the following terms.

1. plasma cell ——

———

2. antigen ——

———

3. memory cell ——

———

4. antibody ——

———

5. allergy ——

———

MULTIPLE CHOICE Write the correct letter in the blank.

———— 1. Which of the following are *not* lymphocytes?

    a. memory cells   **b.** helper T cells   **c.** macrophages   **d.** B cells

———— 2. Bone marrow is considered part of the immune system because it

    a. filters pathogens from blood.   **c.** produces white blood cells.
    b. drains into the lymphatic system.   **d.** produces plasma cells.

———— 3. B cells

    a. are involved with the humoral immune response.
    b. kill infected cells.
    c. mature within the thymus.
    d. are derived from plasma cells.

———— 4. Interleukins are secreted by

    a. cytotoxic T cells.   **b.** helper T cells.   **c.** plasma cells.   **d.** All of the above

———— 5. Cell-mediated immune responses require

    a. production of antibodies.   **c.** B cells.
    b. helper T cells.   **d.** a secondary immune response.

SHORT ANSWER Answer the questions in the space provided.

1. What signals does a T cell require in order to divide? _____

_____

_____

2. How do vaccinations produce immunity? _____

_____

3. How do antibodies provide defense from viruses? _____

_____

4. **Critical Thinking** Would you expect defective T cells or defective B cells to be the primary

cause of autoimmune diseases? Explain your answer. _____

_____

_____

STRUCTURES AND FUNCTIONS Use the figure of the immune response below to answer the following questions.

1. Label each part of the figure in the spaces provided.

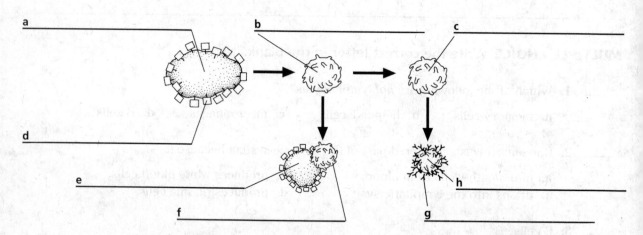

2. What event triggers the chain of events shown in the figure? _____

_____

_____

3. How would an enzyme that destroys cytokines affect both the cell-mediated and humoral

immune responses? _____

_____

_____

SECTION 47-3 REVIEW

HIV AND AIDS

VOCABULARY REVIEW Explain the relationship between the terms in each of the following pairs of terms.

1. helper T cells, AIDS _____

_____

2. AIDS, HIV _____

_____

3. opportunistic infection, AIDS _____

_____

MULTIPLE CHOICE Write the correct letter in the blank.

_____ 1. A diagnosis of AIDS is made when a person has

    a. an HIV infection.   **c.** few T cells.
    b. few B cells.   **d.** All of the above

_____ 2. Which of the following is a route of HIV transmission?

    a. breathing air in a room with a person with AIDS
    b. touching a person infected with HIV
    c. sharing of hypodermic needles
    d. insect bites

_____ 3. The most common means of HIV transmission is

    a. sexual intercourse with a person infected with HIV.
    b. blood transfusion.
    c. shaking hands with a person with AIDS.
    d. performing experiments with HIV.

_____ 4. Vaccines against HIV are difficult to design because HIV

    a. is a retrovirus.   **c.** changes rapidly.
    b. is difficult to isolate.   **d.** is not detectable.

_____ 5. HIV begins to reproduce

    a. when AIDS occurs.   **c.** months after infection.
    b. shortly after infection.   **d.** All of the above

SHORT ANSWER Answer the questions in the space provided.

1. Is HIV the primary cause of death in people with AIDS? Explain your answer. _____

   _____

   _____

2. Can a person be infected with HIV but not exhibit AIDS? Explain your answer. _____

   _____

   _____

3. List two ways that HIV can be transmitted. _____

   _____

4. **Critical Thinking** Could people become exposed to HIV during an organ transplant or skin graft

   operation? Explain your answer. _____

   _____

   _____

STRUCTURES AND FUNCTIONS Use the graph below to answer the following questions.

The graph shows a decrease in the number of helper T cells in a person with HIV over time.

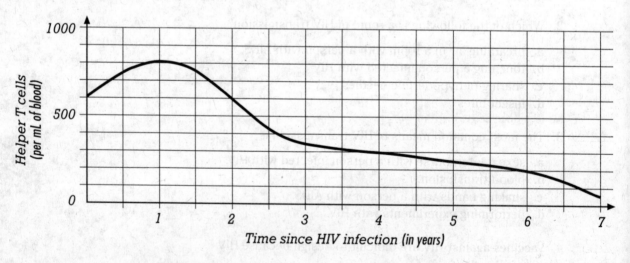

1. In this person, how many years after infection did the onset of AIDS occur? _____

   _____

2. The person tested positive for HIV six months after infection but tested negative for HIV six years

   later. Explain how this might happen. _____

   _____

SECTION 48-1 REVIEW

NUTRIENTS

VOCABULARY REVIEW Answer the questions in the space provided.

1. What are the six basic nutrients? _____

_____

_____

2. What is an unsaturated fat? _____

_____

3. What is the function of vitamins? _____

_____

4. How does dehydration affect the body? _____

_____

_____

MULTIPLE CHOICE Write the correct letter in the blank.

_____ 1. Which of the following is *not* an organic nutrient?

    a. vitamins   **b.** lipids   **c.** carbohydrates   **d.** minerals

_____ 2. Carbohydrates are important sources of

    a. monosaccharides.   **c.** legumes.
    b. nonessential amino acids.   **d.** glycerol.

_____ 3. Essential amino acids are obtained from

    a. animal products.   **b.** plant products.   **c.** legumes.   **d.** All of the above

_____ 4. Saturated fats

    a. are found in most plant oils.   **c.** are found in animal fats.
    b. have double bonds.   **d.** do not have a glycerol molecule.

_____ 5. Which of the following statements is *true?*

    a. Potassium is a component of ascorbic acid.
    b. Potassium is required for the formation of red blood cells.
    c. Bananas are good sources of potassium.
    d. It is not necessary to consume foods containing potassium.

Name _____ Class _____ Date _____

SHORT ANSWER Answer the questions in the space provided.

1. Explain the difference between essential amino acids and nonessential amino acids. _____
   _____
   _____

2. Describe the importance of simple sugars for normal body functioning. _____
   _____
   _____

3. List two reasons that water is an important nutrient. _____
   _____

4. **Critical Thinking** What characteristic is common to all of the nutrients? _____
   _____
   _____

STRUCTURES AND FUNCTIONS Use the food pyramid below to answer the following questions.

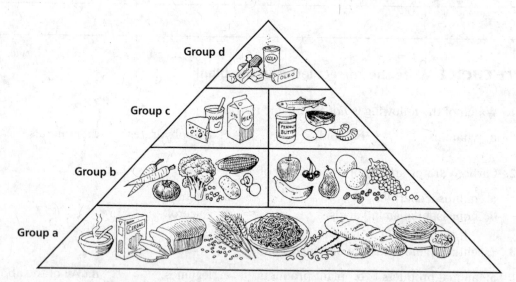

1. Based on the organization of the pyramid, which food group does the body need and use the

   most? What is the primary nutrient in this group? _____

   _____

2. Which food group contains all of the essential amino acids? Is this the only group that contains

   essential amino acids? Explain your answer. _____

   _____

SECTION 48-2 REVIEW

DIGESTIVE SYSTEM

VOCABULARY REVIEW Explain the relationship between the terms in each of the following pairs of terms.

1. pharynx, epiglottis _____

_____

2. ulcer, gastric fluid _____

_____

3. peristalsis, colon _____

_____

4. pyloric sphincter, chyme _____

_____

5. villus, gastrointestinal tract _____

_____

MULTIPLE CHOICE Write the correct letter in the blank.

_____ 1. The gastrointestinal tract includes the

    a. liver.   **b.** large intestine.   **c.** pancreas.   **d.** All of the above

_____ 2. Bile is

    a. released into the small intestine.   **c.** stored in the gallbladder.
    b. produced by the liver.   **d.** All of the above

_____ 3. Chemical digestion involves

    a. the molars.   **c.** the hard palate.
    b. saliva.   **d.** the incisors.

_____ 4. Which of the following is a component of both the respiratory system and the digestive system?

    a. esophagus   **b.** salivary glands   **c.** pharynx   **d.** peristalsis

_____ 5. Ulcers are linked to breakdown of the

    a. pyloric sphincter.   **c.** stomach lining.
    b. gallbladder function.   **d.** common bile duct.

Name _____ Class _____ Date _____

SHORT ANSWER Answer the questions in the space provided.

1. What is the function of mucus in the stomach? _____
   _____

2. What is the primary role of pepsin in digestion? _____
   _____

3. How does the pancreas aid digestion? _____
   _____

4. **Critical Thinking** Which part of the gastrointestinal tract should have the highest concentration
   of blood capillaries? Explain your answer. _____
   _____
   _____

STRUCTURES AND FUNCTIONS Use the figure of the gastrointestinal tract below to
answer the following questions.

1. Label each part of the figure in the spaces provided.

a _____

b _____

c _____

d _____

e _____

f _____

g _____

2. Which organ is not part of the gastrointestinal tract? How does this organ aid digestion?
   _____
   _____

3. In which organ does absorption take place? What structural features make this organ particularly
   well-suited for absorption of nutrients into the blood? _____
   _____
   _____

SECTION 48-3 REVIEW

URINARY SYSTEM

VOCABULARY REVIEW Define the following terms.

1. nephron _____

_____

2. urethra _____

_____

3. renal medulla _____

_____

4. excretion _____

_____

5. urea _____

_____

MULTIPLE CHOICE Write the correct letter in the blank.

_____ 1. Most reabsorption within a nephron occurs in the

    a. Bowman's capsule.   **c.** collecting duct.

    b. duodenum.   **d.** proximal convoluted tubule.

_____ 2. Which of the following is *not* part of the nephron?

    a. glomerulus   **b.** loop of Henle   **c.** ureter   **d.** Bowman's capsule

_____ 3. Which of the following substances would *not* normally be collected in the Bowman's capsule?

    a. small proteins   **b.** glucose   **c.** erythrocytes   **d.** vitamins

_____ 4. The renal pelvis

    a. empties into the renal vein.   **c.** is a part of the nephron.

    b. is an extension of the ureter.   **d.** All of the above

_____ 5. During the process of reabsorption, components of the filtrate are

    a. actively transported out of the nephron.

    b. transferred to the capillaries surrounding the nephron.

    c. separated from waste products.

    d. All of the above

Name _____ Class _____ Date _____

SHORT ANSWER Answer the questions in the space provided.

1. Describe the importance of filtration in urine production. _____

_____

2. How do the kidneys contribute to homeostasis? _____

_____

3. Why are nephrons considered the structural and functional units of the kidney? _____

_____

_____

4. **Critical Thinking** How is ammonia related to kidney functioning? _____

_____

_____

STRUCTURES AND FUNCTIONS Use the figure of a nephron and the information below to answer the following questions.

About 99 of every 100 mL of filtrate
are reabsorbed into the blood, and
about 1,500 mL (1.6 qt) of urine are
excreted per day.

c _____

d _____

e _____

a _____

f _____

b _____

1. Label each part of the figure in the spaces provided.

2. In which structure is the filtrate collected? _____

3. Based on the amount of urine excreted daily, about how many milliliters of filtrate would be

produced daily by a pair of normally functioning kidneys? _____

SECTION 49-1 REVIEW

NEURONS AND NERVE IMPULSES

VOCABULARY REVIEW Define the following terms.

1. dendrite _____

_____

2. axon terminal _____

_____

3. action potential _____

_____

4. neurotransmitter _____

_____

5. synapse _____

_____

MULTIPLE CHOICE Write the correct letter in the blank.

_____ 1. Myelin sheaths surround

    a. dendrites.   **b.** the spinal cord.   **c.** axons.   **d.** synapses.

_____ 2. The initiation of an action potential

    a. causes the membrane potential to become more negative.
    b. requires sodium ions move into the neuron.
    c. originates in Schwann cells.
    d. happens at axon terminals.

_____ 3. A typical neuron has more than one

    a. nucleus.   **b.** axon.   **c.** dendrite.   **d.** All of the above

_____ 4. Action potentials require

    a. sodium ions.   **b.** gated channels.   **c.** diffusion.   **d.** All of the above

_____ 5. In a neuron, neurotransmitters are stored in

    a. the cell body.   **c.** vesicles within dendrites.
    b. the cytoplasm of the nucleus.   **d.** vesicles within axon terminals.

Name _____ Class _____ Date _____

SHORT ANSWER Answer the questions in the space provided.

1. Describe how a neurotransmitter can affect the activity of a postsynaptic neuron. _____

_____

2. Describe the relative concentrations of sodium and potassium ions inside and outside a neuron

at resting potential. _____

_____

3. Explain why action potentials move through axons in only one direction: away from the cell body,

toward the axon terminal. _____

_____

4. **Critical Thinking** In myelinated axons, ions can cross the cell membrane only at the nodes of

Ranvier. How does myelination increase the speed of an action potential? _____

_____

_____

STRUCTURES AND FUNCTIONS Use the figures below to answer the following questions.

The figures below represent the cell membrane of an axon at different states of activity.

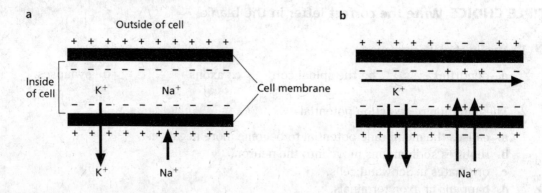

1. Explain why sodium ions do not cross the cell membrane in figure *a*. _____

_____

2. Describe what is happening in figure *b*. _____

_____

3. What are two factors that cause the movement of sodium and potassium ions as shown in figure *b*?

_____

_____

SECTION 49-2 REVIEW

STRUCTURE OF THE NERVOUS SYSTEM

VOCABULARY REVIEW Explain the relationship between the terms in each of the following groups of terms.

1. brain stem, medulla oblongata _____

_____

2. somatic nervous system, autonomic nervous system _____

_____

3. central nervous system, peripheral nervous system _____

_____

4. thalamus, hypothalamus _____

_____

MULTIPLE CHOICE Write the correct letter in the blank.

_____ 1. Each cerebral hemisphere is divided into

    a. four lobes.
    b. right and left halves.
    c. the cerebral cortex and the corpus callosum.
    d. All of the above

_____ 2. Which of the following is *not* a component of the brain stem?

    a. midbrain   **c.** medulla oblongata
    b. thalamus   **d.** pons

_____ 3. A spinal reflex requires

    a. the spinal cord to be separated from the brain.
    b. involvement of the diencephalon.
    c. neurons in the body but not the brain.
    d. only afferent neurons.

_____ 4. The cell bodies of neurons are located within the

    a. ventricles.   **b.** nerves.   **c.** corpus callosum.   **d.** gray matter.

_____ 5. The sympathetic division of the autonomic nervous system

    a. is part of the central nervous system.   **c.** stimulates body systems.
    b. inhibits body systems.   **d.** All of the above

SHORT ANSWER Answer the questions in the space provided.

1. Describe the function of the limbic system. _____

_____

2. What kind of information is carried in the ventral roots of spinal nerves? _____

_____

3. How does the body respond to stress or danger? _____

_____

_____

4. Which part of the peripheral nervous system is most important for homeostasis? Explain

your answer. _____

_____

5. **Critical Thinking** Do the central nervous system and the peripheral nervous system function

independently of one another? Explain your answer. _____

_____

STRUCTURES AND FUNCTIONS Use the figure below of a cross section of the spinal cord
with a spinal nerve to answer the following questions.

1. Which of the identified structures contains cell bodies of neurons? _____

2. How would cutting at point *B* affect the functioning of the central nervous system?

_____

_____

3. How would cutting at point *D* affect the functioning of the central nervous system?

_____

_____

SECTION 49-3 REVIEW

SENSORY SYSTEMS

VOCABULARY REVIEW Define the following terms.

1. papillae _____

_____

2. rod _____

_____

3. retina _____

_____

4. cone _____

_____

MULTIPLE CHOICE Write the correct letter in the blank.

_____ 1. Which of the following statements is *false?*

    a. Rods and cones are specialized neurons.
    b. Rods and cones lie deep within each retina.
    c. Cones respond to dim light, whereas rods are stimulated by bright light.
    d. Rods and cones are photoreceptors.

_____ 2. The perception of taste

    a. depends on sensory receptors in the nasal passages.
    b. is based on chemicals dissolved in food.
    c. does not involve the thalamus.
    d. is a function of the digestive system.

_____ 3. The olfactory epithelium

    a. is located in the pharynx.   **c.** is responsible for taste sensations.
    b. contains chemoreceptors.   **d.** contains papillae.

_____ 4. Bones of the middle ear

    a. vibrate the tympanic membrane.
    b. transfer sound vibrations to the inner ear.
    c. contain hair cells.
    d. All of the above

_____ 5. Which of the following is associated with the semicircular canals?

    a. balance   **b.** taste   **c.** hearing   **d.** vision

SHORT ANSWER Answer the questions in the space provided.

1. How does the cochlea detect and transmit sound signals? _____

_____

_____

2. What is the *first* event that is required for the detection and perception of sound? _____

_____

3. Describe the path that visual information takes from the eyes to the brain. _____

_____

_____

4. Discuss the role of the thalamus in hearing, vision, taste, and smell. _____

_____

_____

5. **Critical Thinking** More of the neurons in the cerebral cortex are involved with body parts that have complex, or "important," functions—such as the fingers, which make fine, detailed movements and interact with the environment—than with body parts that have less-complex functions. What advantage is gained by this variable representation of body parts in the nervous system?

_____

_____

STRUCTURES AND FUNCTIONS In the table below, write the type of sensory receptor—mechanoreceptor, photoreceptor, thermoreceptor, pain receptor, or chemoreceptor—that is associated with each sensory system. There may be more than one answer for each system.

Sensory System	Receptor Type
Vision	1.
Balance	2.
Hearing	3.
Smell	4.
Touch	5.
Temperature	6.
Taste	7.

SECTION 49-4 REVIEW

DRUGS AND THE NERVOUS SYSTEM

VOCABULARY REVIEW Explain the relationship between the terms in each of the following groups of terms.

1. psychoactive drug, stimulant _____

_____

2. tolerance, addiction _____

_____

3. addiction, withdrawal _____

_____

4. nicotine, emphysema _____

_____

MULTIPLE CHOICE Write the correct letter in the blank.

_____ **1.** Emphysema is

    a. an inflammation of the bronchi and bronchioles.

    b. an infectious lung disease similar to pneumonia.

    c. a degenerative lung disease in which alveoli lose their elasticity.

    d. caused by using smokeless tobacco.

_____ **2.** Which of the following is an example of a drug?

    a. aspirin   **b.** iodine   **c.** penicillin   **d.** All of the above

_____ **3.** Blood alcohol concentration, BAC, can be fatal at

    a. 0.50   **b.** 0.30   **c.** 0.10   **d.** 0.08

_____ **4.** Reuptake receptors

    a. transfer neurotransmitters from one neuron to the next.

    b. reabsorb neurotransmitters for later use.

    c. are more efficient in the presence of drugs such as cocaine.

    d. None of the above

_____ **5.** Codeine, heroin, and opium are examples of

    a. depressants.   **b.** stimulants.   **c.** narcotics.   **d.** hallucinogens.

SHORT ANSWER Answer the questions in the space provided.

1. Describe how tolerance to a drug develops. _____

_____

_____

2. List the symptoms of drug withdrawal. _____

_____

_____

3. Summarize how cocaine functions at the synaptic level. _____

_____

_____

4. **Critical Thinking** Is the relationship between body weight and blood alcohol concentration direct or inverse? Why do you think body weight would affect blood alcohol concentration?

_____

_____

_____

STRUCTURES AND FUNCTIONS Organize the following terms and phrases into two groups: *Group A* for those associated with smoking tobacco, and *Group B* for those associated with drinking alcohol. Write your answers in the table below.

throat irritation   drowsiness
slows respiratory system   emphysema
tars   addiction
liver damage   heart attack
fetal alcohol syndrome   chronic bronchitis

Group A	Group B

HORMONES

VOCABULARY REVIEW Define the following terms.

1. target cell ——
——

2. second messenger ———————————————————————————————————————
——

3. prostaglandin ———
——

4. hormone ——
——

MULTIPLE CHOICE Write the correct letter in the blank.

—————— 1. Amino acid–based hormones are

    a. protein hormones only.   **c.** considered as second messengers.
    b. derived from cholesterol.   **d.** None of the above

—————— 2. Because steroid hormones are fat-soluble, they can

    a. synthesize new enzymes.
    b. activate DNA synthesis.
    c. diffuse through the cell membrane of target cells.
    d. act as a first messenger or a second messenger.

—————— 3. Cyclic AMP

    a. is produced in response to amino acid–based hormones.
    b. appears in cycles.
    c. is produced in response to steroid hormones.
    d. attaches to DNA to control mRNA transcription.

—————— 4. Glands do *not* secrete

    a. hormones.   **b.** mucus.   **c.** prostaglandins.   **d.** saliva.

—————— 5. A steroid-hormone-receptor complex

    a. binds to cyclic AMP.   **c.** binds to DNA in the nucleus.
    b. acts through cell-surface receptors.   **d.** All of the above

SHORT ANSWER Answer the questions in the space provided.

1. How does a first messenger affect a target cell? _____

_____

_____

2. How are hormones transported throughout the body? _____

_____

3. Are sweat glands considered to be endocrine glands? Explain your answer. ___

_____

_____

4. **Critical Thinking** Why might the cells of two different organs respond differently to cyclic AMP

activation? _____

_____

_____

STRUCTURES AND FUNCTIONS Use the information given and the figure at right to answer the following questions.

Protein hormone

The diagram at right shows an amino acid–based hormone (a protein) that has been divided into four segments—A, B, C, and D—with an enzyme that cuts up proteins. In the experiment, each segment was physically isolated from the others, and a specific antibody was raised against each segment. The antibodies are identified according to the segment to which each of them binds. Cultured target cells of the hormone were then exposed to a mixture of the complete protein hormone and one of the antibodies. The responses of the cells are presented in the data table at right.

1. Which of the antibodies prevented the action of the

hormone? _____

2. In general, does the binding of an antibody prevent the

hormone's action? Explain your answer. _____

Antibodies	Cell Response
Anti-A	normal
Anti-B	normal
Anti-C	none
Anti-D	normal

_____

_____

3. What do these observations suggest about the hormone's action on its target cells?

_____

_____

SECTION 50-2 REVIEW

ENDOCRINE GLANDS

VOCABULARY REVIEW Explain the relationship between the terms in each of the following pairs of terms.

1. hypothalamus, pituitary gland _____

_____

2. epinephrine, norepinephrine _____

_____

3. follicle-stimulating hormone, luteinizing hormone _____

_____

4. insulin, diabetes mellitus _____

_____

5. estrogen, testosterone _____

_____

MULTIPLE CHOICE Write the correct letter in the blank.

_____ 1. Which of the following endocrine glands is *not* controlled by the pituitary gland?

    a. testes   **b.** thyroid gland   **c.** adrenal cortex   **d.** adrenal medulla

_____ 2. Thyroxine is important to the control of

    a. cellular metabolic rates.   **c.** diabetes mellitus.
    b. sex-hormone production.   **d.** calcium uptake.

_____ 3. Which of the following is a sex hormone?

    a. norepinephrine   **c.** progesterone
    b. cholesterol   **d.** cortisol

_____ 4. Lethargy and low body temperature are symptoms of a defect in the

    a. adrenal medulla.   **c.** pancreas.
    b. islets of Langerhans.   **d.** thyroid gland.

SHORT ANSWER Answer the questions in the space provided.

1. List two hormones that regulate the concentration of calcium in the blood and describe their effects. _____

_____

_____

2. Name the two posterior-pituitary hormones, and describe their actions and sites of production.

_____

_____

3. **Critical Thinking** In a person with goiter, would the blood level of TSH be below normal, normal, or above normal? Explain your answer. _____

_____

_____

STRUCTURES AND FUNCTIONS Use the figure of a feedback mechanism below to answer the following questions. In the figure, the number of hormone molecules represents the relative blood concentrations of *hormone A* and *hormone B*.

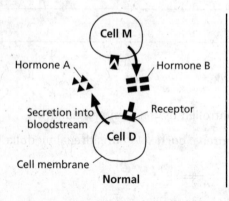
Normal

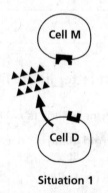
Situation 1

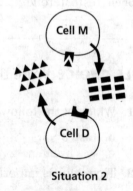
Situation 2

1. Which cell is defective in *Situation 1?* What happens to the hormone concentrations as a result of this defect? _____

_____

_____

2. Which cell is defective in *Situation 2?* What happens to the hormone concentrations as a result of this defect? _____

_____

_____

SECTION 51-1 REVIEW

MALE REPRODUCTIVE SYSTEM

VOCABULARY REVIEW Define the following terms.

1. semen _____

_____

2. testes _____

_____

3. ejaculation _____

_____

4. seminiferous tubules _____

_____

5. epididymis _____

_____

MULTIPLE CHOICE Write the correct letter in the blank.

_____ 1. A human sperm

    a. does not have a nucleus.
    b. has the haploid number of chromosomes located in the midpiece.
    c. has a small amount of cytoplasm.
    d. All of the above

_____ 2. The vas deferens connects the epididymis to the

    a. seminal vesicles.   **c.** urethra.
    b. bulbourethral glands.   **d.** seminiferous tubules.

_____ 3. The prostate gland is important to the

    a. proper functioning of the scrotum.   **c.** ejaculation of normal semen.
    b. completion of meiosis.   **d.** maturation of sperm.

_____ 4. After sperm move through the vas deferens, they enter the

    a. seminal vesicles.   **b.** urinary bladder.   **c.** urethra.   **d.** All of the above

_____ 5. A sperm tail consists of

    a. a nuclear envelope.   **c.** mitochondria.
    b. enzymes used to penetrate an egg.   **d.** a flagellum.

SHORT ANSWER Answer the questions in the space provided.

1. Describe the path that sperm take in leaving the body. _____

_____

2. Describe the composition of semen. _____

_____

3. Describe two differences between seminiferous tubules and the vas deferens. _____

_____

_____

4. How is the structure of a sperm suited for fertilization? _____

_____

5. **Critical Thinking** Is there an advantage for cells that secrete androgens (particularly testosterone) to be located within the testes instead of in other areas of the body? Explain your answer.

_____

_____

_____

STRUCTURES AND FUNCTIONS Use the figure below to answer the following questions.

1. Label each part of the figure in the spaces provided.

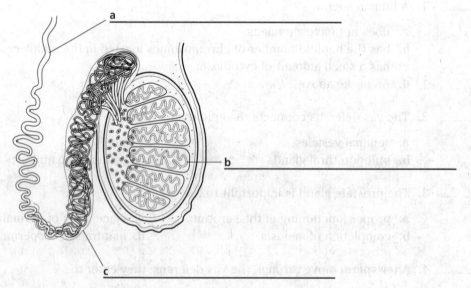

a _____

b _____

c _____

2. For each labeled structure, indicate whether sperm would be immature or mature. _____

_____

_____

SECTION 51-2 REVIEW

FEMALE REPRODUCTIVE SYSTEM

VOCABULARY REVIEW Explain the relationship between the terms in each of the following pairs of terms.

1. ovulation, ovary _____

_____

2. menopause, menstruation _____

_____

3. uterus, cervix _____

_____

4. menstrual cycle, follicular phase _____

_____

5. corpus luteum, luteal phase _____

_____

MULTIPLE CHOICE Write the correct letter in the blank.

_____ 1. How many mature eggs does each complete meiotic division yield?

     a. one   **b.** two   **c.** three   **d.** four

_____ 2. Fallopian tubes are connected to

     a. the corpus luteum.   **c.** the vagina.
     b. the urethra.   **d.** the uterus.

_____ 3. Which stage of the menstrual cycle is characterized by thickening of the uterine lining?

     a. follicular phase   **b.** luteal phase   **c.** menstruation   **d.** ovulation

_____ 4. Which of the following hormones initiates ovulation?

     a. progesterone   **c.** luteinizing hormone
     b. follicle-stimulating hormone   **d.** oxytocin

_____ 5. Which of the following hormones acts directly on the uterine lining during the menstrual cycle?

     a. estrogen   **c.** follicle-stimulating hormone
     b. luteinizing hormone   **d.** testosterone

SHORT ANSWER Answer the questions in the space provided.

1. Does the male or female gamete contribute more chromosomes to the fertilized egg? Explain

your answer. _____

_____

2. Describe two structural differences between a mature sperm and a mature egg. _____

_____

_____

3. **Critical Thinking** What does the onset of menopause indicate about the number of immature

eggs remaining in the ovaries? _____

_____

_____

STRUCTURES AND FUNCTIONS Use the figures of the menstrual cycle below to answer
the following question.

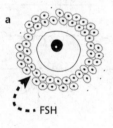

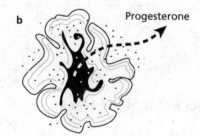

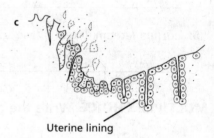

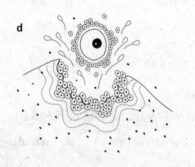

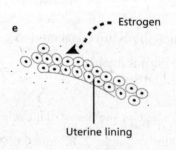

Briefly describe what is depicted in each figure. _____

_____

_____

_____

SECTION 51-3 REVIEW

GESTATION

VOCABULARY REVIEW Define the following terms.

1. human chorionic gonadotropin _____

_____

2. implantation _____

_____

3. chorionic villi _____

_____

4. umbilical cord _____

_____

5. amniotic sac _____

_____

MULTIPLE CHOICE Write the correct letter in the blank.

_____ 1. Fertilization occurs in the

    a. vagina.   **b.** uterus.   **c.** fallopian tubes.   **d.** ovaries.

_____ 2. The morula is

    a. the outer cell layer of a rupturing follicle.
    b. an unfertilized egg.
    c. formed after the fusion of sperm and egg nuclei.
    d. attached to the uterine lining after implantation.

_____ 3. Which of the following organ systems begins to form during the first trimester?

    a. nervous system   **c.** digestive system
    b. circulatory system   **d.** All of the above

_____ 4. Afterbirth includes

    a. amniotic fluid.   **c.** unfertilized eggs.
    b. the placenta.   **d.** ruptured ovarian follicles.

_____ 5. A zygote is a(n)

    a. implanted fertilized egg.   **c.** fertilized egg.
    b. ovulated egg.   **d.** blastocyst.

SHORT ANSWER Answer the questions in the space provided.

1. Explain why ovulation does not occur during pregnancy. _____

_____

2. Describe how the placenta, chorionic villi, and allantois are functionally and structurally related.

_____

_____

3. Explain the importance of estrogen during pregnancy. _____

_____

4. What events must be completed before implantation is successful? _____

_____

_____

5. **Critical Thinking** If you were asked to design a pregnancy test that was based on hormones,

which hormone would you select to indicate a pregnancy? Explain your answer. _____

_____

_____

STRUCTURES AND FUNCTIONS Use the figure of part of the female reproductive system below to answer the following questions.

1. Label each part of the figure in the spaces provided.

a _____

b _____

c _____

d _____

2. Use the letters of the labeled structures to indicate where the following would normally be found during pregnancy:

_____ blastocyst   _____ corpus luteum

_____ zygote   _____ morula